IN THE SERVICE OF GOD AND HUMANITY

In the Service of God and Humanity

Conscience, Reason, and the Mind of Martin R. Delany

Tunde Adeleke

THE UNIVERSITY OF
SOUTH CAROLINA PRESS

© 2021 University of South Carolina

Published by the University of South Carolina Press
Columbia, South Carolina, 29208

www.uscpress.com

30 29 28 27 26 25 24 23 22 21
     10 9 8 7 6 5 4 3 2 1

Library of Congress Cataloging-in-Publication Data
can be found at http://catalog.loc.gov/.

ISBN: 978-1-64336-184-0 (hardcover)
ISBN: 978-1-64336-185-7 (ebook)

S | H
M | P

The Sustainable History Monograph Pilot

Opening up the Past, Publishing for the Future

This book is published as part of the Sustainable History Monograph Pilot. With the generous support of the Andrew W. Mellon Foundation, the Pilot uses cutting-edge publishing technology to produce open access digital editions of high-quality, peer-reviewed monographs from leading university presses. Free digital editions can be downloaded from: Books at JSTOR, EBSCO, Hathi Trust, Internet Archive, OAPEN, Project MUSE, and many other open repositories.

When you cite the book, please include the following URL for its Digital Object Identifier (DOI): https://doi.org/10.48172/9781643361857

We are eager to learn more about how you discovered this title and how you are using it. We hope you will spend a few minutes answering a couple of questions at this url: **https://www.longleafservices.org/shmp-survey/**

More information about the Sustainable History Monograph Pilot can be found at https://www.longleafservices.org.

In Memory of
Ralph Archibald Legall (1925–2003)
and
Gerald A. Burks (1947–2009)

Both Martin Delany Enthusiasts!

CONTENTS

Few nineteenth-century Black leaders traveled as extensively as Martin Robison Delany (1812–1885). From the time he left Pittsburgh, Pennsylvania, at the invitation of Frederick Douglass to serve as coeditor and roving lecturer for the *North Star* in 1847, Delany's life was one of constant motion. These travels initially took him to all corners of the Black communities in the North and Midwest. By the 1850s, with his turn to emigration and Black nationalism, his travels expanded globally (Canada, Africa, and Britain). Delany's experiences and adventures while traveling nationally and internationally exposed him to the exigencies and complexities of the Black experience, which he meticulously documented, thereby creating a rich legacy for posterity. Needless to say, his travels were not for personal gain or pleasure but were undertaken primarily in furtherance of the Black struggle. This was a preoccupation Delany gladly and enthusiastically embraced with love but with little to no expectation of personal compensation. Most often, especially in the early phase, he relied on the kindness and charity of strangers and abolitionists—men and women alike who raised donations. Some offered him shelter and cared for his horse; others gave him rides in stagecoaches. Through it all, Delany was never on anyone's permanent payroll. His work involved many sacrifices, as he underscored, in the service of God and humanity.

As a Martin Delany student and scholar, I can venture the contention that we are yet to fully explore and appreciate the wealth of Delany's legacy. The more we probe his writings, the more we are exposed to new insights, with rich and varied perspectives and viewpoints. Personally, studying and researching Martin Delany has been the most intellectually enriching and rewarding of endeavors. Through it all, I have been fortunate to benefit from the knowledge and expertise of other colleagues, friends and scholars many of whom I have acknowledged in several of my previous publications. For this study however, I will acknowledge two key individuals, both now deceased and in whose memories the work is dedicated: Ralph Archibald Legall (1925–2003) and Gerald A. Burks (1947–2009).

I first met Ralph by chance encounter at a bus stop on the corner of Richmond and Dundas in downtown London, Ontario, in the fall of 1980, shortly after my arrival in Canada. We struck up a friendship, and I quickly discovered his depth of knowledge of Black history. Ralph was very generous. He invited me to his apartment on countless occasions, and over sumptuous meals (Ralph was a chef), we would engage in spirited but friendly discourses on the state of the Black struggles in America and across the globe. He was particularly passionate about developments in the Caribbean. Ralph was born and raised in St. Michael, Barbados, and had partaken of the experiences and struggles that the late renowned West Indian writer Austin Clarke described in his memoir *Growing Up Stupid Under the Union Jack*. Austin Clarke also hailed from Barbados and was a schoolmate of Ralph's at Harrison College. I soon discovered that Ralph had also written a master's thesis on aspects of the Black struggles in the Caribbean for the University of Winsor. Ralph was instrumental in helping to shape and frame my early thoughts about Martin Delany. Ralph was not just a personal friend, he was a family friend. He was very kind and generous to my wife and our son, Tosin. I lost contact with Ralph after completion of my studies and returned to Nigeria in 1985. We reconnected briefly by phone when I moved to New Orleans in 1991. He was then working as a Tennis instructor for the Kinesiology Department of the University of Windsor in Ontario, Canada. I did not hear from Ralph again until I read his obituary in 2003. In all our meetings and socializing, Ralph never once mentioned his stellar athletic accomplishments prior to immigrating to Canada. Ralph had won the Trinidad and Tobago Table Tennis singles title in 1949; he played basketball and soccer for both Trinidad and Tobago and Barbados, West Indian Cricket for Trinidad in the 1940s and 1950s, Davis Cup tennis for the Caribbean team against the US and Canada in 1954 and 1956, First Division soccer for the British Army and police in 1947, and cricket for the Lancashire League (England) in 1960 before emigrating to Canada. I found out about all of these after his death. What an amazing feat, and what a humble and unassuming human being!

It was also by chance that I met Gerald Burks. Our paths first crossed in 2007 at the Annual Conference of the Association for African American Historical Research and Preservation in Seattle, Washington. I had the privilege of being recognized as "Honorary Conference Chair" and thus became the focus of attention. During a preconference reception, I shared a table with a group of attendees that included Gerald Burks. It was at this table that Burks shared a volume he had edited containing primary and genealogical sources he had collected in an effort to, in his words, "identify my maternal ancestry and to prove that Martin Robinson (Martin Robison Delany) is part of it."[1] The next day, to my surprise, he presented me with a copy of the book. This was an unexpected gesture of generosity for which I remain eternally grateful. Burks's book is among the truly treasured classics on Martin Delany. I place it alongside the pioneering works of Dorothy Sterling and Victor Ullman. As Burks claimed, "In familial vernacular without the 'greats', I am his [i.e., Delany's] nephew."[2] He referred to Delany as "Uncle Martin." Burks was a consummate Delany buff who spent considerable time and resources in pursuit of validating his ancestry. He traced his "great, great grandfather, James Robinson and great grandfather Harrison Robinson to Shepherdstown, Jefferson County, West Virginia, a few miles north of Charlestown," Martin Delany's birthplace.[3] Based on his finding, and their uncanny resemblance, Burks considered Martin Delany his great-great uncle. This rich volume contains documents from United States census and genealogical data and plantation records dating back to before Delany was born. Burks traveled extensively and spent considerable time in the counties of West Virginia; in the process, he amassed a truly impressive and meticulous record that strongly supported his case. I have no doubt that had Burks not died, the trajectory of his research would have resulted in some form of publication that would have benefitted generations of Delany students and scholars.

I would be remiss not to acknowledge the singular positive influence that has nurtured a most welcoming and endearing environment for me and my family in Ames, Iowa: the Owusu family (Francis, "my little brother," as I fondly refer to him; his lovely wife, Teresa; and their beautiful children). We have been inseparable ever since I met them during my campus visit to Iowa State University. Their home is my second home, and as madam Teresa always reassured me whenever I arrived at their doorstep uninvited and unexpected, "welcome home." This welcome is not empty cliché or rhetoric. It is always accompanied by sumptuous meals rendered with love and affection. In over four decades in academia, during which I have taught in several institutions in the United States and abroad, my stay at Iowa State University is the longest. I attribute this, without equivocation, to the familial welcome and endearing influence of Francis and his family.

I want to acknowledge my immense gratitude to, and appreciation for, the two anonymous reviewers of the manuscript for the University of South Carolina Press. Working independently, they came up with similar suggestions for revision. I am truly grateful for their knowledge, insights, and constructive comments, which helped to enhance and enrich the book. Also, I would like to acknowledge, with gratitude, acquisitions editor, Ehren Foley, for his interest in Martin Delany and the professionalism and efficiency by which he handled the acquisition and review process.

Last, but certainly not the least, I owe immeasurable gratitude to my wife and friend, Gloria, and our children (Tosin, Toyin, and Chinyere). Their presence in my life, and their accomplishments and daily struggles, have sustained my desire to keep trudging on and remain intellectually curious and productive. They are indeed the reason I wake up every day with the deepest and profound gratitude for almighty God's mercy and benevolence.

IN THE SERVICE OF GOD AND HUMANITY

Introduction

WRITING FOR THE *PITTSBURGH COURIER* over eight decades ago, historian W. E. B. Du Bois asked this poignant rhetorical question: "[Martin Delany's] was a magnificent life, and yet how many of us have heard of him?"[1] Du Bois was right. This remarkable person—the man who collaborated with Frederick Douglass to coedit nineteenth-century Black America's leading newspaper, the *North Star*, and considered by some to be second only to Frederick Douglass as a leading Black abolitionist and activist; the man who crisscrossed the country for antislavery, and who in 1849, helped save several lives in the Cholera epidemic that hit Pittsburgh, Pennsylvania, and in consequence received commendations and certificates of appreciation from the city council and board of health;[2] the man who in 1850 became one of three Black students to enter Harvard Medical School, and after being forced out due to racism, led the emigration movement in the second half of the nineteenth century, earning a national and international reputation as a leading Black nationalist and Pan-Africanist;[3] the man who, on the outbreak of the Civil War, President Abraham Lincoln referred to as "this most extraordinary and intelligent Black man" and commissioned him the first Black combat major in the Union army, and who subsequently helped recruit several Colored regiments;[4] and the man who was appointed a sub-assistant commissioner of the Bureau of Refugees, Freedmen and Abandoned Lands (Freedmen's Bureau) after the war,[5] became active in local South Carolina politics, and competed for nomination for the office of lieutenant governor, the second highest political office in the state[6]—had simply and mysteriously been erased from America's collective historical memory. By the 1930s, Martin Robison Delany (1812–1885) and other leading Black citizens of his generation had been buried beneath the weight of the emergent and triumphant New South ideology and Jim Crow culture and historiography, which their accomplishments were sacrificed to consecrate. Fundamentally, this culture and historiography deliberately misrepresented and deemphasized the achievements and contributions of Black Americans, especially of their heroes and heroines whose careers seemed to challenge and contradict the dominant and entrenched tradition of White supremacy.[7]

Not even the Harlem Renaissance of the previous decade could rescue Delany from historical oblivion. The Delany "renaissance" would have to wait for another four decades, when the rise of instrumentalist historiography in the 1960s and the civil rights movement would inspire increased scholarly interests in researching and recovering Black history. This was the historical and cultural context that birthed the Delany rediscovery.[8] Thanks to the efforts of Delany aficionados (Dorothy Sterling, Victor Ullman, Cyril Griffith, Theodore Draper, and Floyd J. Miller) we now know much more about Delany's magnificent life[9] and can confidently answer Du Bois's question. The pioneering works of these Delany scholars have, in the last five decades, been complemented by an outpouring of publications on Delany's life, struggles, and accomplishments.[10]

Martin Delany was born of a free mother in 1812 in Charlestown, Virginia (now in West Virginia), at a time in the nation's history when, for African Americans (slave and free), being free meant nothing. In nineteenth-century America, free Blacks were, according to one historian, "Slaves without Masters."[11] Black Americans generally were considered and treated less than human. Delany grew up witnessing his grandparents and parents suffer the daily inhumanities and horrors of enslavement. This reality compelled young Delany at a very early age to "register his vows against the enemies of his race."[12] Determined to escape the fate of his parents and grandparents, Delany took the momentous decision in July of 1831 (at the age of 19) to relocate from Chambersburg, Pennsylvania (where they had sought refuge after escaping Virginia), to Pittsburgh.[13] It was in Pittsburgh that Delany encountered a growing and thriving community of like-minded Black activists, many of whom had also migrated from other states, working together toward, and committed to, advancing the cause of Black freedom and equality. Here, he continued his education and met leaders who would help shape and guide his career. It was here also that his antislavery career began. He worked part time loading coal and pig iron into barges while pursuing his education at the African Methodist Episcopal Church Cellar School.[14] As secretary of the Philanthropic Society of Pittsburgh, an organization dedicated to aiding fugitives, Delany also began helping with Underground Railroad activities.[15]

Delany attended a convention in Pittsburgh in 1834 at which there was a split between advocates of moral suasion and those in favor of more militant approaches. Moral suasion was then being discussed by the leadership of the emerging National Negro Convention movement which opened in Philadelphia in August of 1831. He sided with the moral suasionists who also pushed for temperance and nonviolence. Shortly thereafter he was appointed secretary of the newly created Temperance Society of the People of Color of Pittsburgh. That same year, he helped found the Young Men's Moral Reform Society of Pittsburgh.[16] By 1837, he had become librarian of the Young Men's Literary and Moral Reform Society of Pittsburgh. In 1839, with increased anti-Black violence in Pittsburgh, Delany became a central figure in organizing resistance efforts. He was appointed by the Mayor to form a biracial vigilante committee for law and order. Subsequently, he was elected to the Board of Managers of the Pittsburgh Anti-slavery Society.[17] Delany's antislavery efforts no doubt endeared him to some of the leading and wealthiest Pittsburgh socialites. In 1843, he married Catherine Richards, daughter of Charles Richards, who was the son of "Daddy" Ben Richards, one of the wealthiest men in Pittsburgh. The union was blessed with eleven children, seven of whom survived (Toussaint L'Ouverture, Charles Lenox Remond, Alexander Dumas, Saint Cyprian, Faustin Soulouque, Rameses Placido, and Ethiopia). The marriage also brought in much-needed income, for Catherine inherited property valued at $200,000.[18] Less than six months after his marriage, Delany began his newspaper the *Pittsburgh Mystery*. He published the *Mystery* until 1847 when he gave it up to join Frederick Douglass as coeditor and roving lecturer for the *North Star*—a move that launched his nationwide antislavery career.[19]

In the two years Delany worked with Douglass (1847–1849), he made numerous trips to Black communities in the North and Midwest to deliver antislavery lectures and propagate moral suasion; the reform strategy Black abolitionists had adopted. Delany, Douglass, and other leading Black abolitionists, believed that through the cultivation of the tenets of moral suasion (thrift, industry, economy, education, and character reform) Blacks would change their condition and thus appeal favorably to the moral conscience of the nation, and thereby, compel concessions of their rights and privileges.[20] The upsurge of anti-Black violence and race riots in several states including Pennsylvania, New York, New Jersey, Rhode Island, Connecticut, and Massachusetts eroded their faith in moral suasion. Free Blacks had thought they would find an atmosphere receptive of and sympathetic to their desires and efforts to change their condition.[21] Instead, they encountered resentments and violence. These race riots and violence targeted successful Black businesses, institutions, and symbols of Black cultural, economic, and social progress (such as churches and schools).[22] The last straw for Delany was the passage of the Fugitive Slave Law in 1850 which convinced him that Blacks would never be given the opportunity to strive for progress in America.[23] The race riots and his experiences of racism during his journeys convinced Delany that however hard Blacks struggled to improve their condition, racism was so rooted and entrenched that their efforts would always be "rewarded" with hostility and violence.[24] He presented a dark and gloomy description of the prospects for Black elevation in America. According to Delany, "The most prominent feature of the American policy is to preserve inviolate the liberty of the WHITES in this country, and to attempt to deny or disguise this, is both unjust and dishonest [emphasis in original]."[25] He referred to the "expulsion" of the Indians from their lands, and "the continued wrongs perpetrated against" them to bolster the contention that Whites would go to any lengths, including nationalizing slavery, in order to preserve and defend their power and privileges.[26] Delany reflected and expressed a growing conviction among Blacks which the "Colored Citizens" of Pennsylvania articulated in their 1848 "Appeal" to the Commonwealth:

> The barrier that deprives us of the rights which you enjoy finds no palliative in merit—no consolation in piety—no hope in intellectual and moral pursuits—no reward in industry and enterprise . . . we may exhaust our midnight lamps in the prosecution of study, and be denied the privileges of the forum—we may be embellishing the nation's literature by our pursuits in science . . . yet with all these exalted virtues we could not possess the privileges you enjoy in Pennsylvania, because we are not "White."[27]

Delany fully agreed and concluded that Blacks had no future in America. He distrusted White abolitionists and denounced their liberal ideas as limited in scope, paternalistic, racist, and phony. Almost a decade before it would become a slogan in the prelude to the Civil War, Delany described the "Cry of Fee Men" by Northern Whites and abolitionists as

> not for the extension of liberty to the black man, but for the protection of the liberty of the white. The liberty of the whites of the North was endangered by the encroachments of the slave power; hence, an alarm was necessary to arouse the North and alarm the South, who determined on the permanent establishment of slavery, as the North is well advised of, is ever ready to compromise, and always able to find one.[28]

He urged Blacks to embrace emigration, and for the next few years (1852–1863) he embarked on a search for an independent Black nationality. This quest took him to Liberia and the Niger Valley of West Africa where, in southwestern Nigeria, he convinced the local chiefs to cede a portion of their lands for his Black nationality. However, this phase of Delany's career ended abruptly with the outbreak of the Civil War.

Like Frederick Douglass and other leading Black Americans, and with re-newed hope and optimism about the prospects for change in America, Delany reversed course and became actively involved in the pursuit of Black integration in America. His renewed integration zeal and dedication to the Union cause led to his appointment as the first combat Black major in the Union army; a rank he held until after the end of the war when he was transferred to the Freed-men's Bureau as sub-assistant commissioner and field agent in Hilton Head Is-land, South Carolina.[29] He was assigned to take charge of several government plantations in Hilton Head. Delany served the Bureau until its demise in 1868 when he thrust himself into the political arena of South Carolina. He would play a pivotal role in both Republican and Democratic Party politics, contesting for lieutenant governor as an "Independent" in 1874.[30] Delany seemed to have won the confidence of both Republican and Democratic state governors, Daniel Chamberlain and Wade Hampton respectively, who appointed him trial justice for the city of Charleston.[31]

Though Delany's political career in South Carolina was marked by conflicts and hostilities provoked in part by the controversial decisions and choices he made, his overall accomplishments were quite remarkable. Against the political wishes and inclinations of fellow Blacks and the ruling Republican Party, Delany persistently pushed for reconciliation with, and compromise toward, the defeated Democrats (the party of slavery).[32] By the late 1870s, his hopes and aspirations for racial reconciliation were dashed, paradoxically, by the ascendance of Democrats to political power (supporters of the ancien régime); the very group he had de-fended and whose support he courted. The "redeemers" as they proudly referred to themselves introduced anti-Black policies designed to undo and reverse the re-forms and progress of the Civil War and Reconstruction. Delany, their one-time vocal defender, did not escape their anger and retribution.[33] Disappointed, frus-trated, and alienated from the mainstream Black leadership, Delany left South Carolina. His integrationist aspirations shattered, Delany reverted to his old na-tionalist back-to-Africa scheme. He joined a resurgent Liberia Exodus Movement, and appealed to the American Colonization Society in Washington, DC, for fi-nancial assistance for the emigration cause. No help came from the Colonization Society. But time seemed to have taken its toll, and Delany had neither the phys-ical ability nor pecuniary resources to relaunch a new initiative. In late 1884, he returned physically and psychologically a broken man to Xenia, Ohio, where his wife and children had relocated. He died shortly thereafter on January 24, 1885.

Martin Delany's life and accomplishments therefore spanned about seven decades of the nation's history (1812–1885). In 1895, just ten years after his death,

Booker T. Washington would address the Atlanta International Cotton Exposition and deliver a speech that would go down in history as the Atlanta compromise.[34] Anyone familiar with Delany's ideas and arguments in furtherance of compromise and accommodation in Reconstruction South Carolina would find nothing new in Washington's Atlanta Exposition speech. Much of his arguments derived almost verbatim from some of Delany's writings and speeches in South Carolina.[35] Ironically, Washington earned the unenviable reputation as a compromiser, while Delany slipped into historical oblivion. Less than fifty years after his exit from the political scene, Delany's accomplishments would almost be completely erased from peoples' memories. Thanks to the works of the aficionados, and those of subsequent scholars for challenging and reversing this Jim Crow historiography. Delany would ultimately be resurrected and valorized as exemplar of uncompromising radicalism. Despite increased publications on, and hence increased knowledge about, Martin Delany, there is still much about him that remains unexplored and unappreciated.

Ironically, the more we know about Delany, the more we yearn for more knowledge. The versatility of his thought, and the fact that his antislavery and nationalist careers spanned five decades (1831–1885), which also coincided with major political developments in the nation's history, underscore and help us better appreciate the complexity and ambivalence that several scholars characterize as possibly the single defining attribute of his life. As Victor Ullman noted, Delany "simply cannot be classified with either the 'good guys' or the 'bad guys.'"[36] His ideas and choices reflected and encompassed multiple and complex ideologies. His life touched on virtually every aspect of American history—slavery, racism, abolitionism, religion, colonization, emigration, Civil War, and Reconstruction. The fact that Delany embodied and experienced so much makes the task of studying him all the more challenging. In essence, what Ullman acknowledged was that you could not compartmentalize Delany or his life within narrow and simplistic ideological categories. The more you explore Delany, and are drawn deeper into his life, the more you are likely to realize how much more there is to learn about him, and the more you would want to probe even deeper the inner dynamics of his erudite and prolific mind. In other words, the more we know about Delany, the more we realize how little we actually know, and thus are motivated to explore him even further.

One area of Delany's life that had escaped scholarly scrutiny, despite the outpourings of publications in the last several decades, relates to the particular dynamics of the ideas he propagated—the political choices he made and defended. While it was clear that Delany made certain controversial decisions and choices, with the exception of the emigration movement about which he wrote extensively, there remains a gap in our understanding of the ideological under-pinnings of his controversial, ambivalent, and quite often provocative political decisions and choices. Overcoming this challenge would require slow and delib-erate reexamination and analysis of his writings and speeches. For instance, we need to understand why he took so many seemingly anti-Black and unpopular choices and decisions in the closing years of Reconstruction in South Carolina. Furthermore, we know from the scholarship that he was not born a nationalist and that, like many of his peers, Delany spent his early life fighting for integra-tion in America. How did he conceptualize and rationalize integration? Some of the strategies he adopted are well documented, but we still do not know much about their rationale. Delany not only actively participated in the Black struggles but also reflected and philosophized at length about the ideas he espoused and strategies he embraced. This book is about interrogating and analyzing Delany's ideas in relation to some of the core themes that infused the nineteenth-century Black struggles in America. The objective is to gain informed understanding of the dynamics of his thought that compelled him to make controversial and seemingly contradictory decisions and choices. The central question this book seeks to answer is: what precisely can help us better understand, if not appreciate, Delany's ambivalent, and at times, counterintuitive decisions and choices? Put differently, the book probes the rationale that motivated Delany to advocate po-litical ideas and choices that at times sharply contradicted, and conflicted with, those of the mainstream leadership.

I have identified four crucial areas—emanating from, or associated with, his long engagement with American history—to which he made significant contri-butions and about which he was passionate. These four areas represent possibly the major dynamics, preoccupations, and strategies of the nineteenth-century Black struggles: religion, education, violence, and politics. Martin Delany had much to say about, and helped shape public opinion on, these subjects. Curi-ously, we know relatively little about his thought specific to each subject. This could be attributed to the fact that, with the exception of politics, in which he actively participated late in his life, Delany was never publicly associated with the other three factors. His participation in state politics in South Carolina was short-lived (1872–1876)—not long and impactful enough to distinguish his po-litical career. It did not earn him recognition as a political theorist either. And yet Delany was no silent political witness. He offered constructive and insightful (if provocative) political ideas; and no discussion of the political participation and Black experience in Reconstruction South Carolina would be complete

without engaging the ideas he espoused. Similarly, Delany was never a minister
or religious prelate. He was not an educator either; and certainly, he did not
openly advocate or lead violent insurrection. Nevertheless, he was very open and
vocal in expressing his opinions and views on religion, education, and violence.
Along with politics, Delany felt very strongly about these particular subjects
that also engaged the attention of other Black leaders, and he left few in doubt
about his views. He reflected deeply about them and, in scattered and piecemeal
writings, in public speeches and addresses, offered insights into the rationale
undergirding the choices and decisions they compelled. This book therefore is
more of an intellectual history and seeks to probe deeper Delany's thoughts on,
and contributions to, four vital areas of the nineteenth-century Black struggles
in America.

The Delany "renaissance," restored him to the historical limelight. It also revealed his multifaceted and complex nature. Such knowledge has only bolstered
interest in probing the dynamics of his thoughts and actions. What were his
views on religion, and more specifically the place of the Black church in the
promotion of the ideology of moral suasion that Black leaders and abolitionists
had adopted as guiding philosophy? What did he think of violence as reform
strategy? The subject of violence dominated discussions in some of the early
Black conventions of the 1830s. Delany was certainly aware of the controversies
that violence generated and possibly was present at some of the deliberations.
Thus far, most scholars have analyzed Delany's conception of violence within
the discourse of the "hemispheric revolution" he mapped in his fictional novel
Blake, Or, The Huts of America (1859). I hope to demonstrate the many other
ways and circumstances Delany manifested his disposition toward violence as
reform strategy. While officially Delany was no educator, he fully embraced and
helped propagate moral suasion which had education as a key component. What
were his views on education? How did Delany conceptualize education in relation to other Black liberation strategies? Though he ascended to a position of
prominence in Charleston, as well as in statewide Republican and Democratic
Party politics in Reconstruction South Carolina, we know relatively little about
the political ideas and theories he espoused. What did Delany think of politics?
What political strategies did he advocate and why?

Scholarship on African American thought and leadership consistently tends
to situate Delany within the discourse of Black nationalism and Pan-Africanism.
His thought has consequently been confined to this theme. Not surprisingly, he
has been, and continues to be, narrowly framed as a Black nationalist. A relatively recent publication on African American Political thought exemplifies this

historiographical anomaly. In mapping the themes of African American political thought from David Walker in the late eighteenth century down to Barack Obama, *The Modern African American Political Thought Reader* (2013), edited by sociologist Angela Jones, identified six broad themes: the antebellum era, rise of abolitionism, Reconstruction and beyond, Black nationalism, Black radical feminism, modern Black conservatism, and the new Black moderate. Consistent with prevailing scholarship, Jones associated Martin Delany with Black nationalism.[37] In reality, as this study will demonstrate, Delany could rightly be identified with all six themes. His life span and antislavery activism coincided with every major episode in American history. He actively participated and voiced his opinions. In his writings, Delany touched upon a wide variety of subjects and themes, including Black nationalism, Pan-Africanism, abolitionism, religion, education, women, violence, astrology, freemasonry, ethnology, political economy, and politics. Unfortunately, because of the ideological slant of the era of Delany's rediscovery, scholars have narrowly focused on his nationalist and supposedly antiestablishment ideas. Yet, the nationalist ideas were only a dimension; minute reflection and representation of the versatility and complexity of his thoughts. This book is an attempt to challenge the ideological and skewed representation of Delany and argue instead for engaging and acknowledging other aspects of his thoughts (religion, violence, education, and politics). Probing these other dimensions would, I hope, yield better understanding of the contexts and dynamics of why he made certain decisions and staked certain positions that at the time seemed counterintuitive. Exploring and tapping into the mind of so versatile a human helps us better understand him and gain greater appreciation of his place in, and contributions to, the Black struggles in America. It also demonstrates how his ideas and thoughts embodied and anticipated some of the broader challenges and problems of humanity with which the world is still grappling: liberation theology, women's education, the ethics of nonviolence, and political bipartisanship.

There are four chapters in this book corresponding with the four themes identified: religion, violence, education, and politics. These four areas preoccupied the attention of Black leaders and abolitionists throughout the nineteenth century. They constituted key elements of the strategies and options they considered and debated as represented in the minutes and records of their many and various proceedings. Since Martin Delany was a major participant, it is imperative to seek informed understanding of his ideas and the choices they dictated. What were his views on religion and the role of the Black Church? What was his position of violence as reform strategy? How did he view education? What political ideas and theories did he advocate and defend? These are the fundamental questions this book addresses.

Chapter 1 discusses and analyzes Delany's ideas about religion and its place in the Black struggle. More directly, it deals with his projection of religion as means of liberation. This chapter is divided into two broad themes. In the first (religion and integration), Delany espoused a "this-worldly" interpretation of Christianity. His main objective was to activate human agency and self-determination. In the second (religion and nationalism), Delany invoked scriptural authority to bolster his call for emigration. His this-worldly theology was directed at encouraging Blacks to actively undertake measures that would enhance their prospects of attaining meaningful freedom, equality, and advancement in America. This was largely in response to what he characterized as the debilitating and destructive consequences of a fatalistic and otherworldly providential theology propagated by some of the leading Black churches. This developed within the broader context of his antislavery and abolitionist travels to propagate the ideology of moral suasion officially adopted as a philosophy at the 1835 National Negro Convention in Philadelphia, Pennsylvania. Moral suasion envisioned change and reform through thrift, industry, economy, education, and character reform. It sought to encourage Blacks to become more active in pursuit of means of improving their condition and elevating themselves. Moral suasion was directed at infusing in Blacks the awareness that they too had a role to play in facilitating change. Cultivating moral suasion was crucial. It was during his travels and lectures to encourage Blacks to actively seek to change their condition that Delany was drawn into a robust controversy and debate on the role of religion and the Black church. During the early phase of his career, therefore, Delany characterized religion as an integrationist tool that, properly cultivated and utilized, could help Blacks become elevated and empowered, and thus enhance their chances of attaining full integration in America. Delany's theory of religion, however, conflicted with and challenged the providential and otherworldly theology propagated by leading Black churches. The chapter is fundamentally about how Delany's engagement with, and involvement in, the Black abolitionist movement exposed a crisis and division within the early Black churches, and between the churches and the abolitionist movement. The second part of the chapter deals with Delany's brilliant attempt to reformulate religion. Having seemingly failed in his integrationist aspirations, Delany now turned to Black nationalism and separatism and found religion also an effective weapon for advancing his quest for an independent Black nationality. In essence, the chapter analyzes how Delany framed religion to advance seemingly conflicting goals of integration and separatism. Due to its subject matter (religion), this chapter is focused on the pre-Civil War epoch. Delany espoused his philosophy of religion most vividly first, in the late 1840s, during his brief stint as roving lecturer for Frederick Douglass's *North Star*; and second, from the mid-to-late 1850s when he used religion to bolster his emigration scheme.

Chapter 2 focuses on Delany's views on violence as a weapon of change. Given the condition of Blacks and the magnitude of the challenges they confronted daily, it should not be surprising that violence appealed to some nor that the subject was featured in the deliberations of several of the early conventions. As much as leading Blacks endorsed and emphasized moral suasion and reform through individual initiatives, violence as an option was never completely ruled out. Delany both experienced violence and was aware of the debates and controversies it generated among Black abolitionists. He was therefore in position to engage the subject and offer his views. Foregrounding the debates on, and controversies generated by, violence in the deliberations of the Negro National and State Conventions of the 1830s and 1840s, I discuss Delany's background and the influences that shaped his views on violence. I address the moral dilemma violence represented and how leading Black thinkers, particularly those who were Delany's ideological mentors, dealt with this dilemma. What they said about, and how they perceived, violence ultimately shaped Delany's own ideas and position on the subject. This chapter, like the first, is focused on the pre-Civil War period. Delany was a leading proponent of the nonviolent philosophy of moral suasion in the 1840s. In the 1850s when he embraced emigration, Delany used the medium of fiction (*Blake*) and his response to John Brown's insurrectionary scheme to reiterate his reservations about violence as a weapon of change. For a very brief period during the Civil War, Delany seemed to embrace violence. He was appointed the first Black combat major in the Union army. But this was in 1865, and shortly before the war's termination (more on this later).

Chapter 3 is about how Delany conceptualized and attempted to formulate a key component of the moral suasion ideology: education. Along with thrift, economy and industry, education was considered a critical area of improvement for Blacks as they sought meaningful freedom and equality. As a leading advocate of moral suasion, Delany not only observed the low and dismal state of education among Black Americans, but also felt compelled to share his views on ongoing debates about the importance of education as well as on what form of education to pursue. His educational philosophy evolved and developed over three decades beginning in Pittsburgh in the late 1830s to South Carolina in the late 1860s. Delany had always prioritized education; first as abolitionist and moral suasion advocate in the 1830s and 1840s, and later as Freedmen's Bureau sub-assistant commissioner in South Carolina in the mid-to-late 1860s. In his antislavery writings and speeches during the 1840s and 1850s, Delany stressed the importance of education. He discussed education in his 1852 publication, *The Condition, Elevation, Emigration and Destiny of the Colored People of the United States.* He would revisit the subject even more extensively in his Bureau reports during the late 1860s. In these yearly reports, Delany commented at length on strategies for enhancing the education of free Blacks: curriculum, pedagogy, classroom management, teacher-pupil relationship, women's education and race. Clearly, Delany was way ahead of his time on these aspects of education. Some of his ideas and suggestions would resurface in the thoughts and policies of future generations of Black educators. Delany's thoughts on education, therefore, intersected the pre-and post-Civil War eras.

Chapter 4 is an attempt to give form and shape to a very difficult and controversial aspect of Delany's career: his political thought. Though there is much information on, and knowledge about, Delany's nationalist ideas and activism as well as his political activities in post-Civil War and Reconstruction South Carolina, we know relatively little about his political ideas and the rationale undergirding the controversial and provocative political choices and decisions he made. I attempt to develop our understanding of Delany's political thought by foregrounding his early nineteenth-century involvement with promoting moral suasion. This was the springboard for much of the political ideas that he advocated in the postbellum period. In 1848 Delany identified two factors that determined and shaped his political decisions and choices. They represented the dynamics of his political thought: *conscience* and *reason.* Writing in an article in the *North Star,* Delany boldly proclaimed; "I care little for precedent, and therefore, discard the frivolous rules of formality . . . conforming always to principle, suggested by *conscience,* and guided by the light of *reason* [emphasis added]."[38] Here Delany was unambiguous in identifying the two ideological underpinnings of his philosophy of life. However, their political implications and ramifications would not become fully manifested until Delany became actively involved in politics in Reconstruction South Carolina. It was here that a crucial dimension of Delany's political thought emerged: political conservatism. Delany advocated political strategies and solutions, made choices and forged alliances dictated by his *conscience* and *reason.* Curiously, the dictates of Delany's *conscience* and *reason* oftentimes mirrored contradictory and counterintuitive ideas and choices. The political ideas and values Delany proposed and defended during Reconstruction in South Carolina (1870–1876) contradicted those he had earlier proffered and defended as a Black nationalist (1852–1863). It would seem that the reforms of the Civil War and Reconstruction profoundly impacted Delany's political ideas and thoughts in ways that proved detrimental to the image and reputation he had earlier cultivated as an avowed advocate and defender of the rights of Blacks. Fundamentally, this chapter is about authenticating the conservatism of Martin Delany's thought, a subject that seemed at odds with the historical reputation he had garnered. Delany's political thought, like his ideas about education, intersected both the pre-and post-Civil War epochs. Much of his political writings occurred in the 1850s. It was, however, during the Reconstruction that Delany became actively involved in politics and thus had the opportunity and context to formulate, and attempt to implement, his political ideas.

Delany's was indeed a magnificent life, as Du Bois rightly observed. With the possible exception of Frederick Douglass, and some would, with justification, contest this exception, no other nineteenth-century Black leader contributed and sacrificed as much for his race. Whatever Delany accomplished, it was rendered as labor of love in the service of "God and humanity" (the phrase with which he ended several of his correspondence). Regardless of whether or not he received compensation, and in most situations, he did not, Delany comported himself with grace and humility. From the time he left his parents in Chambersburg in 1831 through his early start in Pittsburgh to his collaboration with Douglass, down to his emigration and Civil War and Reconstruction endeavors, Delany blazed a trail of selfless service and sacrifices. In the process, he espoused certain ideas, made choices and decisions; and formed alliances that were controversial, provocative, perhaps even counterintuitive, prompting some to question his motivation. Yet, it would be difficult to deny Delany's immense contributions. This book is about probing and understanding the intellectual and philosophical reasoning infusing those decisions, choices, and alliances.

CHAPTER I

Religion

Integration and Black Nationalism

D ELANY BEGAN HIS ANTISLAVERY CAREER an advocate of moral
suasion. In fact, apart from the American Moral Reform Society
founded in 1835 and whose crusade for moral suasion effectively ended
in 1841, it was Delany, along with Frederick Douglass, through the medium of
the *North Star*, who would take the moral suasion crusade far deeper into Black
communities across the nation. In its push for Blacks to become much more
active and self-deterministic, moral suasion encouraged the pursuit of worldly
gains and acquisitions. This conflicted with the otherworldly and compensatory providential theology propagated by some of the early and leading Black
churches. As a moral suasion abolitionist, therefore, Delany had to engage the
subject of religion, for it was challenging to activate the human agency and
self-deterministic drives of Blacks if at the same time they were being infused
with otherworldly and compensatory theology. Delany therefore assumed this
challenge in the early phase of his antislavery and abolitionist activism. He
expended a considerable amount of time and effort on explaining and theorizing
religion as means of liberation. In fact, religion was a core element of the foundation of Delany's philosophy of the Black struggle. It was the legitimizing force
that gave his programs and strategies simultaneously a conservative and radical
complexion. This notwithstanding, religion is today the least associated with
Martin Delany. His nationalist, Pan-Africanist, and seemingly uncompromising
and militant antiestablishment ideas and idiosyncrasies effectively masked his
religious ideology. In consequence, therefore, there has prevailed a tendency to
discuss Delany's political and nationalist ideas in isolation from the religious
foundation upon which they developed.

Consumed by the search for a radical and instrumentalist history, some critics
ignored the dualistic and complex role religion played in Delany's thoughts. They

focused, and rather selectively, on his perceived "radical" nationalist ideas and programs. Yet, no understanding of the complexities and ambiguities of Delany's life and thought would be complete without acknowledging and engaging his attitude toward and use of religion. Religion played a central role in both the conservative (integrationist) and "radical" (nationalist) phases of his career. In essence, his religious thoughts embodied complex ethos, and were amenable to radical and conservative interpretations. At one point, he used religion as a "militant" and subversive means of encouraging Black/human agency and self-determination to infuse in Blacks a belief in their capacity and responsibility for change. The goal was to demonstrate Blacks' compatibility with American values and establish a strong case for integration (conservative end). At other times, under a different set of circumstances, Delany draped religion in nationalist robes. It became the means of justifying and advancing his nationalist ideology of emigration. The objective this time was to create an independent Black nationality abroad (a radical end). In other words, Delany invoked religion in the two phases of his life (integration and emigration). First, he used religion to push for integration in America. When this seemed to fail, he then redefined the same religion to bolster his advocacy of emigration and quest for an independent Black nationality. This chapter is about how religion undergirded both countervailing ideologies of integration and separatism. Delany's use of religion to argue simultaneously for integration and separatism demands clarity and deeper understanding. In the integrationist phase, Delany vigorously challenged what he characterized as the misuse and abuse of religion by some of the leading Black churches to stymie Black efforts. He argued instead that religion be used as a means for Black liberation. The rationale he defended anticipated much of what modern scholars associate with liberation theology. He portrayed Christianity as a religion concerned with much more than spiritual salvation. It was, he would insist and attempt to justify, also about securing the secular and material well-being of humanity.

Based on his upbringing, Delany seemed destined for a career in the church. In spite of the experience of slavery (perhaps because of it) his maternal grandparents remained devout Christians. His mother Pati, was raised on Christian values, becoming "a most exemplary Christian."[1] In turn, she infused in her offspring a strong sense of moral values. In early youth Delany espoused total abstinence, and throughout his life, avoided tobacco and liquor.[2] His religious horizon broadened in the 1830s in Pittsburgh when he joined the African Methodist Episcopal Church and the Pittsburgh Bible Society. In fact, one can date the beginning of Delany's antislavery career to July of 1831 when he left his parents in Chambersburg and headed for Pittsburgh.[3] Though only nineteen, the move reflected his developing consciousness since Pittsburgh was then a major hub of antislavery activism in Pennsylvania.[4] He became involved in plans to improve the material and moral conditions of Blacks. In 1834, he was appointed Secretary of the Temperance Society of the People of Color of Pittsburgh and subsequently helped found the Pittsburgh Young Men's Literary and Moral Reform Society.[5] Through public lectures and medium of the *Pittsburgh Mystery*, Delany condemned slavery, popularized moral suasion, and advanced the cause of reform in Pennsylvania.[6] To fully understand the role of religion in Delany's life and thought, it is necessary to examine how religion shaped, fractured, and problematized early nineteenth-century Black abolitionism—a movement of which Delany was both founding and contributing member. While leading Black abolitionists and institutions (church, newspapers, and self-help and fraternal societies) seemed to agree on goals, they disagreed sharply on strategy.

The reformist atmosphere of Jacksonian America, especially the Second Great Awakening, seemed to thrust upon the church (religion) a major role in helping to transform society for the good of everyone. There was a pervasive optimism about, and belief in, human agency—that is, the human capacity and obligation to help change society for the good of everyone. This was the central message of the evangelical reform movements of the time.[7] Black abolitionists embraced and welcomed this challenge. It infused in Blacks a sense of responsibility and a desire to become active agents of change. In its formative years, the Black church also welcomed this challenge. Yet, despite the reformist impulse within the Black church, controversies surfaced over strategies, and the broader goals of the Black abolitionist movement. This chapter addresses not only the controversial and problematic responses of the Black church to antislavery, but also the countervailing religious ideas Martin Delany developed in order to configure and promote his twin ideologies of integration and separatism (emigration). It is an analysis and exposition of how Delany used religion to promote American middle-class values and steer the Black struggle along the path of reconciliation with mainstream society, and when this failed, he reconfigured it to justify his push for an independent Black nationality. As a prelude, it is necessary to examine the broader context of the crisis religion provoked within the early Black abolitionist movement—a cause Delany would spearhead.

The Black Church and Antislavery

In August of 1848, two prominent Black abolitionists, William Wells Brown of Kentucky and Charles Lenox Remond of Massachusetts, were invited to address a gathering of the Black community in Philadelphia. The city had just hosted the annual meeting of the Eastern Pennsylvania Anti-Slavery Society, which generated so much interest in, and enthusiasm for, antislavery. Anticipating a large turnout, a committee was charged with the task of applying to some of the leading Black churches for permission to use their halls for this important antislavery gathering. Surprisingly, all the requests were rejected. As a last resort, the abolitionists turned to the "Philadelphia Institute" on Lombard Street described as "a very small place."[8] Though the churches refused the use of their facilities, prominent Black preachers and pastors attended the meeting. Among them were Rev. Daniel Scott of the Baptist church and Rev. Stephen H. Gloucester of the Second Colored Presbyterian Church. The latter had in fact established quite "a distinguished" reputation "for his zealous opposition to antislavery."[9] It was not surprising, therefore, that the attitude of the Black church towards antislavery featured prominently in the deliberations. In their speeches, Brown and Remond strongly condemned the churches and openly challenged Revs. Scott and Gloucester to explain the justification for their churches' actions. For unspecified reasons, both pastors refused to offer any explanations, but instead proposed to debate Brown and Remond on the subject of the relationship of the Black church to antislavery at a later date. They promised that during that debate they would prove that, in the words of Reverend Gloucester, "there is not a colored 'pro-slavery' church in Philadelphia."[10] Accepting the challenge, Remond then asked if they would make their churches available for the debate. Both pastors declined.[11]

Reverend Gloucester was no stranger to controversy. In January of 1848, a Scottish correspondent for the *Liberator* had published a letter about Gloucester's visit to Britain and his addresses to both the British and Foreign Anti-slavery Society and the Free Church of Scotland. Among abolitionists, the latter had the unsavory reputation of being proslavery. Gloucester reportedly distanced himself from the abolitionist movement which he characterized as "violent, impolitic and detrimental to antislavery."[12] Enraged, Black abolitionists back home were unsparing. Frederick Douglass denounced Gloucester as "one of the vilest traitors of his race."[13] Martin Delany was more vicious: "that miserable person, Stephen H. Gloucester, has proved himself a traitor worthy of the deepest and most lasting execration. Let the burning indignation of a misrepresented and insulted people lash him naked through the world."[14] Delany then called for the summoning of a meeting "in every place by the friends of the slave, irrespective of color, for the exposure of the deed of this clerical assassin."[15]

These denunciations notwithstanding, Reverend Gloucester had not always been antagonistic to antislavery. He was born a slave in 1802 in Tennessee. At fourteen, his father purchased his freedom, and subsequently the family relocated to Philadelphia, Pennsylvania, where Gloucester immersed himself in community and antislavery activism, specifically the Underground Railroad. He would also contribute to advancing literacy.[16] Furthermore, he was one of eight Blacks including James W. C. Pennington and Samuel E. Cornish, who founded the American and Foreign Anti-Slavery Society in May of 1840.[17] But, Gloucester changed when his church, the Second Colored Presbyterian, was destroyed during the August 1842 Moyamensing riot when anti-abolitionist mobs attacked and destroyed institutions and symbols of Black progress.[18] A contemporary portrayed this riot as "a prime example of Whites denouncing Blacks for their degradation while simultaneously destroying those institutions which sought to eradicate that degradation."[19] It should be noted that the Second Colored Presbyterian was a brick building that had cost the congregation nearly ten thousand dollars; a debt that took eighteen years to repay.[20] Its destruction could explain why subsequently Reverend Gloucester wisely avoided public endorsement of antislavery. The episode compelled rethinking of his antislavery activism. He became "cautious, defensive and accommodating," and while soliciting funds to rebuild the church, publicly disavowed abolitionism.[21]

This "cautious and accommodating" disposition was not uniquely Gloucesterian. In a related development in June of 1850, a biracial meeting of Philadelphia citizens was summoned at a Black church. The lower part of the building was reserved exclusively for Whites who had objected to an integrated seating.[22] Rev. Samuel R. Ward, a leading Black abolitionist, consented to the arrangement and agreed to address the gathering. His sanctioning of the reservation of a "Whites only" pew in a Black church to appease the racist sensibilities of Whites angered fellow abolitionists. Frederick Douglass denounced Ward's action as "the most cowardly, contemptible and servile specimen of self-degradation."[23]

The aforementioned episodes exemplified the crisis and contradictions that informed the responses of some of the early Black churches to antislavery. By 1848, the absence of a coherent Black church response to abolitionism had become an established and troubling reality. Reporting on the Philadelphia incident to Frederick Douglass and Martin Delany, coeditors of the *North Star*, one "W. W." wrote:

> The battle now having begun, it ought to be continued on until its termination, until the church shall be able to vindicate the purity of her motives in regard to her opposition with the Anti-slavery movement, her freedom from the venom of pro-slavery and put accusers forever to rest, or failing to do this,

her accusers may be able to arrest her withering influence, and say to her. Hitherto hast thou domineered over the hearts and consciences of men, but no further-here let thy proud waves be stayed, so that we may see her, with all her lofty pretensions, recoil in obedience to the high behest of truth[24]

The battle line appeared drawn: the Black church versus antislavery. It is uncertain, however, if the debate proposed by Revs. Scott and Gloucester happened. The one certainty was that the Black church did not enthusiastically embrace antislavery. As a Philadelphian and noted Black abolitionist Geo W. Goines lamented, "Thousands of Blacks flock to the churches to hear anything but antislavery. . . . The majority of *the churches are so connected with slaveholding* [emphasis added] that they have forgotten that this is a land of slaves."[25]

Though the Black church originated in protest against the segregationist policies of mainstream White churches, it did not develop a coherent and unified policy vis-à-vis the pervasive racism of mainstream society. Instead of standing solidly in support of antislavery, several Black churches seemed stymied by an otherworldly and compensatory theology, as well as other legal, socioeconomic, cultural, and political constraints.[26] Consequently, these churches refused to host abolitionist lectures and events resulting in conflicts with the values and ideologies of the mainstream Black abolitionist movement. At its core, this conflict revolved around the meaning and efficacy of moral suasion as reform ideology. While everyone seemed to agree on the need for moral reform, not everyone endorsed the strategies embedded in moral suasion.

The Moral Suasion Challenge

The ambivalence of the early Black churches to antislavery was most evident in their response to moral suasion. Moral suasion embodied the universalistic vision and aspirations of the early nineteenth-century Black abolitionists. It reflected their collective decision to give environmental and situational causalities precedence over race and racism. Essentially, Black abolitionists attributed the challenges Black confronted to environmental (condition) factor. They were therefore optimistic that the problems could be remedied by moral reforms. A deep and abiding faith in the redemptive and progressive character of American political culture bolstered their optimism, as reflected in this declaration by delegates at the 1832 Second National Negro Convention in Philadelphia:

We yet anticipate in the moral strength of this nation, a final redemption from those evils that have been illegitimately entailed on us as a people.

We yet expect by due exertions on our part . . . to acquire a moral and
intellectual strength . . . that would unshaft the calumnious darts of our
adversaries, and present to the world a general character, that they will feel
bound to respect and admire.[27]

In her recent publication *Force and Freedom*, Kellie Carter Jackson contends
that Black abolitionists in the early 1830s confronted a choice between a "se-
ditious and revolutionary" call for resistance to antislavery espoused in David
Walker's *Appeal* (1829) and William Lloyd Garrison's ideology of moral suasion,
which emerged with the founding of his paper the *Liberator* and subsequently
the New England Anti-slavery Society and the American Anti-slavery Society.[28]
Carter Jackson argues that Black leaders confronted a choice between violence
and a moral suasion approach that endorsed "compromise" and cooperation
with White abolitionists (like Garrison) who had jettisoned their earlier support of colonization for "immediacy" abolition.[29] Blacks chose to embrace moral
suasion and reposed faith in the redemptive capacity of the "moral strength of
the nation." In his study, Eddie Glaude Jr. describes the appeal of moral suasion as essentially about the "politics of respectability" which stressed reform of
"individual behavior and attitudes both as a goal in itself and as a strategy for
reform of the entire system of American race relations."[30] Blacks were encouraged to "embrace temperance, to work hard, and in short, to assume a general
sense of self-regulation and self-improvement along moral, educational and economic lines."[31] Moral suasion, they believed, would pave the way to elevation, "to
a proper rank and standing among men."[32]

The evolution of moral suasion can be traced to a combination of circumstances. First, between 1831 and 1835, Blacks organized five Negro National
Conventions to develop consensus on antislavery strategies. Meeting in Pennsylvania and New York, delegates discussed the importance of moral reform,
self-improvement, temperance, and the pursuit of knowledge.[33] Second, in December of 1833 a group of White abolitionists and four Blacks met in Philadelphia to launch the American Anti-Slavery Society. They pledged to seek reform
utilizing moral suasion.[34] Third, delegates at the 1835 Negro National Convention in Philadelphia launched the American Moral Reform Society (AMRS)
and formally adopted moral suasion as reform strategy.[35] Reflecting the values of
its founding leader William Whipper, the AMRS adhered to the belief that "we
are all made in the image of God, and are endowed with those attributes which
the Deity has given to man."[36] Consequently, as Glaude explains, Whipper and
his colleagues were willing to bury "in the bosom of Christian benevolence all

those natural distinctions (and) complexional variations that have hitherto marked the history, character and operations of men; and now boldly plea for the Christian and moral elevation of the human race."[37]

Moral suasion advocates therefore believed that improvements in the moral and material conditions of Blacks would disprove the proslavery contention that Blacks were inherently inferior, lazy, unintelligent, and morally decadent. Such improvements, they hoped, would appeal favorably to the moral conscience of Whites. The faith Blacks reposed in moral suasion also derived from verbal promises and reassurances by prominent White abolitionists. In August of 1837, the Moral Reform Society of Philadelphia hosted a "Moral Reform Convention" attended by delegates of "Colored Citizens" from "various states, cities and towns" across the nation "to device the best method and to procure and promote the best means, for the moral, social, and political elevation of Colored Americans."[38] A "distinguished" Quaker lady, also described as "a tried philanthropist" addressed the gathering on "moral and intellectual culture," and implored the delegates to "Make yourselves a character of EMINENCE in moral, intellectual, and social virtues, and we [i.e., Whites] shall lose sight of your color."[39] The promise of this Quaker lady notwithstanding, moral suasion was not a reactive ideology that Black abolitionists developed in order to satisfy the whims of some White paternalists. Regardless of how one interprets the "moral," Manisha Sinha rightly notes that moral suasion embodied resistance. "Moral reform and racial uplift were," she suggests, "constitutive of rather than an alternative to the politics of resistance."[40] Blacks did not simply embrace "bourgeois values" embedded in moral suasion just to appease Whites, or "prove Black worthiness in White eyes." Moral suasion entailed what Sinha describes as "complementary strategies to challenge slavery and the community-wide problem of racism and poverty."[41]

Moral suasion therefore embodied the goal of abolitionism, and was part of a much broader reform efforts. Black abolitionists organized conventions and created institutions (churches, newspapers, and self-help and mutual aid societies). These institutions and structures were, according to John Ernest, directed at challenging attempts by the dominant society to impose upon Blacks a "collective identity" of negation and negativity. Resisting this attempt, Blacks sought to wrest control of defining themselves from "within" their community based on their "shared cultural practices, community affiliations, and the joys and responsibilities of family, work, and self-governance."[42] Moral suasion was therefore about a group taking charge of defining itself and its values. This was the driving force that propelled the Black abolitionist movement. Furthermore, moral suasion, as Carter Jackson stresses, assured Blacks that an appeal to the nation's moral conscience would ultimately obliterate the unmitigated violence and dehumanization they experienced. Unfortunately, this assurance was shattered, Carter Jackson suggests, by the surge of violence and the fear it unleashed, exemplified by the insurrection of Nat Turner, the violent rhetoric of David Walker's *Appeal*, and the murder of White abolitionist Elijah P. Lovejoy.[43] While Carter Jackson is correct in highlighting the violence that defined the context of moral suasion, this should not mitigate the fact that Black abolitionists who embraced moral suasion in the early 1830s truly believed in the ideology, and never seriously considered violence as a viable option.

Fundamentally, moral suasion was an inward-looking ideology which encouraged Blacks to believe in themselves. In response, Blacks evinced confidence that they too possessed both the capacity and wherewithal for change. Moral suasion also represented Blacks' subscription and commitment to broader nationwide reform initiatives and movements. The immediate challenge was how to spread the tenets of moral suasion across Black communities, and all major institutions and organizations (churches; self-help, fraternal, and mutual aid societies; newspapers; and abolitionists) embraced this challenge. However, almost from the start, there emerged disagreement over implementation, and it was Martin Robison Delany who would undertake the task of spreading moral suasion and in the process unearthed what could be termed, in the words of Henry Mitchell, the "Long-Hidden" reality of the early Black church: ambivalence to antislavery. In 1847 Delany had the opportunity to expand the scope of his activism nationwide when Frederick Douglass embarked upon an independent Black abolitionist course, and traveled to Pittsburgh to solicit his assistance.[44] Both shared a passionate commitment to antislavery and understood the strategic importance of an independent Black abolitionist path. When Douglass launched his paper the *North Star* in Rochester, New York, in 1847, Delany joined him as coeditor and lecturer. This inaugurated the activist phase of his moral suasion career. It was during this period that he confronted the "Long-Hidden" reality.[45] From 1847 to 1849, as coeditor and roving lecturer for Frederick Douglass's paper, the *North Star*, Delany embarked on tours of Black communities in the Midwest and Northeast to deliver antislavery lectures and propagate moral suasion.[46]

Delany had not anticipated any hostile reactions to his lectures. Quite the contrary, he expected favorable receptions from Black churches since he thought he would essentially be "preaching to the converted." He and Douglass had hoped that embarking on an independent Black abolitionist path would energize the Black community. They had also expected the church to assume leadership role in antislavery and help educate Blacks on the values of industry, self-help, economy, and character reform. In fact, the preponderance of those whom historian Benjamin Quarles characterized as "Clergymen-Abolitionists" in the leadership of the abolitionist movement made church endorsement of moral suasion seemed like a foregone conclusion.[47] Also, the fact that the independent Black church had risen out of "the desire by the Negro to share more fully in the shaping of his own destiny" made such expectation even more realistic.[48]

Engaging "Illiberal" and Liberal Churches

Delany began his antislavery and moral suasion lectures in Pennsylvania by visiting several Black churches in Pittsburgh, Philadelphia, and Allegheny. It should not surprise anyone that he began in Pennsylvania, since it was in Philadelphia that Black churches had refused the use of their facilities for antislavery meetings. There was an estimated ninety-six Black churches in Pittsburgh and Allegheny suburbs. Yet, reflective of the Philadelphia episode, Delany reported that it was difficult to organize antislavery lectures because the "antislavery tide" was equally at "low tide."[49] He observed that Blacks in these cities seemed more interested in religious revivalist gatherings. In several Black churches in Pittsburgh, Delany encountered those he characterized as "ignorant" and "gullible" pastors who refused the use of their facilities and encouraged their congregations instead to seek heavenly rewards through religious revivalism.[50] His arrival in Pittsburgh coincided with a great revivalist worship organized by one Rev. Thomas Lawrence. Delany denounced this pursuit of "religious orthodoxy" and neglect of temporal challenges and problems. He accused these religious leaders of forgetting that "the well-being of man, while upon earth, is to God of as much importance as his welfare in heaven."[51]

Other Black churches opposed to moral suasion included the African Methodist Episcopal Church, and the St. Mary Street Colored Presbyterian Church in Pittsburgh, the Wesley Church in Allegheny, the Baptist Church, and the Colored Presbyterian Church in Philadelphia. These "illiberal" churches, as Delany characterized them, denied him the use of their facilities.[52] However, there were other churches led by those Delany described as "liberal" pastors who would gladly have made their facilities available but for the opposition of their "elders and trustees." One such was Rev. B. F. Templeton, pastor of the Colored Presbyterian Church in Philadelphia. Delany confirmed that both pastor and congregation embraced antislavery and seemed eager for his lectures. However, the "so-called elders and trustees" disagreed.[53] He noted, with dismay, that congregants were being brainwashed into believing in, and relying on, divine providence.

In Lancaster city and Harrisburg Delany observed that otherworldly theology was so entrenched that some Blacks declared that they would rather remain enslaved than engage in any activities, movements or causes that could jeopardize their prospect for heaven. In Harrisburg, with a population of between seven and eight hundred, only an average of fifty attended antislavery meetings and several arrived very late. This was in sharp contrast to attendance at religious revivalist gatherings.[54] Delany had a mixed reception in Lancaster city. The clergies of the leading Black churches gladly opened their doors and attended the meetings. However, the youth and entire congregation displayed "indifference" and "restlessness" and seemed uninterested in antislavery. He ascribed this to "the grievous doctrine" instilled into Black preachers by "their pro-slavery and slaveholding oppressors," designed to maintain Blacks in "servility and subjection."[55] According to this doctrine, God supposedly designated Blacks his earthly "suffering servants" in order for them to inherit his heavenly kingdom. Adherents, therefore, "readily declined" when asked to host antislavery meetings, convinced that antislavery lectures compromised the peoples' preparedness for heavenly inheritance.[56]

Some churches boldly and openly embraced antislavery. One such was the Shiloh Church in Philadelphia, which made available its facility. Delany, however, lamented that in some of the churches in Philadelphia, congregants came late and would often display disruptive behaviors such as "running in and out."[57] Similarly, in York County, the Reverend John T. Moore opened his church doors. There were also other "liberal" pastors in Pennsylvania who, Delany believed, would willingly and happily have endorsed antislavery, but for the stiff opposition of "the leading Christians of their churches." Among such pastors were Rev. M. M. Clark of the African Methodist Episcopal Church in Pittsburgh and Reverend Stevens of the Wesley Church in Allegheny. The elders of their churches objected to their antislavery sympathies and accused both pastors of "concerning themselves too much *with the things of the world* [emphasis in original]."[58] They were told to desist or "risk losing their usefulness as ministers of the gospel." The "elders" believed that the "*things of this world*," which the pastors emphasized in their worship could not "be reached by *preaching* but by *lecturing* [emphasis in original]."[59] They were informed that their primary duty was to *preach* and not *lecture*. *Lecture*, in the opinion of the "elders" encouraged worldly material pursuits.

Delany's visit to Pennsylvania was not entirely a failure. In West Chester, for example, proslavery influence was so entrenched that the only Colored church in town was located some distance beyond the city limit.[60] Nonetheless, the Colored residents yearned for Delany's lectures and hosted several meetings and lectures in private homes. He attributed the success of these house meetings to the influence of longtime resident and abolitionist A. D. Shadd.[61] Delany also held successful antislavery meetings in private homes in other locations including Carlisle, Harrisburg, Lancaster, Reading, York, and Lewiston. He cherished the opportunity "to arouse our people . . . to a greater sense of their own condition in this country, and the means necessary to change that condition."[62] In Allegheny County, Delany appealed to Rev. A. R. Green, a pastor and editor of one of the leading religious papers in the county the *Church Herald*, "to be more useful" by paying equal attention to "the temporal welfare of our people."[63] He urged the pastor/editor to focus "upon our moral elevation and temporal reformation—upon our education, morals, manners and progress of our people in Pittsburgh and Allegheny."[64] Delany then described Christianity as a religion of morality and conscious *reflection*. *Reflection* would lead Christians to greater knowledge and understanding of the essence and mission of Christianity. He believed that humans must first be sensitive to wrongs (*reflection*) before they can have a proper conception of rights. This mandated improving the lives and conditions of less fortunate people. Every step taken toward "morality and improvement" constituted, in Delany's words, "a step gained toward Christianity, and there is no work more rightfully and legitimately that of the minister of the gospel than the elevation of man and woman temporally as well as spiritually."[65]

Delany encountered mixed reactions in Ohio. In Cleveland, there were two dominant Black churches: the Methodist and the Baptist. The Methodist, the larger and comprised of prominent members of the community was an affiliate of Old Mother Bethel. It was not fully independent. Delany found the church plagued by internal crisis. He attributed much of the crisis to the "ignorance" and "intolerance" of the leadership and called for the appointment of "a good and efficient pastor." He described the current pastor as an intolerant "illiberal person," who opposed "every manner of moral improvement."[66] Delany denounced the Methodist Conference for placing such individuals in charge of Black congregations and accused the Conference of deliberately promoting "ignorance and degradation" among Blacks.[67]

Writing from Hanover, Ohio, Delany reported that he was refused the Friends (Quakers) Meeting House in Columbiana and thus had to deliver lectures in the private home of "our friend, Lot Holmes, whose doors were flown open" with over a hundred in attendance.[68] Delany wondered how these "misnamed Friends would reconcile themselves to their cause?"[69] Their action contradicted the spirit of Christianity which, Delany insisted, was inconceivable "where there is no humanity."[70] He was also denied access to the "Methodist and Disciples' Churches." Leaders of the respective churches accused Delany of "infidelity." As he noted, "It was enough for them to know that I was a moral suasion abolitionist to ensure opposition."[71] Delany however observed a disconnection between church leadership and congregation. The majority of the people "desired to hear antislavery lecture and were disappointed when the churches shut their doors."[72] Most of the disappointed were "Presbyterians" who subsequently made their private homes available for antislavery meetings. There was, however, the exception of one Mr. Sloan, "a staunch friend of the slave who made his Presbyterian Church available."[73]

Delany had a mixed reception in Cincinnati. He held several meetings here including at the Harrison Street Church, the Sixth Street Methodist Church, the Union Baptist Church, and Baker Street Church. There were about five to six Black churches in Cincinnati, some of independent denomination, others affiliated with "the White church government."[74] The Baker Street Baptist Church had its own pastor who was Black and the congregation "possessing full ownership in the property."[75] The Sixth Street Methodist Church, on the other hand, had a White pastor, and the church, according to Delany, "belongs to the White Methodist conference."[76] Most of the Black churches in Cincinnati responded favorably to antislavery. There was an incident at the Fifth Street Congregational Church (formerly Reverend Blanchard's). Being of "liberal" persuasion, the pastor, Reverend Boyinston, readily made the church available for Delany's lecture. Anxious listeners of both races (men and women) filled the building to capacity. In spite of a slight illness, Delany delivered a powerful lecture in which he exposed the evils of slavery and urged Blacks to strive for self-elevation through moral suasion.[77] Due to the enthusiasm of the audience, Delany sought and got approval from the pastor for two more lectures. However, the trustees of the church, who Delany described as "THE RULERS OF THE PEOPLE," [emphasis in original] objected. They were dissatisfied with the themes of his earlier lectures which they characterized as "too liberal."[78] Apparently, the Fifth Street Congregation Church was White-controlled. Delany believed that the trustees objected to the moral suasion and antislavery contents of his lectures, especially since he encouraged Blacks to become active agents of their own salvation. He concluded therefore that; "So long as we are conservative . . . we may get their churches, but a declaration of truth through the channel of liberal sentiments, is certain to meet with religious execration."[79]

Delany spent one week in Chillicothe, Ohio, and delivered lectures on the subject of "moral elevation" at the African Methodist Episcopal Church and at the "Union Township Settlement" nine miles out of town. He also lectured to a large gathering of women at the Colored Baptist Church, as well as at a Methodist Church, two and half miles out of town, and at the town of Frankfurt, about twelve miles east of Chillicothe.[80] He also held several meetings in private homes.[81] However, proslavery influences provoked hostilities in Columbus, New Lisbon, and Springfield. In Dayton, despite a pervasive proslavery atmosphere, Delany succeeded in organizing several meetings. He described Dayton as "a very pro-slavery community," rampant with mob spirit. Notwithstanding, his meetings attracted "a general audience."[82] To illustrate the "mob spirit," Delany described what happened to one Dr. Adams Jewett, an abolitionist who had boldly displayed notices of the meetings in the front porch of his house. Dr. Jewett "was four or five times mobbed . . . having his windows broken to atoms."[83] Delany also had good audience "with the ladies and gentlemen" at a small church. Due to "the anxiety of the people" for more lectures, and the building being small, Delany secured permission to use the city hall for three more meetings. An estimated 1,100 people attended these meetings. Subsequently, he lectured to the Colored congregation at the True Wesleyan Church, under the pastorate of one C. Clemence described as "a nice gentleman, Oberlin graduate."[84] Delany left Dayton on Saturday, 10th of June 1848, and arrived in Springfield, Ohio, to discover that "people and clergy were rather too pro-slavery to obtain a church."[85] Since no church would host his meetings, Delany applied to the sheriff for permission to use the courthouse. It was "readily granted." However, "the court being in session, it could not be used."[86] He extended his stay in Springfield hoping for a speedy adjournment of the court. After four days of waiting without adjournment, Delany left in frustration. And then the court promptly adjourned shortly after his departure![87]

Delany encountered slavish characteristics and the absence of "zeal for the higher incentive of life" among Blacks in Wilmington, Delaware. He attributed this to the fact that the leading Black churches: the AME, the Zion AME, the Union AME, and the Zion Methodist were all White controlled.[88] Nonetheless, there are indications that Delany succeeded in organizing several meetings. He praised two "liberal" pastors—Rev. Abram Cole of the Wesley Church and Reverend Smith of the Bethel Church—for "the success" of his mission in Wilmington.[89] The meetings in Reverend Cole's church were well attended, with many unable to gain entry. In Detroit, Michigan, Delany had access to the Baptist, Presbyterian, and Episcopal churches. However, the Methodist, the largest of the Colored churches, vehemently opposed antislavery and shut its doors. According to Delany, the pastor was against "every manner of moral improvement."[90] In New York, Delany seemed to have encountered overwhelmingly "liberal" churches and leadership, since he reported no opposition to his lectures, which were well attended.

Delany's Materialist and This-Worldly Theology

Generally, Delany's reports suggested the dominance of "illiberal" churches whose growing influence alarmed antislavery activists. Undoubtedly, this reality shocked and disappointed him. Nothing had prepared him for such counterintuitive experience. Why would a Black church oppose antislavery? The Reverend Stephen Gloucester himself suggested an answer when he claimed that in spite of his and other churches' refusal to host antislavery lectures, "there is not a colored 'pro-slavery' church in Philadelphia."[91] As indicated above, Reverend Gloucester helped establish the American and Foreign Anti-Slavery Society. Nevertheless, he and the "illiberal" churches he represented had distinct notions of the role of the church in antislavery. While they were not opposed to antislavery per se, they had misgivings about the demands and mandates of moral suasion. Their conception of antislavery and the role of the church derived from two interrelated factors and circumstances: first, otherworldliness and scriptural injunctions, and second, their fragile and compromised independence.

A good number of antebellum Black churches preached otherworldly and compensatory theology which confined the churches' function to helping their congregants psychologically endure temporal injustice in preparation for heavenly inheritance.[92] "Illiberal" churches had misgivings about moral suasion and its seeming disruption of otherworldly ethos. Specifically, they opposed moral suasion for the following reasons. First, in its bid for the moral regeneration of Blacks (which the churches endorsed), moral suasion also encouraged the drive for material wealth which, to some of the churches, jeopardized Blacks' chances of realizing the divine promise.[93] Second, moral suasion implied doubts in God's promise. These churches preached that God had sanctioned the injustices Blacks experienced in order to better prepare them for His heavenly kingdom. Therefore, instead of direct action aimed at changing their condition, Blacks were expected to prioritize religious revivalism which supposedly would bolster their capacity to psychologically and physically endure temporal injustices. Delany highlighted three dominant religious injunctions that undergirded the revivalist ethos. The first was, "First seek ye the kingdom of Heaven and its righteousness, and ALL other things shall be added [emphasis in original]."[94] He lamented that many Black church leaders wrongfully appropriated this injunction, convinced that it offered solutions to all the challenges Blacks confronted. Delany argued instead that the injunction was meant solely for the disciples, those whom Jesus Christ had called to propagate the gospel. It was necessary to reassure them of a living. The second, "Stand till and see the salvation of God," was also, Delany contended, misconstrued as a command to wait for, and anticipate, God's intervention. The third, "Give us this day our daily bread," taught reliance upon God, through prayers, for daily sustenance.[95] Delany denounced reliance on this particular injunction as "a spiritual blunder."[96] Like the others, this was meant for the disciples who "were taught to daily ask to be fed with the bread of heaven upon which to feast their soul, to fit and prepare them," for preaching the gospel.[97] He ascribed all three injunctions to the false religious dogmas slaveholders and their sympathizers infused in ignorant and gullible Black preachers. Delany opted instead for what John Ernest describes as "a motivated Black approach to religion." He wanted Blacks to "make your religion subserve your interest, as your oppressors do theirs. . . . They use their scriptures to make you submit, by preaching to you the texts of 'obedience to your masters' and 'standing still to see the salvation.'"[98] He advocated a different understanding of, and orientation to, the Bible "so as to make it of interest to us."[99]

Delany denounced providential determinism as "a great mistake" resulting from "a misconception of the character and ways of the Deity."[100] The attainment of meaningful freedom and elevation was, therefore, contingent upon an informed knowledge of God. Otherwise, Blacks would forever confine themselves to inaction and poverty. While acknowledging the necessity of religion, Delany lamented the fact that being "susceptible" to a proslavery religion had demonstrably stymied Black initiatives. His critique of Black religious disposition is worth quoting at length:

> The colored races are highly susceptible to religion; it is a constituent principle of their nature. . . . But unfortunately for them, they carry it too far. They usually stand still—hope in God, and really expect him to do that for them, which it is necessary they should do for themselves, . . . We must know God, that is understand his nature and purposes, in order to serve him; and to serve him well, is but to know him rightly. To depend for assistance upon God, is a duty and right; but to know when, how and what manner to obtain it, is the key to this great bulwark of strength, and depository of aid.[101]

He assumed the task of revealing the "nature and purposes," the hidden and submerged side of God—the side that held the key to Black elevation *in this world*.

Delany theorized that contrary to the injunctions and divine promises, the challenges Blacks confronted could not be remedied by heavenly intercession. In fact, he was confident that God Himself had not mandated divine solution to human problems. Rather, God meant for humans to seek temporal and earthly solutions, and He had provided the wherewithal. He created the earth and its fullness "for high and mighty purposes—the special benefit of man." To truly enjoy the benefits of God's providence, therefore, humans had to *appropriate* and *possess* the resources. Such accumulation would also enable them accomplish God's injunction to help the less fortunate.[102] Delany reasoned therefore that it was only through the *appropriation* and *possession* of material wealth would humans execute God's command to assist the poor and needy. Instead of heavenly inheritance, therefore, God had given humans an earthly mission. Delany used the divine precepts therefore to underscore the compatibility of religion and materialism. God intended for humans to acquire mastery "over the earth, *to possess its' productivity* and *enjoy them* [emphasis added]."[103] Given this mandate, Christianity was inconceivable, Delany concluded, absent material possession and compassion for the less fortunate.[104]

In the alternate theology Delany preached, God functioned by *means* not *miracles* and had given humanity all the necessary *means*. Unfortunately, false religious teachings had misled Blacks into seeking divine solutions.[105] Delany contended that there had never been a "grosser and more palpable absurdity." He urged Blacks to focus instead on pursuing occupations that would improve their conditions here on earth. Such preoccupation was fundamental because "Prayers and praises only fill one's soul with emotions, but can never fill his mouth with bread, nor his pocket with money."[106] Delany identified three distinct laws through which, according to him, God ruled the destinies of humans: *spiritual*, *moral*, and *physical*. These laws were "as invariable as God Himself, and without a strict conformity to one or the other nothing can be affected."[107] A physical or temporal goal cannot be achieved utilizing spiritual means and vice versa. Consequently, being a spiritual means, and in conformity with spiritual law, prayer could only be used to achieve spiritual not physical or temporal goals. Delany cited as indisputable evidence that prayers were not meant for "temporal and physical ends," the contrast between the wretched and impoverished conditions of *prayerful* Blacks, and the wealth and affluence of the wicked, sadistic, and *prayer-less* slaveholders.[108] Delany drew attention to a fundamental contradiction; "how can you reconcile yourselves to these facts—facts, which challenge, and defy contradiction, that the slave who prays, has not only got nothing, but dare not lay claim to his own person-to the affections of his own wife and children; while the wicked master, the infidel wretch, who neither prays, nor believes in the existence of God, possesses power, almost unlimited, means of all kinds, lands, money and wealth in abundance, besides owning the very bodies and souls, as it were, of the people who depend upon prayer as a means?"[109]

Instead of praying or "standing still to see the salvation of God," Delany proposed as alternative; "NOW is the accepted time, TODAY is the Day of salvation [emphasis in original]." God intended salvation *here* and *now*, and not *hereafter*.[110] Based on his ideas, it could be inferred that Delany anticipated modern day liberation theology, which John Ernest depicts as "the theological core of nineteenth-century African-American Christianity" exemplified by James W. C. Pennington who "linked intellectual life with question of biblical interpretation and then placing both within the context of governance, both human and divine"[111] Furthermore, liberation theology "calls for attention to social order and disorder in determining the proper reading and application of the Bible. God is identified with the condition of the oppressed and specifically with the historical expression of oppression and the struggle for liberation."[112]

It should be acknowledged however that Delany's experiences as described in his travel reports cast doubt about the "theological core" of liberation theology in the nineteenth-century Black church. Not every Black church embraced and endorsed "liberation theology." If there was a "theological core" at all in the nineteenth century, it would be "Providential determinism."[113] And yet, even this viewpoint is questionable. Eric Lincoln and Lawrence Mamiya complicate any attempt at superimposing a single "ideological core." In their study of the Black church they criticized the "otherworldly-this-worldly" binary, or what they termed "single nondialectical typology" that had dominated the historiography and argued for a dialectical and "Sociological perspective" that highlights the conflicting viewpoints that permeated the churches. They believed that this "dialectical model" of analysis would "lead to a more dynamic view of the Black churches along a continuum of ideological tension, struggles and change."[114] They identified four major ideological tensions reflective of conflicting theological viewpoints such as priestly vs. prophetic (worship and spiritual life versus political and secular concerns); otherworldly vs. this-worldly (concerns with heaven and eternal life versus involvement in the affairs of the world); universalism vs. particularism (universalism of the Christian message versus particularism of the larger society); and resistance vs. accommodation (willingness to pursue change versus engaging society as cultural broker and "mediating institution").[115]

These ideological viewpoints and conflicts notwithstanding, from the perspective of Martin Delany, the dominant tradition he encountered and had to counteract was the otherworldly and providential. There were, however, other factors besides providential determinism that shaped the contexts within which the several Black churches he encountered functioned which also undermined effective support for antislavery. At best, some of these churches had fragile independence. They remained under the control of the White churches against which they had rebelled.[116] Even where Blacks seemed in control of their churches, Whites continued to exert influence in pastoral appointments. Many therefore found the themes of Delany's lectures unsettling. To host lectures critical of slavery would most definitely have created a problem for the churches vis-à-vis their more powerful and dominant White affiliates. As suggested earlier, Delany condemned slavery in his lectures and highlighted the hypocrisy of White religious leaders. He enjoined Blacks to explore every available means to uplift and free themselves both psychologically and physically. Such lectures would definitely ruffle feathers, especially of those who would rather maintain Blacks in perpetual subordination.

The "radical" and potentially disruptive nature of Delany's lectures received coverage in local newspapers. The *Anti-Slavery Bugle* (Ohio) editorialized that Delany condemned slavery and "the absurdity of prejudice against color and urged the expediency of emancipation."[117] Similarly, the *Cincinnati Herald* described Delany's lecture at the Sixth Congregational Church as "forcible . . . bold and manly denunciation of the religious and political hypocrisy of the times."[118] Delany ended this particular lecture with a scathing rebuke of the government and the oppressive system. According to a reporter, Delany declared, "in the language of Frederick Douglass," that he would "welcome the bolt, whether from Heaven or Hell that shall strike down and severe a Union that is built upon the liberties of the people."[119] A resident of York, Pennsylvania, who identified simply as "M C" informed Douglass on how "the people in this part of the vineyard have been invigorated by a discourse, long eloquent and argumentative, by your manly and distinguished colaborer, M. R. Delany."[120] In his lectures, delivered over three evenings, according to "M C", Delany talked about, and did "ample justice" to, "the present condition of the colored people."[121]

Given the content and tone of Delany's lectures, it should not surprise anyone, therefore, that Black churches with tenuous independence would be concerned about retaliatory measures from their affiliate White churches. As Henry Mitchell contended, "prior to 1800, *no* Black churches evolved north or south without some form of White denominational recognition, trusteeship of land title, and or certification to the government by respected Whites that Blacks involved would cause the slave system no trouble."[122] Regardless of how they evolved, Black churches were "always" subordinate to White "sponsoring" institutions.[123] This was "inevitable," Mitchell argued, due to "a legal requirement for White sponsors and guarantors." Absent this sponsorship and guarantors, "government prohibited Blacks from gathering for mass worship."[124] Mitchell further explained that "in the north and south in the early years, and continued in the south up to the Civil War," Black congregations were obligated to accept White "assistance" and pastoral supervision.[125] This "supervision" included the superimposition of White preachers, if only for the monthly service of Holy Communion. This was true of Bethel African Methodist Episcopal Church in Philadelphia, where Blacks were considered incapable of serving as full pastors and thus denied ordination. This was the church founded by Rev. Richard Allen and his followers, and it was financed by Whites who retained control of ordaining key functionaries.[126]

There were also several instances where Black church buildings were on leased lands, and titles to church sites held by White trustees.[127] In one of his reports, Delany mentioned the situation in Wilmington, Delaware, where Whites exercised control over several Black churches. This underscored the precarious "independence" of these churches, and thus constrained their antislavery engagements. It is also important to acknowledge the broader hostile anti-abolitionist environment within which these early Black churches functioned. The Moyamensing riot mentioned earlier was not an isolated occurrence. Antislavery and anti-abolitionist violence was a widespread and recurrent phenomenon in the early nineteenth century.[128] Black church buildings and symbols of Black progress were targeted and destroyed by anti-abolitionist mobs in New York, Pennsylvania, Massachusetts, Connecticut, and Rhode Island.[129] This explained the reluctance of many of these churches to engage in, or endorse, efforts to undermine a system Whites, North and South, seemed determined to protect.

It was obvious that despite the prominence of pastors and preachers in the antebellum Black struggles, their churches did not solidly embrace antislavery. Several of the churches refused to support measures which directly or indirectly questioned prevailing doctrinal teachings, and could potentially alienate their more powerful, and still influential, White sponsoring or "parent" affiliates.[130] This was why Delany made the issue of religion and freedom the centerpiece of his antislavery lectures. The religious injunctions he condemned prioritized providential determinism which, in the judgment of "illiberal" churches, rendered moral suasion irrelevant. The injunctions supposedly embodied the goals of antislavery. "Illiberal" churches, therefore, envisioned change in the Black condition resulting not from any temporal, secular or human agency, but from divine intercession. These churches encapsulated moral suasion within what could be termed "the moral economy of God." Moral suasion was about seeking out, and adhering to, divine injunctions that would ease the pathway to the promised heavenly inheritance. Delany disagreed and insisted that those who relied on divine intervention condemned themselves to perpetual poverty and dependence. He denounced "illiberal" churches for misrepresenting Christianity and misleading their congregations.[131] He offered scriptural evidence to complicate and disrupt providential determinist discourse and insisted that God's plan for humanity mandated a this-worldly materialistic disposition. Delany's counter narratives notwithstanding, the moral suasion ideology was inherently and fundamentally flawed. It implied that the challenges Blacks confronted could be eradicated through self-improvement. It also presumed that moral suasion could appeal favorably to the moral conscience of the nation. Both proved wrong. In essence, moral suasion was predicated on a false perception of slaveholders and their supporters as people who possessed a moral conscience.

Notwithstanding the false premise of moral suasion, and despite the opposition of several Black churches, Delany had encountered economically successful, educated, and morally upright Blacks. Yet, their accomplishments failed to gnaw the moral conscience of Whites. Instead, they became victims of White hostility and violence. It became evident that the challenges Blacks confronted had less to do with "moral" shortcomings. There was another for more troubling cause as the "Colored Citizens" of Pennsylvania underlined in their 1848 *Appeal* to the Commonwealth: "The barrier that deprives us of the rights which you enjoy finds no palliative in merit—no consolation in piety—no hope in intellectual and moral pursuits—because we are not 'White.'"[132] None was more troubled by this conclusion than William Whipper, the acclaimed "universalist" and among the leading and prominent advocates of moral suasion. It must have been particularly disheartening for Whipper to admit publicly that:

> We have been advocates of the doctrine that we must be elevated before we could expect to enjoy the privileges of American citizenship. We now utterly discard it, and ask pardon for our former errors. The Declaration of Independence and the laws of God had made all men equal. It was not lack of elevation, but complexion that deprived the man of color of equal treatment. Religious morals and intellectual elevation would not secure full political privileges . . . because we are Black.[133]

Delany fully concurred, and by 1849, just two years into his partnership with Douglass, he had reached a critical crossroads. He had witnessed and experienced enough of the troubling and violent reality that daily defined Black existence in America. In a report he sent from Pittsburgh, Pennsylvania, in February of 1849, Delany had detailed in graphic and horrifying manner how Blacks then experienced America. This document captured his disillusionment with America and heralded the end of the integrationist aspirations and visions he and Douglass once shared. Perhaps for maximum effect, Delany juxtaposed two contradictory emotions and realities. He reminisced about the almost two decades he had traversed the beautiful and serene landscapes of the Alleghany Mountains, marveling at "the beauty, picturesque, grand and sublime scenes."[134] This environment, as he experienced it, allowed the human soul to "expand in the magnitude of its nature, and soar to the extent of human susceptibility."[135] The mountains afforded Delany a place, sheltered from the atrocities of the outside world, in which he could appreciate:

> His existence as a man in America, my own native land. It is there and there my soul is lifted up, my bosom caused to swell with emotion, and I am lost in the wonder at the dignity of my own nature. I see in the work of nature around me, the wisdom and goodness of God. I contemplate them, and conscious that he has endowed me with facilities to comprehend them, I then perceive the likeness I bear to him.[136]

Delany then contrasted this positive vision of the human potential with the stark reality of the denial to Blacks the right to fully realize that potential. Blacks generally were denied the opportunity to fully share the American experience; prompting Delany to wonder; "What being is man!—of how much importance—created in the impress image of his maker and how debased is God, and outraged his divinity in the person of the oppressed colored people of America?"[137] Using his personal experience, Delany both exposed and denounced the dissonance between the promises of Black humanity (embedded in God's reflection) and the reality of entrenched slavery, racial bigotry, and intolerance. He characterized the abuse and debasement of Blacks he both witnessed and experienced as a violation and abuse of God's essence. Echoing David Walker, Delany denounced America and predicted that: "The thunder of his mighty wrath must sooner or later break forth, with all its terrible consequences and scourge this guilty nation, for the endless outrage and cruelty committed upon an innocent and unoffending people. I invoke the aid of Jehovah, in this mighty work of chastisement."[138] Delany then prayed that God would unleash on the nation, "for mocking Him in the person of three millions of his black children, . . . the fiery dragons of heaven, bearing with their approach the vengeance of an angry God!"[139] Delany concluded that moral suasion had failed. However determined Blacks pushed for change, it would not happen. He discerned an entrenched, pervasive, and seemingly indestructible cancer of racism. This conviction prompted Delany to reverse course and this marked the start of his gravitation toward emigration and Black nationalism, leaving Douglass, still optimistic, hanging tightly to moral suasion.[140]

Religion and Emigration: 1850–1863

Disappointment with moral suasion and a turn to emigration did not mean that Delany was done completely with religion. Disillusionment with the ambivalent responses of Black churches to antislavery could not diminish or obliterate Delany's belief in the potency of religion. In fact, the turn to emigration inaugurated a new chapter and phase in his antislavery career—one in which religion would play an equally crucial role. Though emigration was a political strategy designed to create avenues for further enhancing and advancing the fortunes of oppressed, impoverished, and enslaved Blacks, it would not be easy convincing Blacks to leave a nation they had grown accustomed to for the unknown, particularly for a place that had been given mystifying, conflicting, and negative attributes. The immediate challenges for Delany were first how to convince a population steeped in religious and providential determinism that emigration was consistent with their worldview, and second how to then encourage the same people to emigrate to Africa—a place that was for them infused with derogatory and dreadful attributes.

In the 1830s, Delany's mentor the Reverend Lewis Woodson had written extensively in support of emigration to the West (Illinois, Michigan, Wisconsin, and Ohio). He based his arguments on utilitarian, existential, and religious considerations. He called on those who encountered life threatening situations to emigrate.[141] Woodson justified his call for emigration on purely the practical and existential need to escape from, and overcome, life-endangering conditions and thus be in position to protest some other day. He believed that the fate of every enslaved person ultimately depended on the survival of the free. Consequently, he posed the rhetorical question: "Strike from the list of the living, the freemen, and what becomes of the slave?"[142] Woodson also invoked religious or biblical justification for his emigration ideas. He contended that "Christ directed his disciples when persecuted in one place to seek refuge in another."[143] He adduced a robust biblical justification for emigration that is worth quoting at length. Writing under the pseudonym "Augustine" in a letter to the editor of the *Colored American* dated May 3, 1838, Woodson wrote:

The principle which prompted a desire to better our condition by emigration, is perfectly sound and good—it was recognized by God, when he caused the immediate descendants of Noah, to leave off building the city and tower in which they had just engaged, and *'scattered them abroad from thence, upon the face of all the earth*;—Among other things, God has here taught us that it is not his will that men should continue together in great numbers, engaged in works that never can result in any practical good. So also, God dealt with Abraham. For when he saw him in Ur of the Chaldees, surrounded by his incorrigibly wicked friends and countrymen, and his moral character continually exposed to the corrupting influence of idolatry, He said unto him, *'get thee out of thy country, and from thy kindred, and from thy father's house, unto a land that I will show you.'* In addition to this, our Blessed Redeemer said to His disciples on a certain occasion, *'when they persecute you in one city, flee ye to another.'* [emphasis in original][144]

Woodson offered possibly the most compelling religious interpretation of emigration at the time, and the fundamentals of his arguments would reappear in Delany's own interpretation. Delany imbibed Woodson's religious ideas—specifically the injunction against exposing oneself to martyrdom in a cause in which survival was crucial for ultimate success. By the early 1850s, with the benefit of his exposure to the religiosity of Blacks, people for whom religion had become, in his words, "alpha and omega," Delany decided it was necessary to seek religious justification for emigration in order to enhance its appeal and acceptance. He found Woodson's arguments compelling and useful.

By the mid-1840s, the failure of moral suasion as a reform strategy was evident. Black efforts at self-improvement (educational, moral, and economic) paradoxically reinforced White resentments and induced further anti-Black violence. Increasingly, Blacks began to demand immediate change and their strategies became much more political. These were reflected in the deliberations and proceedings of the State and National conventions of the late 1840s and early 1850s. The passage of the Fugitive Slave Law (FSL) in 1850 was the final blow on moral suasion. Though aimed at the apprehension of fugitives, it threatened free Blacks with re-enslavement. More significantly, some Blacks, among the most vocal and prominent, Martin Delany, interpreted the law as an ominous sign of the impending nationalization of slavery.[145] As Grant Shreve argues, "By the late 1850s, the territorial advances of US slaveholding interests had convinced a growing class of Black intellectuals that universal bondage was in the offing....

Black emigration was the political movement developing out of these conclusion."[146] This reality shattered their integrationist dream.

Delany was among the most disillusioned. Jettisoning moral suasion, he embraced emigration, and in 1852 launched the emigration movement with the
publication of his book, *The Condition, Elevation, Emigration and Destiny of the
colored People of the United States* (Philadelphia; 1852). The book is a massive tes-
timony to the industrial and commercial capacities of Blacks, and their contributions to the development of America. He presented a compelling case for Black
citizenship and integration. While highlighting Black compatibility with, and
entitlement to, all the rights and privileges of American citizenship, he also emphasized the hopelessness of the situation.[147] In this, Delany would diverge from
the reform paths and strategies of leading and prominent Black abolitionists.
For instance, Sterling Stuckey noted that Delany's path diverged from that of
his one-time partner Frederick Douglass. Unlike Douglass, the consummate integrationist and optimist, Delany concluded that the "struggle in America alone
could never achieve freedom for Blacks . . . though he agreed that free Blacks
should never accept racism, freedom was forever beyond their grasp in America,
unless those of talent migrated to establish a nation for themselves."[148] Delany's
turn to emigration led him also, according to Sterling Stuckey, to renounce the
prevailing Victorian construction of Africa. He now represented Africa in the
most positive lights, and to bolster his call for emigration, drew correlation between African traditions and values and Southern Black life and culture. Stuckey
argued that Delany attempted to convince Blacks that they were really not relocating to an entirely strange and unfamiliar environment.[149] Stuckey is only
partially right. While it is true that Delany developed positive portraits of Africa,
he was not absolute and unequivocal in denunciation and rejection of Victorian
values and worldview. He would later invoke those same values as prescriptions
for "civilizing" aspects of African culture he characterized as primitive.[150]

Delany represented the Fugitive Act as the death knell of the integrationist
dream. All indications, he argued, suggested the strengthening and intensification of slavery and racism. He depicted the United States as a nation whose
stability and survival depended on Black subordination.[151] Delany essentially
described a Herrenvolk political culture in which the rights and privileges of one
group depended on the denial of such rights to other groups. Though slavery was
sectional, racism was national, and very soon, Delany predicted, slavery would
become national.[152] To avoid this imminent disaster, he urged Blacks to emigrate. He believed that the development of an externally situated and economically powerful Black nation would generate the force to undermine slavery and

racism worldwide.[153] Publication of *The Condition* immediately drew a storm of protest from some Blacks, and emigration came under attack in several Black state conventions. Many equated emigration with the loathsome colonization scheme of the proslavery American Colonization Society (ACS). Frederick Douglass, for example, insisted that emigration was tantamount to Blacks' sabotaging "their own cause." They would in essence be conceding "a point which every Black man must die rather than yield—that is, that the prejudice and maladministration toward us are invincible to truths, invincible to continued and virtuous efforts for their over-throw."[154] Many agreed. Even in what had become Delany's adopted state—Pennsylvania—Blacks moved to "remain and fight" in the United States for as long as one Black remained in bondage. Emigration, they emphasized, was tantamount to abandoning the slaves and strengthening the knot of bondage.[155] Meeting at a National Convention in Rochester, New York, in July 1853, convened by Frederick Douglass, Blacks rejected all schemes of repatriation, and resolved instead to "plant our trees on American soil, and repose beneath their shade."[156]

Though publication of *The Condition* formally launched Delany's emigration movement, this was not the first time Blacks experimented with a variant of this strategy. Lott Cary, Paul Cuffee, and a few others had advanced and promoted a similar scheme much earlier.[157] It was, however, the emergence of the controversial and proslavery American Colonization Society in 1816–1817 that paradoxically undermined emigration, since most Blacks conceived the two as synonyms. Delany was well aware of this negative perception of emigration long before he published his book. Moreover, as a Pittsburgh agent of Henry Bibb's *Voice of the Fugitive,* he had attended an antislavery convention in Toronto in 1851, where he and three other United States delegates objected to a resolution that urged American Blacks to emigrate to Canada on the ground that it was "impolitic and contrary to our professed policy—of opposing the infamous Fugitive Slave Law and the scheme of Colonization."[158] In a recent study, Richard Blackett identifies Delany as one of the earliest critics of colonization in Pennsylvania, who publicly denounced the ACS and vehemently opposed colonizing free Blacks in Liberia; a place he described as "a miserable hovel of emancipated and superannuated slaves and deceived colored men, controlled by the intrigue of a conclave of upstarts colored hirelings of the slave power of the United States."[159] To be clear, that was pre-1850. The FSL changed Delany's viewpoint on Liberia. When he embraced emigration, Delany's perception of Liberia and other parts of Africa changed radically.[160] In his earlier opposition to colonization, Delany, as David Brion Davis rightly noted, was careful to distinguish colonization from emigration.

The former was White-inspired, White-led, and proslavery in its vision; the latter was Black-inspired, Black-led, and antislavery in its goal. By the mid-to-late 1850s, however, Delany would abandon his opposition to colonization and began to solicit the assistance of the ACS for emigration. In fact, his first trip to Liberia and the Niger Valley of West Africa was partly funded by the ACS.[161]

Delany's advocacy of emigration, as demonstrated earlier, provoked widespread rejection and condemnation. This must have influenced how he addressed the subject in *The Condition*. It definitely dictated his choice of religion as the medium through which to reformulate emigration. Since emigration *as a political solution,* appeared unpopular, perhaps emigration *as a religious injunction and solution* would appeal favorably to the religious-minded Black community. He quickly mapped the religious foundation of emigration. Emigration was not an aberration, but the logical and divinely sanctioned solution for all oppressed people.[162] To prove its divine character, Delany referred to several biblical migrations—the movement of Dido and followers from Tyre to Mauritania and the exodus of the Israelites from Egypt. He then reminded Blacks of a more recent migration of another religious group, the Puritans, who left the old for the New World.[163] This proved therefore that emigration was historical, legitimate, and divine. Delany underlined the link between capitalism and religion and demonstrated how emigration (divinely sanctioned) would advance the capitalist goal of the Black middle class. Emigration was consequently consistent with God's plan.[164]

To further reassure skeptics, Delany announced that the relocation site had carefully been selected and set aside by God. The "finger of God" had established the entire American continent as a place of refuge for freedom-seeking emigrants, and had specifically set aside Central and South America and the West Indies for Blacks.[165] He characterized the subtropical climate, the rich natural resources, and the preponderance of people of color (constituting the *ruling element* in these regions) as divinely conditioned factors that made these parts of the world ideal for the resettlement of free Blacks.[166] According to him, "God has, as certain as he has ever designed anything, has designed this great portion of the new world for us, the colored races."[167] In a picturesque depiction of divine approval, he declared: "Heaven's pathway stands unobstructed, which will lead us into a paradise of bliss. Let us go on and possess this land and the God of Israel will be our God."[168]

To strengthen the appeal of emigration, Delany introduced a messianic/missionary factor. Emigration would enable Blacks concomitantly to advance themselves and execute a divine function. It was the first step in the fulfillment of a divine promise that "a prince (i.e. power) shall come out of Egypt (from among the

African race) and Ethiopia stretch forth (from all parts of the world) her hands unto God."[169] The movement of Blacks out of the United States was, therefore, a prelude to the redemption of humankind. Free Blacks had been entrusted with a divine mission and responsibility. They were the "instrumentalities" God had created for the redemption of the world. Refusal or failure to undertake the divine responsibility embedded in emigration would, Delany suggested, result in God dispossessing Blacks of whatever little they had and withdrawing his "divine care and protection."[170] Or, as Delany poignantly proclaimed, "as certain as we stubborn our heart, and stiffen our necks against it (i.e. emigration), his (i.e. God's) protecting arm and fostering care will be withdrawn from us."[171] His sermons, however, appealed to very few Blacks.

Emigration remained a minority movement. The majority of Blacks endorsed a cultural pluralistic approach to promoting integration in America. Many objected to a racialist definition of the problem and insisted that *condition* not *race* was the factor and that a change in the *condition* of Blacks through "economy, amassing riches, educating our children, and being temperate" (not emigration) would accelerate integration.[172] Perhaps the most vicious attack against emigration, and pointedly, against Delany, occurred at a State Convention of Colored Citizens of Illinois. Delegates accused Delany of advocating "a spirit of disunion which, if encouraged, will prove fatal to our hopes and aspirations as a people."[173]

Delany denied the charges, and reaffirmed his contention that Blacks had no chance in the United States, and that the nation was inching toward nationalizing slavery.[174] He insisted that "Whites cannot be rationally and morally persuaded out of their prejudice because they have a material stake in Black subordination and because they have too little empathy for what they consider a degraded race."[175] Delany considered emigration imperative since "Blacks cannot compel Whites to treat them as equals, because Whites greatly outnumber and have significantly more power than Blacks."[176] Proceeding with his emigration plan, he summoned his followers to a National Convention in Cleveland, Ohio, in August 1854, where he read a lengthy presentation in which he elaborated on, and justified, his scheme.[177] Again, he strongly appealed to religion. Stressing the imperialistic disposition of Whites, he urged Blacks to "make an issue, create an event, and establish for ourselves a position," by emigrating to the West Indies, Central and South America.[178] Delany characterized emigration as indispensable to the redemption and "effective elevation" of Blacks and to the "pursuit of our legitimate claims to inherent rights, bequeathed to us by the will of heaven—the endowment of God, our common parent."[179]

Delegates at Cleveland, particularly the leadership of the movement, perceived themselves as commissioned by God to spearhead emigration for the national regeneration of Blacks, and therefore, accountable to him "who will surely require the blood of our people at our hands, if they perish in their national bondage."[180] They defined a cause-effect relationship between oppression and emigration—the former usually induced the latter. An oppressed minority must perforce emigrate as a prelude to "entering upon a higher spiritual life and development."[181] Emigration became a purifying and redeeming process. One of them referred to the biblical experience of "the ancient people of God (i.e. Israelites)—(who) after being ground down to dust under the despotism of Egypt, received their new birth by removal," as proof of both the divine and redeeming qualities of emigration.[182] The added burden of accountability imposed a responsibility of immense magnitude upon advocates of emigration. It was their duty to convince other members of the race to emigrate. It was clear that emigration was an unpopular option and a tough sell. In April of 1853, just about one year after the publication of Delany's *The Condition*, Uriah Boston of Poughkeepsie, New York, published a piece in *Frederick Douglass's Paper* critical of what he perceived as the growing separatist inclinations of prominent Black abolitionists. He was particularly troubled by the racial undertone and concerned, as Patrick Rael notes, that the quest for a distinct Black nationality would lend credence to and reinforce "the propriety and necessity of African colonization." Boston did not believe that Blacks could ever constitute "a nation within a nation." He would wish that Blacks would not accentuate the racial differences but "lessen the distinction between Whites and colored citizens of the United States."[183] Boston's integrationist preference directly contradicted Delany's emigration/ nationality scheme. In Delany's judgment, the prospect for Black elevation and racial equality was nonexistent in America. He was very skeptical of, and cynical about, how he felt Blacks had been duped into believing in the doctrine of "universal humanity and natural rights," and thus "we are the same as other people." This was not true. He considered this a red herring designed to lure Blacks into complacency and thus compromise and erode their true identity even as their oppressors advance and promote the doctrine of "universal *Anglo-Saxon predominance* [emphasis in original]."[184]

Delany remained firm in his support of emigration and searched deeper into the Bible for divine corroboration. He found biblical evidence for the demographic factor. Delany estimated the population of people of "pure European extraction" in the West Indies, Central, and South America at 3,495,714, in contrast to a Colored population of 20,974,286.[185] This preponderance of number made the Colored race "the *ruling element,* as they ever must be, of those countries [emphasis in original]."[186] He, therefore, exhorted Blacks to regard "this most fortunate, heaven-designed (and fixed) state and condition of things" as proof of God's desire to elevate them through emigration. Consequently, persistent refusal to emigrate would result in the "universal possessions and control by Whites of every habitable portion of the earth," thus strengthening their strangle hold on Blacks.[187]

Delany also considered emigration an avenue for the assertion of Black "physiological superiority." As he reasoned, God had endowed Blacks with "natural properties" that enabled them to survive in all climatic conditions—temperate, cold, and hot—unlike Whites, whose adaptability, he argued, was confined to temperate and cold environments.[188] A logical implication of this "divinely" conditioned "superiority" was the flexibility and mobility it facilitated whenever conditions in any particular environment became unbearable—as with the North American situation. By emigrating to subtropical West Indies, South America, and Central America, therefore, Blacks would simply be utilizing an option made available by God through their "physiological superiority." As he reiterated: "The creator has indisputably adapted us for the denizens of EVERY soil . . . all that is left for us to do is to MAKE ourselves the LORDS of terrestrial creation [emphasis in original]."[189] Again, his divine rendition of emigration won few converts. A state council of the Colored citizens of Massachusetts expressed the feelings of other Blacks when it equated emigration with colonization and voiced "a strong and unqualified condemnation" of both movements.[190]

Conclusion

Delany's use of religion to justify two contradictory goals—integration and emigration—is fascinating. To advance integration, he situated the "Kingdom of God" temporally (here in the United States) attainable through the pursuit of materialism. To render capitalism more acceptable to Blacks, he clothed it in divine robes. When this failed, he externalized the divine kingdom, realizable this time, through divinely sanctioned and directed emigration. His religious appeals failed in both respects.

In the earlier phase, his religion was a component of the moral suasionist crusade. He used religion in an attempt to affect a convergence of interests and aspirations between Blacks and Whites and render integration mutually acceptable and legitimate. When moral suasion collapsed in the late 1840s, it pulled every auxiliary component along. Emigration is often misconceived as a radical movement. Delany built his emigration platform upon a religious foundation that had been submerged beneath the misguided conception of nineteenth-century Black nationalism, especially its separatist aspect, as a militant, countervailing political and cultural phenomenon. Though he used religion to justify emigration, Delany was careful to emphasize the pervasive power of a ubiquitous God, whose universal law—fixed and immutable—governed humanity, irrespective of geographical or physiological differences. He did not advocate emigration en masse. His constituency was the free Black community of "sterling worth"; the resourceful and wealthy few he hoped would develop the economic and moral force of a foreign land that would induce recognition, respect, and long over-due concessions of freedom and equality. Fundamentally, Delany theorized the external equivalent of moral suasion. The central focus of his emigration scheme was not change in Africa, Central and South America, and the West Indies per se but how that change would influence further changes in an external environment—the United States. Emigration enabled him to externalize the geopolitical setting for the advancement of integration in the United States. However, the limited scope of the emigration call, and more significantly, its correspondence with colonization proved problematic. First, it was difficult to demonstrate to Blacks, beyond verbal promises, how the departure of a few, and their activities elsewhere, could induce positive reforms within the United States. Second, it was even more difficult to convince Blacks that God sanctioned emigration—a scheme that bore similarity to the dreaded and pernicious proslavery colonization movement. Most Blacks conceived of emigration as colonization with a Black face and refused to believe that God sanctioned such a "pro-slavery scheme."

Delany's alienation from the mainstream Black struggle notwithstanding, his ideas attested to his prudence and foresightedness. He was certainly a child of his time. A significant paradox of his theology was its dualistic function—it served both integrationist and emigrationist purposes. His use of religion to advance capitalistic goals underlined his subscription (along with other middle-class Blacks) to the dominant Protestant Work Ethics. But he was also ahead of his time. His utilitarian and secular definition of religion—the contention that religion is only meaningful and relevant to the extent that it addressed secular problems—was revolutionary in the context of the nineteenth-century Black struggle. He can legitimately be counted among the precursors of modern liberation theology.

CHAPTER 2

Violence

Martyrdom vs. Survival

O NE OF THE CHALLENGES Delany confronted in the course of his travels to Black communities as abolitionist and antislavery lecturer was how best to frame his ideas on how Blacks could effectively develop a foundation and culture of empowerment and self-determination at a time when they were also beginning to consider and debate violence as resistance strategy. It should come as no surprise that as overwhelming as the challenges they confronted and, as bleak as the prospect seemed, perhaps because of this reality, some Blacks seriously considered violence as a viable option. Throughout the nineteenth century, Black abolitionists had to confront this matter. The fundamental and nagging question was: how viable and realistic was violence as reform strategy? Attempts to answer this question preoccupied delegates at several of the early national and state conventions. As Delany became involved in the abolitionist movement, he too had to engage this subject, and he offered his views and insights. It was evident from his writings and thoughts that Delany was no blind advocate of violence. Though at some points, he might have considered the necessity of violence, he was also careful to underscore its challenges and constraints.

Violence preoccupied the attention of Blacks in early nineteenth-century Pennsylvania. It would not be an exaggeration to suggest that violence was in the air! Most whispered the subject quietly. A few openly debated it and offered sobering and insightful opinions. In fact, Carter Jackson states the "perennial question" of political thought which Blacks sought to answer as: "Is violence a valid means of producing social change?" The central theme of her book is that violence was very much embedded in the transformation of the nation and the status of Blacks in the antebellum period. Focusing on the activism of Black abolitionists, she contends that there was a noticeable shift in Black leadership orientation in post-1850 toward violence due to the failure of moral suasion.[1] Black leaders now combined "protective violence" (self-defense) with the threat of violence. They had come to the conclusion that, like the violence of slavery, abolitionists needed to apply "force and violence" in response.[2] Carter Jackson ascribes this shift to the noticeable failure of moral suasion; an ideology that implied "the unstated assumption that Black people were equal." White negative responses to Black success belied this assumption.[3] Moral suasion had not stemmed the tide of "disenfranchisement, kidnapping, unemployment, segregation and increased violence."[4] In essence, the anti-Black violence and race riots of the 1830s and 1840s exposed the limitations of moral suasion as well as nonviolence.

The Black community Delany encountered in Pennsylvania in 1831 was therefore starting to view violence differently; agitated no doubt by the 1830 failed Nat Turner's insurrection in Southampton County Virginia. Though it occurred in a distant state and failed, the episode, particularly Nat Turner's bravery, assumed mythic proportions among Blacks in Pennsylvania, as in other parts of the country. Delany immersed himself in the excitement and it was precisely at this time that, according to his authorized biographer, Frances ("Frank") Rollin, Delany "consecrated himself to freedom, and registered his vows against the enemies of his race."[5] This consecration, however, should not be misconstrued as endorsement of violence. As committed to, and as passionate as Martin Delany was about, the quest for Black freedom in America, he was equally clear and unambiguous concerning how far he was willing to go, the limits of the strategy he would adopt, and how much he was willing to sacrifice for that end. In his judgment, though no sacrifice was too high for the cause of Black freedom and equality in America, sacrificing one's life, or recklessly endangering it, was definitely not one of them. This is a reflection of how deeply Delany was influenced by the two individuals who helped shape the ideological contours of the Black abolitionist movement during its early beginnings in 1830s Pennsylvania: the Reverend Lewis Woodson and William Whipper. They were among leading advocates of nonviolence during Delany's formative years in Pittsburgh. In their writings, both Woodson and Whipper argued for and stressed the imperative of survival. They considered survival most crucial to one's ability to advance the cause of Black freedom and empowerment in America. Delany began his education in 1831 at the African Methodist Episcopal Church Cellar School in Pittsburgh cofounded by Reverend Woodson. The year also coincided with the official launching of the Negro National Convention movement which birthed the Black abolitionist movement. These were momentous and exciting times for Blacks. They were not only independently creating their movement and institutions but also several of their leaders began to engage in spirited and productive debates about procedures and strategies and about ideas and ideals for the bourgeoning Black abolitionist movement.

As a young man, Delany gained as much knowledge as possible from these debates. Their ideas impacted him for the first part of his antislavery career, and one might argue, also for the rest of his life; Delany did not deviate from the nonviolence philosophy and strategy they propagated. To underscore this point, Rollin described Delany as someone nature had "marked for combat and victory and not for martyrdom."[6] To understand Delany's attitude and disposition toward violence, one needs deeper understanding of the broader context and ideological debates that shaped those crucial early years of the Black abolitionist movement, which, as pointed out, coincided with Delany's formative years. There is therefore no better starting point than analysis of the controversies over violence in the deliberations of early to mid-nineteenth-century Black national and state conventions. Though, violence generally was not a popular option among Blacks, there were occasions during both national and state conventions when delegates spiritedly debated and considered violence as means of advancing the cause of Black liberation. Nonetheless, for much of the first half of the nineteenth century, Blacks remained faithful to moral suasion and nonviolence as abolitionist philosophy and strategy. In other words, though violence was a minority option; it was never completely ruled out of consideration. As a young observer, and newcomer to the scene who was also struggling to gain education, Delany did not actively participate in, or contribute to, these early deliberations. However, as he matured and as his antislavery zeal blossomed, Delany would assume a pivotal role in the propagation of abolitionist ideas and became a major contributor to the debate and controversies about violence and its place in, and relevance to, the Black struggle.

Debating Violence

Although the subject of violence featured in the deliberations of some of the state and national Negro conventions of the 1830s and 1840s, it came into sharper and more contentious focus at the August 1858 convention of the Colored Citizens of Massachusetts held in New Bedford. Two issues provoked spirited debates among the delegates. The first was the 1850 Fugitive Slave Law (FSL) which pledged federal support for the pursuit, apprehension and return of fugitive slaves. The second, and perhaps more contentious, was the recently rendered Supreme Court decision in *Dred Scott v. Sandford* (1857), which concluded that

Blacks "had for more than a century before been regarded as beings of an inferior order; and altogether unfit to associate with the White race, either in social or political relations; and so far inferior, that they had no rights which the White man was bound to respect; and that the negro might justly and lawfully be reduced to slavery for his benefit."[7] Put simply, Blacks were not considered citizens of the United States and were stripped of all rights. For several days the delegates discussed the implications of the FSL and considered violence as an appropriate response. One consideration was whether free Blacks could and should foment revolutionary ideas among, and incite the insurrection of, slaves. Some delegates thought so. Ohio delegate Charles Lenox Remond was unequivocal and uncompromising. He insisted that the days for talks and resolutions were over. It was time for action. According to the minutes of the meeting, Remond wanted, "a position taken, a defiant position towards every living man that stood against them, towards legislatures, and congresses, and supreme courts."[8] He believed that "the colored people would gain nothing by twiddling and temporizing . . . they were strong enough to defy American slavery."[9] Thus, Remond urged Black men "to stand up for and by themselves."[10] To accomplish this objective, he proposed the creation of "a committee of five . . . to prepare an address . . . to the slaves of the South to create an insurrection."[11] He urged slaves to "rise with bowie-knife and revolver and muskets."[12] According to one delegate, violence was "by far the most spirited discussion of the convention."[13] Passions ran high. However, when Remond's proposal was put to vote, it lost by a wide margin.[14]

As hinted earlier, this was not the first time Blacks debated whether or not to use violence as a weapon of change. It had featured prominently in the deliberations of at least three previous National Negro Conventions—Buffalo and Troy, New York, in 1843 and 1847 respectively, and Cleveland, Ohio, in 1848.[15] In fact, at the 1843 convention, delegates considered a motion to adopt as a platform, Henry H. Garnet's incendiary address to the slaves proclaiming, "Let your motto be Resistance! Resistance! Resistance! No oppressed people have ever secured their liberty without resistance."[16] The motion lost by one crucial vote cast by Frederick Douglass, who was, at that time, according to one authority, "a revolutionary who opposed violence."[17] Also, at the 1848 convention in Cleveland, Ohio delegates lamented that Blacks were "far behind the military tactics of the civilized world" and therefore resolved to "recommend to the Colored Freemen of North America to use every means in their power to obtain that science, so as to enable them to measure arms with assailants *without* and invaders within [emphasis in original]."[18] They further resolved to "appoint Committees in the different States as Vigilant Committees to organize as such where the same may be deemed practicable."[19] These declarations suggested that there was recognition among Blacks of the need for some form of violent resistance. Yet, they were also very cautious. Despite their frustrations and alienation, Blacks would not fully commit to violence. Still in its formative years, the Black abolitionist movement was very much driven by integrationist aspirations, and Black abolitionists were overwhelmingly optimistic. Consequently, they embraced moral suasion which emphasized nonviolent change through hard work, thrift, education, and character reform; values rooted in the Protestant Work Ethics (PWE). Moral suasion became the philosophy of the Black abolitionist movement in its early phase.[20] Developments in the 1850s, however, changed the dynamics. The Fugitive Slave Law and the Dred Scott decision raised the profile of violence in both State and National Negro Conventions.

In 1858 in Massachusetts, however, legislative reversals notwithstanding, most Blacks remained skeptical of violence. Josiah Henson, a Canadian delegate, then resident of Ontario, Canada, cautioned against Remond's suggestions. Born and raised of slave parents in Charles County, Maryland, in 1789, it would not be an exaggeration, therefore, to infer that slavery was no fairy tale to Henson. He had experienced and witnessed operations of the South's *peculiar institution* in all its inhumane and brutal dimensions. It was no surprise, therefore, when in 1830 he escaped to the small town of Dawn, close to Dresden in Kent County, Ontario (Upper Canada), where he established the Dawn settlement, which became a magnet for fugitive slaves from the United States.[21] Subsequently, Henson became active in the Underground Railroad and, according to one estimate, assisted over two hundred slaves in their escape to Canada.[22] At its height, and under the management of the Henson family, the Dawn Settlement became economically self-sustaining, with a population of over five hundred fugitives.[23] It seems plausible to suggest therefore that contrary to popular Uncle Tom mythology, Henson was no coward. His actions required tremendous courage.[24] In 1858 in Massachusetts, however, his was the voice of caution. He urged delegates not to embark rashly and hastily upon a strategy which, he was convinced, would fail and with disastrous consequences for slaves. Though Henson believed it was appropriate for Blacks to express public outrage against the injustices of slavery and racism, he deemed the call for violent confrontation unreasonable because, in the event of a failure (a very high probability), he had no doubt that Blacks, particularly the slaves, would be subjected to unspeakable reprisals.

Standing firmly against violence, and rejecting Remond's accusation of cowardice, Henson cautioned that "he didn't want to see three or four hundred thousand men hung before their time . . . everything would be lost."[25] He doubted if free Blacks like Remond who talked tough and uttered violent rhetoric could be trusted to stand by, and with, the slaves if and when violence actually erupted.[26] "When I fight," Henson boldly affirmed, "I like to whip somebody."[27] In this declaration, Henson advanced a utilitarian and existential theory of violence. For him, the choice of violence had to come with the certainty of victory—and victory meant physical survival, triumph, "whipping somebody." Anything short of this assurance, particularly if engaging violence had the potential of one being the "whipped," which could mean defeat and possibly death; then, violence was to be approached with the utmost caution, and avoided at all cost. Another delegate, Captain Henry Johnson who also opposed insurrection, informed the delegates: "If an insurrection occurred, he wouldn't fight."[28] Reacting to Remond's violent rhetoric, Johnson opined: "It was easy to talk, but another thing to act." His assessment of the power dynamics led him to one conclusion: "If we were equal in numbers, then there might be some reason in the proposition."[29] In other words, Blacks simply did not have the "numbers" to launch a successful violent insurrection. What happened in Massachusetts in 1858 reflected a nationwide dilemma. Though some delegates endorsed violence as a weapon of change, the thought of failure compelled caution. They considered violence viable only with the certainty of victory. Blacks must engage violence from a position of strength; in which *they* would be doing the "whipping." Thus, a certain survivalist and existential ethos informed Black responses to violence in the nineteenth century. In fact, many known advocates of nonviolence insisted they were not inherently opposed to violence, but only apprehensive of its failure. They would embrace violence if it would succeed.

Delany, Moral Suasion, and Violence

Few nineteenth-century Blacks embodied this utilitarian and existential conception of violence as Martin R. Delany. His philosophy of violence reflected deep personal experiences. As suggested earlier, being a "free" Black did not protect him from the brutalities and inhumanities that defined Black lives in Jeffersonian Virginia.[30] Like other "free" Blacks, therefore, Delany grew up frustrated, angry, and alienated. His paternal grandfather Shango, who was captured in Africa and enslaved in Virginia, had once escaped with his family to Toronto, Canada, before being apprehended and returned to the United States. He was later killed in "an encounter with some slaveholder, who attempted to chastise him into submission."[31] His father, Samuel Delany, bore a permanent scar on his face, the result of injury caused by a large stone hauled at him by a posse of nine men, including the sheriff, sent to arrest him for daring to resist "one Violet, as he was endeavoring to inflict bodily punishment on him."[32] According to Rollin, Delany witnessed the "mark of brutality" and "humiliations and bestial associations to which (his) hapless race was subjected," with growing sense of bitterness and a determination to "root out every fiber of slavery and its concomitants."[33]

Delany's own encounter with violence, or one might say "baptism of fire" occurred on the evening of Wednesday the 28th of May 1848 in the small Ohio town of Marseilles. Accompanied by Ohio native John Mercer Langston, Delany had come to organize and deliver an antislavery lecture as part of his Western lecture circuit for Fredrick Douglass's paper, the *North Star*. They were greeted by an angry mob of anti-abolitionists composed mostly of "the principal men of the place," who lined the main street and shouted "darkie burlesque" repeatedly.[34] This was accompanied by the beating of "drums, tambourines, clarinets, violin, jaw-bone of a horse and other instruments." Someone in the crowd called for "tar and feathers" and shortly thereafter a burn fire was started in the town square.[35] The crowd outside grew increasingly restive with repeated chants of "Burn them alive—kill the Niggers! They shall never leave this place—bring them out!"[36] This went on for over four hours with Delany and Langston confined to their hotel rooms and terribly scared. The drumming and festive atmosphere continued through the night. As Delany surmised, this "exceeded anything I have ever witnessed."[37] Late into the night, the pandemonium subsided and the crowd dispersed, several vowing to return in the morning. This gave Delany and Langston the opportunity to slip safely out of town.

Delany's background and experiences notwithstanding, he attained intellectual maturity in an environment that shaped a very conservative mindset and consciousness. As mentioned earlier, he began his education in Pittsburgh, Pennsylvania, in the early 1830s at the AME Church Cellar School and was immediately thrust into an atmosphere dominated by spirited discourses among leading Blacks in search of a philosophy for the emerging and burgeoning Black abolitionist movement. In fact, Delany was educated and mentored by a leading discussant—one whose ideas helped shape the conservative thrust of the early Black abolitionist crusade—the Reverend Lewis Woodson. Woodson was a highly respected educationist who had cofounded the AME Church Cellar School.[38] He and another Black leader, William Whipper, lectured and spoke at length about strategies for the Black struggle. Both evinced strong faith in moral suasion and campaigned passionately against violence.

In his writings, Woodson rejected violence because of his belief in the essential goodness of America. He believed that Blacks were denied and underprivileged because of individual conditional and situational deficiencies which could be remedied though moral reform. Success in this regard would enhance the cause of integration.[39] But more significantly, Woodson opposed violence because, in his view, it violated a fundamental law of nature—survival. He declared "self-preservation" to be "the first law of nature."[40] In order to succeed in their struggles, according to Woodson, Blacks would have to prioritize survival. As he poignantly affirmed, "I can do more by living than by dying, especially in our cause."[41] Woodson also invoked the scriptures to argue that escape from life-threatening locations and condition was consistent with God's injunction. According to him, "Christ directed his disciples when persecuted in one place to seek refuge in another."[42] Then, he posed a rhetorical and existential question: "As Christians . . . have we morally the right to allow ourselves to be deprived of life, rather than suffer the infliction of a physical wrong?" His answer was unequivocal: "We are morally bound by the sacred scriptures, to answer in the negative. The scriptures nowhere inculcate the idea that a man may deprive himself, or suffer others to deprive him, of life, in order to escape the infliction of physical evil."[43] Escape from violent and life-threatening situations, therefore, was a divine injunction. Invoking religion to bolster his philosophy of nonviolence, Woodson claimed that God's policy "shows that it is better to bear our wrongs in silence than to aggravate them by fruitless attempts at their overthrow."[44]

Whipper equally wrote at length on nonviolence. He characterized nonviolence as divine; it drew humans closer to the divine nature, whereas violence reflected irrationalism, which drew humans closer to animals. To be nonviolent, therefore, he suggested, was to manifest *reason*, a divine quality.[45] Whipper described violence as a product of "the rude passion" that animates humans, denying them peace and stability. He believed that humans possessed the capacity to expunge this "rude passion" through the exercise of *reason*.[46] To be violent, according to Whipper, was to risk alienating God—the only power able to rescue Blacks from their predicaments. Furthermore, violence exemplified disorder, a violation of "nature's first law: Order."[47] He opined that Blacks could not end slavery and racism through vengeance: only through the exercise of *reason*, which linked humans to God, who alone is able to end human suffering. Thus, Whipper sought to enlighten Blacks on the divine and ennobling power of patience and nonviolence. Further invoking scriptural authority, the Messiah, he declared, "commands us to love our enemies, bless them that curse you, pray for them that despitefully use you, and persecute you." Violence, therefore, constituted a violation of "moral and divine law."[48] Both Woodson and Whipper characterized violence as self-destructive and insisted that the Black struggles of their times had no place for martyrdom. They deemed risking one's life for a cause, however justifiable, ill-advised. Nonetheless, Woodson affirmed the right of the individual to self-defense, especially when attacked. However, this was not an absolute right either. Self-defense should carefully be balanced with consideration for one's safety and survival. Rather than defend yourself and risk death, Woodson endorsed emigrating to a safer environment.[49]

The ideas Woodson and Whipper espoused profoundly shaped Delany's formative years. It was no coincidence therefore that moral suasion and nonviolence became the central tenets of his abolitionist philosophy. He began an active abolitionist career in the late 1830s a dedicated moral suasionist who had been properly schooled in the Woodson-Whipper philosophy of nonviolence. Throughout the 1840s, Delany emphasized and prioritized moral suasion in his antislavery lectures.[50] From 1843, when he launched his short-lived newspaper the *Pittsburgh Mystery* to 1847 through 1849 when he served as coeditor of Frederick Douglass's paper, the *North Star*, Delany helped spread the gospel of moral suasion to free Black communities in the Midwest, Northeast, and across the nation. The 1840s was a crucial period in the Black abolitionist movement when delegates at state and national Negro conventions debated, among many other subjects, the utility of violence. In his contributions, Delany advised Blacks to prioritize moral and character reform.[51] In both state and national conventions, during public lectures, and in many of his publications, he argued passionately for the adoption of moral suasion as reform strategy. Success in moral and character reform would constitute "truths as evident as self-existence ... beyond the shadow of a doubt," which would radically transform not just the Black condition, but the entire nation.[52] Ironically, his moral suasion convictions notwithstanding, Delany soon developed a radical reputation. This was no doubt due to the "radical," "violent," and vitriolic contents of his antislavery lectures. For this, some mistook him for a violent character, someone who would not hesitate to pick up arms against injustice and oppression. This was only partially true. Even the near-death experience in Marseilles, Ohio, could not dent Delany's faith in moral suasion abolitionism, and he would continue his antislavery lecture circuitry for another year. This was however about to change. Circumstances would soon compel Delany to rethink his views on moral suasion and nonviolence.

Delany, the Fugitive Slave Law, and Violence

The late 1830s through the 1840s were particularly violent years for free Blacks attempting to survive in so-called free Midwestern and Northern states. Not even "liberal" Pennsylvania was spared the virulent and rampant anti-Black violence. Pittsburgh was among the cities hardest hit. Delany became actively involved in organizing resistance to protect Black institutions (churches, schools, and cooperative societies), businesses, and private dwellings.[53] This development seemed to reflect a statewide attempt to deny Blacks their due rights and privileges. At a state reform convention in 1837, the state constitution was amended granting suffrage to poor Whites, while excluding Blacks who owned property and paid taxes. The introduction of the word "White" in the Third Article of the constitution effectively eliminated Blacks as citizens.[54] Outraged, Delany joined other Blacks to protest. In March of 1837, he participated in a meeting organized by Blacks in Allegheny County to deliberate on further actions. The intensification of anti-Black violence, especially in Pittsburgh, led to the organizing of resistance to protect Black institutions and property. The mayor sought Delany's assistance in organizing a biracial vigilante committee for law and order.[55] Delany gave further hints of his evolving views on violence as reform strategy at the 1848 National Convention in Cleveland, Ohio. As chair of the Business Committee, Delany helped to draft several resolutions, one of which, referenced earlier, clearly recommended the consideration of violence and it is worth recalling verbatim. Resolution 22 read thus: "Whereas, we find ourselves far behind in the military tactics of the civilized world, therefore, *Resolved*, that this convention recommend to the colored freemen of North America to use every means in their power to obtain that science, so as to enable them to measure arms with assailants without and invaders within; therefore, *Resolved*, that this convention appoint committees in different states as vigilant committees, to organize as such where the same may be deemed practicable [emphasis added]."[56]

The passage of the Fugitive Slave Law (1850) seemed to finally change Delany's view of violence. The law was part of the Compromise of 1850 meant to diffuse the growing sectional conflict over the expansion of slavery. Among its provisions, the law guaranteed federal support for the pursuit, apprehension and return of fugitives. It now made it illegal for a state not to assist with enforcement. The law, in Carter Jackson's words, "resurrected" the abolitionist movement that had been dormant. She describes it as the "final turning point in a failed campaign for moral suasion."[57] It immediately enhanced the appeal of violence as an appropriate response.[58] Furthermore, she contends, the law "radicalized Black abolitionists" and nurtured the growth of nationalist ideas and sentiments. It also made "violence the new language for the oppressed."[59] It ignited mass protests in several cities and Black abolitionists vowed to use violence in defense, if necessary. In several Black conventions, according to

Jackson, resolutions were passed which reflected Black frustrations and determination to resist. The resolutions sanctioned violence by both fugitives and abolitionists. Black leaders therefore manifested a resolve to render the law unenforceable.[60] Blackett argues that the law galvanized resistance in Ohio, New York, Pennsylvania, Massachusetts, Illinois, and Michigan. Gripped by fear of "invasion of slave catchers" and probability of being re-enslaved, many "scrambled to evade recapture" by escaping to a distant place like Vermont; some going as far as Canada.[61]

Delany interpreted the law as indisputable proof that Blacks would never be granted their due rights and privileges in America.[62] In a lengthy critique, he concluded:

> By the provisions of this bill, the colored people of the United States are positively degraded beneath the level of the Whites—are made liable at any time, in any place, and under all circumstances, to be arrested—and upon the claim of any White person, without the privilege, even of making a defense, sent into endless bondage. Let no visionary nonsense about *habeas corpus*, or a *fair trial*, deceive us; there are no such rights granted in this bill. . . . [emphasis in original][63]

Delany concluded that the law was a racist proslavery law designed to rid the nation of free Blacks and vowed to resist its implementation with violence if necessary. At a gathering of Allegheny County officials, including the mayor, senators, and congressmen, he vented his frustrations by threatening violence against anyone, regardless of authority, who ventured into his space in pursuit of fugitives. His justification of violence is worth quoting at length:

> Honorable Mayor, whatever ideas of liberty I may have; have been received from reading the lives of your revolutionary fathers. I have therein learnt that a man has a right to defend his castle with his life, even unto the taking of it. Sir, my house is my castle; in that castle are none but my wife and my children, as free as the angles of heaven, and whose liberty is as sacred as the pillars of God. If any man approaches the house in search of a slave,--I care not who he may be, whether constable or sheriff, magistrate or even judge of the supreme court—nay, let it be he who sanctioned this act to become law, surrounded by his cabinet as his bodyguard, with the Declaration of Independence waving above his head as his banner, and the constitution of this country upon his breast as his shield,--if he crosses the threshold of my door, and I do not lay him lifeless corpse at my feet, I hope the grave may

refuse my body a resting place, and righteous heaven my spirit a home. O, no! he cannot enter my house and we both live.[64]

In the passage above, Delany invoked the Constitution, Declaration of Independence and America's revolutionary heritage to affirm the legitimacy of violence in defense of personal liberty. These were not empty words or bravado. Delany was now willing openly to confront violence if necessary. As secretary of the Philanthropic Society of Pittsburgh, an organization committed to helping fugitives, Delany became actively involved in operations of the Underground Railroad. According to one estimate, within one year, the society helped close to three hundred fugitives escape to Canada.[65] By mid-1853, Delany had helped create a very active anti-Fugitive Slave Law vigilante committee in Pittsburgh. Delany, John Peck, W. M. Webb, and Thomas Burrows became the public face of this committee. They vowed to resist implementation of the law by forcibly intervening to prevent the recapture and return of fugitives. The committee made national and international news when it rescued a young Jamaican boy who had been decoyed from his homeland and was being taken through Pittsburgh for enslavement in Tennessee. The boy's freedom secured, he was placed in Delany's custody.[66] The influx of emboldened slave catchers and bounty hunters to Ohio, Kentucky, Pennsylvania, and New York galvanized what Manisha Sinha characterizes as "Abolitionist Underground" of vigilance committees.[67] These committees existed, in the words of William Still, "not only to rescue self-emancipated slaves from being re-enslaved but also to free slaves brought by their masters to the North."[68]

These fugitives (or self-emancipated slaves) inspired and radicalized Black abolitionists, notably Martin Delany.[69] Not surprising, his state of Pennsylvania had the highest number of runaways and thus became the epicenter of vigilantism.[70] Kidnappers, bounty hunters, and slave catchers who came to Pennsylvania encountered hostile environment of the Vigilance Committee and Fugitive Aid Society.[71] Carole Wilson highlighted this point in another study of vigilantism and the enforcement of the FSL. She noted that "one store in Pittsburg [sic] sold, in one day, last week, over thirty revolvers from four to six barrels each and twice as many bowie knives, to the colored people and their friends."[72] Two years after the passage of the FSL, Delany published his seminal work *The Condition, Elevation, Emigration and Destiny of the Colored People* (1852) in which he advocated emigration, arguing, on the basis of the FSL, that America was irredeemably racist and predicted the imminent nationalization of slavery. Slavery, he opined, would become national in scope as it spreads into, and consumed, the

North.[73] He also discussed the role of slavery as a unifying economic institution; the glue that held both sections of the nation.[74] Delany's conclusions were not baseless. In fact, as Blackett contends, the crises, anxiety and instability and displacement of Black lives that the FSL exemplified occurred simultaneously in an environment of opposition to Black presence, "symbolized by the state promotion of colonization."[75] This was clear message that Blacks were not wanted.

Martin Delany was one of those in leadership position who thought it was time for Blacks "to turn their back on America for a future elsewhere."[76] He presented emigration as the only means by which Blacks, as a people currently living in a country in which they did not "constitute an essential part of the *ruling element* (and) would be able to both "secure their liberty" as well as "control their own political destiny."[77] The Delany who had once condemned and opposed colonization, and described by Blackett as Pennsylvania's "most ardent opponent of colonization," the ACS and its Liberia scheme, was now loudly and openly advocating what to many seemed like a similar scheme.[78] David Brion Davis also asserted that previous opposition to Liberia and colonization did not deter Blacks in the 1850s from embracing emigration.[79] However, many, like Delany, were careful to distinguish emigration from colonization. Emigrationists like Delany argued that "the elevation of Blacks depended on removing at least some . . . from a malignantly prejudiced environment."[80] This was what led Delany to declare by 1852 that Blacks were excluded permanently from the laws and privileges of the country, as represented by the FSL. He likened the status of Blacks to that of marginalized and oppressed European minorities such as Poles, Hungarians, and Jews, and even far worse than these.[81]

Delany's forceful defense of emigration in *The Condition* provoked rebuke from the renowned White abolitionist William Lloyd Garrison who accused Delany of fomenting separatist consciousness. Underlining what he discerned as the racial essentialist undertone of the book, Garrison portrayed Delany "'the author of this work,' as both 'Black and comely' . . . so Black as to make his identity with the African race perfect." He then lamented Delany's "tone of despondency," and what he characterized as "an exhibition of the spirit of caste."[82] Delany responded with a strong affirmation of his existential right to resist oppression. "Were I a slave," he wrote, "I would not live to live a slave, but boldly STRIKE for LIBERTY, for FREEDOM or a martyr's grave [emphasis in original]."[83] Were Delany a slave, based on his vitriolic reactions to the Fugitive Slave Law, it is reasonable to infer that he would most likely have been the "Nat Turner" type. But he was never a slave. Delany was a free Black. Yet, despite the relative latitude that came with being a "free Black" in America, he did not actively engage in any violent subversive plots. He valued his "freedom"—the freedom to be alive and thus in position to organize and plot against the system in ways that did not endanger his life. Survival was paramount for Delany. Put differently, as a "slave" Delany possibly would have risked martyrdom than have his liberty trampled upon. As a "free Black," however, he ruled out martyrdom. He would not risk death. His life and thought evinced an existential aversion to violence, especially one that seemed doomed to failure. In the Hensonian sense, and consistent with the contention of his authorized biographer cited above, Delany would rather "whip" someone else than be "whipped." One episode in his life which clearly underscored his aversion to, as well as ambivalence on, violence was his response to John Brown's revolutionary scheme.

Delany, John Brown, and Violence

John Brown, the fiery and "crazy" White abolitionist had concluded that only a violent revolution would upstage slavery, and with just a handful of die-hard revolutionaries, he believed that he could initiate and lead a movement that would destroy slavery.[84] Brown was born in 1800 in Torrington, Connecticut, into a poor but religious home. His father, Owen Brown, was "earnestly devout and religious," a quality young John Brown seemed to imbibe.[85] He embraced the lifestyle of an ascetic and like Delany, avoided hard liquor and disdained tobacco. "If I had the money that is smoked away during a single a day in Boston," Brown once lamented, "I could strike a blow that would make slavery totter."[86] His religious convictions strengthened after 1805 when the family relocated to Ohio where he became actively involved in local church activities. Brown's entire life was marked by a crisis of direction as he struggled to gain viable and permanent employment. As Brown matured, his family was plagued by tragedies that seemed to push him to the brink of total alienation from society. The seemingly unending quest for gainful employment kept Brown constantly on the move. Through such movements, he gained broader perspectives on slavery which he came to regard as contrary to God's plan. His understanding of the Bible further reinforced his conviction that God wished the destruction of slavery, and that he, John Brown, would be the instrumentality for actualizing that end. Most objective analysts considered Brown's revolutionary scheme reckless, suicidal, and insane. But he would not be deterred.

Convinced of the justness of his cause, Brown surged ahead and actively solicited the support of leading Blacks in the United States. Unfortunately, his expectations were dashed. After careful consideration, most Black leaders, including

Frederick Douglass, wisely kept Brown at a respectable distance.[87] In fact, Brown met Douglass on several occasions to discuss his scheme and solicit support. The first meeting, according to Douglass, was at Brown's home in Springfield, Massachusetts, in 1847. Douglass left this meeting sympathetic to Brown's contention that "Slavery could only be destroyed by bloodshed."[88] In subsequent meetings in Douglass's home in Rochester, New York, several years later, Brown elaborated his plan which, to Douglass, now seemed reckless and foolhardy. What had happened? According to Douglass, Brown's initial plan had not included an attack on the United States. It was simply a scheme to spread disaffection among slaves. By the late 1850s, however, Brown's plan had morphed into open assault on the United States government, a move Douglass deemed ill-advised and suicidal.[89] As he explained, "I at once opposed the measure . . . such measure would be fatal to . . . slaves . . . fatal to all engaged in doing so."[90] Douglass was equally troubled by the demographic disadvantage; "The slave is a minority, a small minority, the oppressors are an overwhelming majority. The oppressed are three million; the oppressors are several millions. The one is weak; the other is strong. The one is without government; the other possesses every advantage in these respects; and the deadly aim of their musketry holds the slave down."[91] Invoking Hensonian existential theory of violence, Douglass insisted he was willing "to combine, and even to conspire against slavery" but only "when there is a reasonable hope of success."[92] In other words, Douglass, like Josiah Henson, would fight only if *he* would be doing the "whipping." Convinced that Brown "would never get out alive" and that his plans would "rivet the fetters more firmly than ever on the limbs of the enslaved," Douglass calmly and wisely rejected Brown's entreaty.[93]

Not easily deterred, Brown then turned to Delany, who at the time was living in Chatham, Canada West, believing that he would endorse his scheme without hesitation and unconditionally. Brown had become convinced that he would find a receptive audience to his violent scheme among fugitives in Canada; those who had daringly and bravely manifested their disdain for slavery by escaping. He was optimistic that none would be more receptive than Martin Delany. During their very first meeting, according to Delany, Brown informed him that he had been advised by "distinguished friends of his and mine, that, if he could but see me, his object could be attained at once."[94] Brown therefore seemed to hinge everything on Delany's support. As he reiterated during their meeting, "I have come to Chatham expressly to see you. . . . I have much to do but little time before me. If I am to do nothing here, I want to know it at once."[95] Delany was astonished by "the conclusion to which my friends and himself had arrived."[96] Nonetheless, he assisted in summoning and organizing Brown's Constitutional

Convention in Chatham in May of 1858, which was supposed to serve as the recruiting platform for his revolutionary army. In principle, Delany seemed to endorse Brown's proposal for violence against slavery. The role he played in helping to organize the Chatham convention led many to believe Delany was deeply involved in the conspiracy. As one aggrieved Virginian surmised, "Delany . . . with other fugitive negroes and American White abolitionists and cut-throats, conspired and planned to attack and conquer the Southern States by means of servile insurrection and massacre."[97] Also, survivors of the raid and other close associates of Brown confirmed Delany's supportive role.

Delany however denied explicit knowledge of Brown's violent intention and insisted that Brown was very secretive and that it was not clear at the convention what exactly he was up to. As Delany contended, the Harper's Ferry raid contradicted the spirit of the convention, which was primarily to reorganize and strengthen the Underground Railroad by diverting fugitives to Kansas instead of Canada. No one anticipated violence. Had Brown been open about his violent scheme, Delany was "doubtful of its being favorably regarded."[98] The deliberations of the convention, however, clearly suggested that Delany did not enthusiastically support the scheme.[99] Delany's claim that Brown was secretive about violence is, however, contradicted by eyewitnesses who remembered Delany "as having objected to many propositions favored by Captain Brown as not having the chance of success," prompting Brown to react disappointingly: "Gentlemen if Dr. Delany is afraid, don't let him make you all cowards."[100] Delany's attempt to deny knowledge of Brown's violent intention is understandable given that in the aftermath of the failed raid on Harper's Ferry, Virginian authorities went after anyone remotely associated with Brown. Most Black leaders, including Douglass who once sympathized with, and offered, Brown moral support, publicly disavowed any knowledge of, or association with, the scheme. Nonetheless, Delany's denial is difficult to sustain, given that Brown went to Canada to confer with him, and he subsequently helped summon the convention. It was evident however that Brown had misjudged Delany's "radical" disposition. However deeply opposed he was to slavery, there was a limit to the risk Delany was willing to take in demonstrating his opposition. Endangering or sacrificing his life was not an option. Little wonder then that when Brown found himself outnumbered and outgunned at Harper's Ferry by a formidable United States government force, Delany, nurtured in the Woodson-Whipper School of self-preservation, tactfully retreated and, consistent with the Woodsonian injunction, opted for the relative security and comfort of relocation (emigration).[101] He was in distant Africa!

Delany was no John Brown! Self-preservation had become the foundation of Delany's philosophy of life and struggle. In order to be an effective agent of change, a Black leader must, a priori, stay alive. Thus, while Delany vehemently defended the individual's right to self-defense, he would not embrace any organized violent scheme that seemed reckless and doomed. Consistent with the teachings of his mentor, Rev. Lewis Woodson, Delany believed that the individual must first guarantee and secure his physical survival in order to be in a position to struggle on behalf of other Blacks. Such survival resulted from the avoidance of strategies which endangered life. The organized use of violence by Blacks was doomed. Like Douglass, Delany was troubled by the demographic imbalance—what he characterized as the "numerical feebleness" of Blacks.[102] Here Delany was no doubt responding to the growing sentiments in some of the state and national Negro Conventions of the late 1840s and early 1850s during which some delegates seriously considered violence as a response to the FSL. Proceedings of several of the conventions underscored growing sympathies for some form of militant resistance.[103] Delany spoke against what he discerned as a suicidal strategy and urged Blacks to consider instead the safety and comfort of emigration— of relocating to a safer environment rather than risking it all in suicidal violence.

The only organized violence Delany would endorse was one that he was convinced was divinely sanctioned and thus had the possibility of success. Like many of his contemporaries, therefore, Delany upheld the right to utilize violence when personally cornered and affronted—self-defense. He was however opposed to collective acts of organized violence, unless it was in cooperation with Whites and, ipso facto, from a position of strength which guaranteed success. In this situation, Blacks would not be the principal actors, but constituents of a broader and stronger force aimed at a goal that had a chance of succeeding. This was Delany's conception of Black participation in the Civil War, which he fully endorsed.[104] He not only embraced the war and campaigned forcefully for Black enlistment; he too enlisted and was commissioned the first combat Black major in the Union army. One of his sons also enlisted in the 54th Massachusetts Colored Regiment.[105] In fact, he described the Civil War as an act of divine intervention. Soon after the assassination of President Abraham Lincoln, a delegation of Black leaders, which included Frederick Douglass, had petitioned his successor Andrew Johnson for the expansion of Black political rights. In a letter to the delegation, Delany counseled caution and moderation and urged the leaders: "Do not forget God. Think, O think how wonderfully he made himself manifest during the war.... He still lives. Put your trust in him.... Wait! Stand still and see his salvation."[106]

Delany's ambivalent response to violence was not unique. This was a defining attribute of nineteenth-century Black abolitionists. Though they acknowledged the necessity for violence, Black abolitionists generally refused, or were reluctant, to endorse violent schemes. Due to the demographic disadvantage, Black leaders considered violent confrontation irresponsible and unwise, however justifiable. The only violence worthy of execution was the one that ensured victory, the one induced by a providential deterministic agency. The subsuming of violence within providential determinism thus became a pervasive feature of nineteenth-century Black leadership discourses on reform strategies. There was a conscious attempt to situate violence outside the orbit of human causality. The process entailed a curiously ambivalent formulation that combined acknowledgement of the theoretical relevance of violence, and the ascription of violence to some external divine agency. What this established, however, was that although theoretically the Black experience called for, and justified, violent response, violence was both empirically impracticable and unethical, and Blacks lacked the capacity to execute successfully and unaided. David Walker and Henry Garnet, two acclaimed Black militants, reflected this ambivalence in their writings. Theoretically, both conceded that the conditions of Blacks justified the adoption of violence. But they made equally strong and compelling case for conceding to divine intervention.

David Walker's powerful book, *Appeal to the Colored Citizens of the World* (1829), provoked angry reactions among Southerners and proslavery advocates nationwide. Walker denounced White Americans in violent terms, and predicted, sans repentance, their imminent destruction. As he warned: "O Americans! Americans!! I call God—I call angels—I call men, to witness, that your DESTRUCTION *is at hand*, and will be speedily consummated unless you RE-PENT [emphasis in original]."[107] Some critics have interpreted this, and similar denunciations in the book, to suggest that Walker endorsed the violent overthrow of slavery. Yet, nowhere in the book did he explicitly call for violence. Instead, in several passages, Walker utilized a biblical sermon style to denounce America. He predicted that Whites would suffer divine retribution and punishments if they failed to change. Walker made it clear that it was not the responsibility of Blacks to wreck vengeance and punishment on Whites, but God's.[108] However angry and militant Walker sounded, he did not call upon Blacks to unleash violent attacks against the proslavery establishment. Blacks were incapable of initiating and successfully executing such violence without divine intervention.[109]

The same was true of Henry Garnet's famous "An Address to the Slaves of the United States" (1843) which was equally hailed as a call for violent rebellion.

This was not Garnet's intention. Though he urged slaves to adopt as their motto "Resistance, Resistance, Resistance" as Harry Reed noted, the violent rhetoric in Garnet's "Address" was conceived within a providential determinist *Weltanschauung*. According to Reed, "The most militant assertions of Garnet were quickly followed by disclaimers of the expediency of an armed revolt."[110] Although Garnet insisted that "no oppressed people have ever secured their liberty without resistance," he did not suggest violence as a strategy. He left the very nature and timing of this resistance open, telling Blacks: "What kind of resistance you had better make, you must decide by the circumstances that surround you and according to the suggestion of *expediency* [emphasis added]."[111] Then, he pleaded with them to "Trust in the living God."[112] In fact, as noted above, Garnet's "Address" to the slaves was voted on at the 1843 Negro National Convention in Buffalo, New York, and lost by one vote, a margin that, some suggested, reflected popular support for violence. The vote, however, was not whether or not to endorse violence as a strategy, but simply whether to adopt the speech as part of the conference memorandum. This is significant. Had the delegates been asked to vote on the adoption of violence as a strategy, the margin of rejection would most certainly have been much wider. Even as Blacks in Pennsylvania, and other parts of the North experienced increased anti-Black violence, they did not completely abandon moral suasion. Rather, they chose to emphasize political and immediatist strategies as well.[113]

Like most free Blacks of his generation, therefore, Delany unequivocally affirmed the individual's right to self-defense. He would risk anything, including his life, in defense of his personal liberty. But like most other Blacks, he was equally opposed to acts of organized violence despite the fact that his and their collective freedom was very much circumscribed by the violence of slavery. Though "free" Black leaders manifested "bravery" in defense of personal liberty, but these "brave" leaders were most reluctant, even with the latitude of freedom, to initiate collective acts of violence against slavery. Two important questions beg for consideration: First, why the reluctance and refusal of free Blacks to embrace violence as a reform strategy? Second, how did free Blacks view the utility of violence? The answer to the first is fairly obvious, and many free Black leaders directly or indirectly answered the question. Douglass, for example, made it clear in his *The Life and Times of Frederick Douglass* (1882), and in his response to John Brown. Douglass considered the individual's right to self-defense inviolable, and thus acknowledged the legitimacy and necessity of self-defense. Yet, he was reluctant to endorse collective acts of violence, which he regarded as both impracticable and suicidal. In his fight with the infamous slave-breaker Covey,

Douglass fully exercised his right to self-defense. He also agreed in principle with John Brown that violence against slavery was justified. Yet, he would not go along with Brown because of the probability of failure, in the event of which, Douglass believed, and rightly so, that Blacks would suffer the worst reprisals.[114] Blacks viewed the utility of violence in existential terms: violence was functional only if it did not threaten life; its adoption had to include the certainty of survival (i.e., triumph).

Delany's *Blake*: Violence and Providential Determinism

In the late 1850s, Delany began serializing his fictional work, *Blake, Or, The Huts of America*, in the *Weekly Anglo-African Magazine*. In 1970, Floyd Miller published the first edited volume which for decades was the standard edition most scholars relied on for study and interpretation of the novel. It should be noted that the Miller edition was not complete. It was missing the closing chapters, and many suggest, concluding part of the novel's plot. Recently, Jerome McGann has published a "corrected" edition, which also is missing the closing chapters. In essence, *Blake* remains incomplete. The missing chapters may never be found. Notwithstanding, in my judgment, the serialized and published chapters contain the core of Delany's thesis: to demonstrate the challenges and problematic nature of violence as reform strategy. In *Blake*, Delany developed a much more robust contextual and moral defense of nonviolence and emigration.[115] As I argue in this study fiction offered Delany an alternative and effective medium for dramatizing the limitations of violence as a weapon of change. The late Ronald Takaki underscored that the fictional medium served as a "less intimidating" avenue for articulating nonfictional political views. "Much more than editorial, letters or autobiographies," Takaki wrote,

> fiction ... permits the writer to express dreams and deeply felt emotions he may have not been able or willing to articulate in speeches or nonfictional writing. Under the guise of fiction, Delany may have felt less intimidated in telling the truth, especially to Whites and perhaps even to himself. Delany's *Blake* seems to reveal more about the father of Black Nationalism than all of his political essays and tracts.[116]

Takaki was right. In *Blake*, Delany was much more forthright about his political beliefs, especially his views on violence. Yet, most modern critics ignore Delany's central thesis: that though violence seemed an appropriate response to the challenges confronting Blacks, its adoption and ultimate success depended on divine intervention and agency. Instead, critics have interpreted *Blake* through the prism of Delany's "radical" nationalism. *Blake* is popularly interpreted as a plot for a hemispheric uprising and revolution. For instance, in Vincent Harding's view, *Blake* "demonstrates that Delany carried the stream of Black radicalism deeper than almost any other man of the post-David Walker generation."[117] Another critic, John Zeugner, identifies the central message in *Blake* as "insurrection, violent purification through insurrection."[118] The fictional hero, Henry, according to Zeugner, constructs revolution as a three-way process: alienation, organization, and violence.[119] In Jean Yellin's analysis, *Blake* both celebrates "The Nat Turner Figure" and outlines "the organization of a guerilla army of Black liberationists."[120] Addison Gayle describes Delany as anti-accommodation and Henry as the "first Black revolutionary character in Black fiction."[121] In his review, Roger Hite represents Henry as a radical who cried "revolution now!"[122] These interpretations are rehearsed in more recent studies and analyses of the book. Some scholars have highlighted Delany's construction and utilization of geographical space, to reinforce the regional and global reaches of the "revolution" in *Blake*. This use of space, Judith Madera for example, argues, enabled Delany to "romanticize the scope of transnational antislavery resistance, with Blacks from the United States, the Guinea Coast, and Cuba brought in alliance."[123] Similarly, Martha Schoolman describes *Blake* as "the quintessential North American geographic novel"—a novel whose spatial purview interlaced Canada, the United States and Africa.[124] While it is true that resistance and revolution permeate the novel, they are not the raison d'être. I argue that in fact the plot of revolution serves more as a conduit for the far more profound message Delany sought to convey: the imperative of focusing on and prioritizing emigration. *Blake*, I contend, is autobiographical. It is the fictional dramatization of Delany's real-life experiences and the economic, political, and cultural ideas and programs he espoused and defended.

In *Blake*, Delany chose a hero with whom he shared qualities. Henry Blacus was very Black and also intelligent. Unlike Delany, however, Henry was a slave, who had been decoyed from his country, Cuba, and enslaved to one Colonel Steven Frank of Natchez County, Mississippi. Like Delany, Henry abhorred slavery, against which he declared total war after Colonel Frank sold Henry's wife into slavery. He vowed to destroy slavery through the instigation of servile insurrections. He planned to travel through the length and breadth of the American South inciting insurrection among slaves. Embarking upon his scheme, Henry attacked religious determinism. Reacting angrily to the pleas of his aged in-laws to leave everything to God and "stand still and see his salvation," Henry retorted,

"Don't tell me about religion! What is religion to me? Put my trust in the Lord! I have done so all my life and of what use is it to me?"[125] Henry was angry because religion, in his estimation, subverted Black consciousness. Nevertheless, he was not an atheist. As he quickly pointed out, "I do trust the Lord as much as ever: but I now understand him better than I used to."[126] His better understanding taught him that God was opposed to injustice and oppression. God's own natural law sanctioned equality of rights. Henry, therefore, rejected the precept "stand still," because it induced complacency and indifference.

By denouncing "stand still," Henry, mimicking Delany of the late 1840s, sought to liberate Blacks from the mental shackles of a religious worldview that rationalized slavery on the promise of a better world beyond: the otherworldly gospel. He urged Blacks instead to struggle for their rights here: "I want a hope on this side of the vale of tears. I want something on this earth as well as a promise of things in another world."[127] He described Black liberation as the central mission of true Christianity. This was in fact the subject of a series in Delany's reports on his Western lecture tour in the 1840s.[128] In that series, Delany deplored what he characterized as a domineering and pervasive otherworldly religion which he blamed for subverting the self-deterministic aspirations of Blacks.[129] At every stop in his journey through the heart of American Slavery, *Blake*'s hero, Henry, infused in slaves a defiant self-deterministic consciousness, just as Delany had done during his tour for the *North Star* discussed earlier.[130] He found slaves generally receptive to his revolutionary scheme. In Cuba, where the search for his wife eventually took him, Henry became commander-in-chief of a "revolutionary movement," organized by aggrieved Blacks.[131] Paradoxically, towards the end of his trip, Henry suddenly changed course and urged the slaves not to revolt but instead to "stand still and see the salvation of God"[132] This about-face surfaced earlier during a visit to New Orleans where one overzealous old slave proclaimed, "War Now!" but Henry quickly cautioned:

> My friend, listen a moment to me. You are not yet ready for a strike; you are not yet ready to do anything effective. You have barely taken the first step in the matter-and you must have all the necessary means, my brother-you must know **WHAT, HOW AND WHEN** to do. Have all the instrumentalities necessary for an effective effort before making the attempt. Without this, you will fail, utterly fail! [emphasis added][133]

But the old man was indignant. He wanted War "dis night" because "if we got wait all dat time, we neveh be free! I goes in for dis night. I say dis night." Unfortunately, the other slaves seemed not quite ready.[134] Meanwhile, news of the "revolutionary" plan leaked to the government which responded with full scale harassment and intimidation of Blacks. Also, in Nashville, Tennessee, where, according to Henry "the harvest was ripe and ready for the scythe," he counseled moderation, advising the slaves to "Stand still and see the salvation!"[135] Many were disappointed. None more so than another old man, Daddy Luu:

> "How long me son, how long we got wait this way?" he inquired.
>
> "I can't tell exactly, father," Henry replied, "but I suppose in this, as in other good works, the Lords own anointed time."
>
> "An, how long dat gwine be honey? Case I's mighty tired waiting dis wey!" Daddy Luu persisted.
>
> "I can't tell you how long, father," Henry responded, "God knows best."[136]

Critics of *Blake* have failed to explain why, despite his alienation, Henry repeatedly urged caution and moderation. Unlike Nat Turner, Henry's abhorrence of slavery did not result in any violent attempts at its overthrow. Why? The answer lies in his attitude to violence and religion, and in his strong faith in an alternative to revolutionary violence: emigration.

Personally, Henry loathed violence. In a discussion with Charles and Andy, two other slaves of Colonel Frank, soon after his Southern trip, Henry confessed his inability to use violence against his master for selling his wife. "The most I could take courage directly to do," he admitted, "was to leave him." (i.e., emigrate)[137] In fact, he had returned to Mississippi to convince other slaves to escape (emigrate) to a more favorable environment (Canada). Henry confronted a dilemma: "mature reflections" justified the use of violence against slavery. Since slavery depended on violence, its destruction could and should come through violence. But, Henry lamented, "I cannot find it in my heart to injure an individual."[138] Emigration, therefore, enabled him to resolve this dilemma. He also regarded violence as against God's plan and incompatible with Christianity. In the course of a debate on violence, the "Revolutionary Council" in Cuba split into two conflicting ideological camps: radicals and conservatives. Tired of incessant police harassments, the radical group opted for "revolution now."[139] No one expressed this determination better than Gondolier—the quarter master general of the movement. In a veiled criticism of Henry, the commander-in-chief, he opined:

> We ought to by this time be able to redress our grievances. Some men are born to command and others to obey, and it is well that this is the case, else I might be a commander, and if I was, I might command when orders should not be given.[140]

Another concerned member, Ambrosima, daughter of Montego, a leading conservative, advocated revolution: "I wish I was a man, I'd lay the city in ashes this
night," she lamented.[141] Her father, Montego, however, disagreed: "We should
not hate our fellow man, as God made us all."[142] He opposed indiscriminate
violence, arguing that not all Whites hated Blacks; "there are some good ones
among them."[143] Violence, insisted another conservative, "would precipitate us
into more trouble." The conservatives opted for caution, moderation and Christian love. They conceived of violence as immoral and impracticable. They seemed
to have won the debate.[144]

Through the entire debate, Henry (commander-in-chief), sat "grave and
sober" and silent. His preference for the conservative option was unmistakable.[145]
Blake underscored the futility of violence. Each time Blacks organized, whether
on the plantations in the Southern states, or in Cuba, the state responded with
brutal force. The use of force and intimidation by both state and federal authorities reflected the pervasive nature of racism. Right at the beginning of the book,
the reader is impressed with the issue of national consensus on Black inferiority.
During a visit to Natchez, Mrs. Arabella Ballard, wife of a prominent Northern
judge, assured Colonel Frank and his wife that, especially on the subject of slavery, Northerners were in sync with Southerners. Her husband, Judge Ballard,
owned plantations in Cuba, and consequently had a strong economic interest in
sustaining slavery. He too pledged his fidelity to Southern values and declared
unconditional support for the Dred Scott decision.[146]

Delany used the Ballards, a prominent Northern family, to highlight an issue
he had repeatedly drawn attention to in his earlier political writings: the economic and moral bonds uniting both sections of the country. In his view, this
shared interest in slavery committed both to upholding the institution. Consequently, he challenged the myth of the liberal North. With such "marriage of
minds" the odds in the event of a revolution favored Whites. *Blake*, nonetheless,
did not completely rule out revolutionary violence. For the integrationists, that
is, those who, in spite of the odds, chose to remain in the United States, revolution might succeed if, and only if, divine providence interceded. In Cuba,
the "revolutionary" movement began and ended all its meetings with calls for
divine aid and guidance, emphasizing the centrality of God to the revolution
and, equally important, the compatibility of religion with freedom.[147] Within
this context, therefore, the farthest Blacks could go was prepare themselves
mentally and psychologically for freedom, be conscious of freedom and of their
self-deterministic capacity. However, the *timing* and the *nature* of the strike depended ultimately on the divine will. Only God knew the "What, How and

When" of the struggle.[148] Therefore, Henry advised Blacks to turn to nature for signs. Addressing a session of the "revolutionary" council, he informed members that "the time to strike was fast verging upon them," and he urged everyone to be vigilant and watch for signs, stressing: "Nature being exact and regular in all her fixed laws, suspended nor altered them to suit no person, circumstance, nor thing."[149] He did not elaborate on the exact timing and nature of the sign. However, if the prevailing modus operandi of contemporary Black activists and "revolutionaries" were any indication, such signs, were they to manifest, would probably have advised inaction, as demonstrated by the "Twelve Knights of Tabor." Organized in 1846 in St. Louis, Missouri, by twelve Blacks from the states of Ohio, Georgia, South Carolina, North Carolina, Virginia, Alabama, Louisiana, Mississippi, and Tennessee, the "Knights" were sworn to secrecy and dedicated their lives to the violent overthrow of slavery.[150] A leading scholar described the movement as "one of the strongest and most secret of any organization ever formed by men."[151] By 1856, the name had changed to the Order of Twelve, with a membership of about 47,000 "Knights of Liberty," all pledged and dedicated to "breaking the bonds of our slavery."[152] By 1857, with military subdivisions and cells created in several states, membership had grown to 150,000 composed largely of "well-armed men . . . prepared to spread death and destruction through the South."[153] They collected ammunitions and held regular drills in readiness for the ultimate assault on slavery.

At the summoning of their commander-in-chief, the Knights were to converge in Atlanta where the mayhem would commence. However, something extraordinary happened in 1857. The commander scanned the horizon for signs and found a clear and unambiguous message: Do nothing! God was about to intervene! In essence, "stand still for his salvation"! According to a report, "it was plainly demonstrated to him (i.e., the commander-in-chief) that a higher power was preparing to take a part in the contest between the North and South."[154] As I surmised elsewhere, "what would have been the bloodiest insurrection by free Blacks in American history was abruptly aborted by the specter of divine intervention."[155] This should not have surprised anyone. The Knights' ideology allowed for escape into an alternate universe of providential determinism, one in which a higher power assumed leadership of the "revolution." Their "revolutionary" zealotry notwithstanding, it was a cardinal belief of the Knights "that the lord God was on the side of right and justice, our faith and trust was in Him, and that He would help us in our needy time."[156] It is not clear if Delany was aware of the Knights. Was he involved? No one knows. But the timing of *Blake*'s serialization, occurring contemporaneous with the Knights of Tabor, would lead one to infer some awareness in Delany of the existence of the organization. Nonetheless, the central message in *Blake* underscores a coincidence of conviction. Delany shared the Knights' faith in divine intervention.

In *Blake*, Delany clothed revolutionary violence in divine robes to highlight a point he had made repeatedly: that left alone Blacks could never successfully launch a revolution. Only God knew the appropriate time for the revolution and the form it would take. Those who chose revolutionary violence, therefore, must "stand still" and wait for God's salvation. They were to watch for some mysterious signs from nature. This mystification is not coincidental. It symbolizes the visionary nature of the violent option. It should be acknowledged that this intersection of *revolution* and *religion* was not unique to Delany's *Blake*. Several critics have also noted with respect to David Walker's *Appeal*; most notably Eddie Glaude Jr., that Walker "explicitly called for armed Black resistance against the institution of slavery (resistance sanctioned by the Grace of God) and prophesized America's fall and destruction unless the nation repented for this evil."[157] Eddie Glaude further contends that Walker coupled violence with divine intercession: "the two went hand-in-hand: for African Americans couldn't wait for God to liberate them. They had to act for themselves" and yet "such action had to emanate from him." Human aggression and agency alone would be ineffective.[158] Underlining this intersection of revolution and religion, Grant Shreve argues that "most accounts of the Black nationalism on display in *Blake* discounts its theological investment by granting Delany a sweeping political imagination, but neglecting his religious creativity." Counteracting this, Shreve draws attention to "the religious experimentalism animating and shaping not only the novel but also Delany's nationalism more broadly" and contends that "*Blake*—its strange history and missing final chapters notwithstanding—is the fullest expression of the metaphysical and political-theological possibilities of emigrationist thinking, a novel that reimagines the relationship between religious beliefs and public life as a strategy for contending with the global dispersion of racial discourse."[159] In Shreve's view, therefore, emigration, an unpopular and failed option in the 1850s, nonetheless "produced" a discourse that was "endowed with unique speculative capacities that find their most charged expression in *Blake*. Delany's novel aspired to think at the outer limit of the Exodus paradigm to reveal what a Canaan for African Americans was for and to envision what such a new order might actually be."[160]

Henry's preference, like Delany's, was unmistakable: emigration. I argue therefore that though violence is a central theme in *Blake*, it is not the thrust of the novel. Delany introduced the idea of violence in order to demonstrate its impractical, unviable, and visionary nature. The disagreement between Montego and his daughter represented generational conflict over violence. Yet, the fact that moderation ultimately triumphed suggested the problematic nature of the violent option. Ultimately, *Blake* made emigration an attractive and viable strategy. Though Henry (like Delany) moved to Canada, it was temporary. His destination was Africa. Members of the "revolutionary" movement in Cuba discussed the immense economic potentials of Africa. During one meeting, Placido urged his colleagues to endeavor to:

> Prove not only that the African race is now the principal Producers of the greater part of the luxuries of enlightened Countries . . . but that Africans are among the most Industrious in the World and before long must hold the Balance of commercial power . . . and the race will at once Rise to the first magnitude of importance in the world.[161]

But Madame Cordora questioned the possibility of Africa ever "becoming a great country [*sic*]."[162] Placido reassured her that "not only hope, but undoubted probabilities existed for that, and, at no distant day."[163] He further emphasized that the foundation of all great nationalities depended on three principles: territory, population, and staple commodities; and Africa possessed all in abundance.[164] Here is a strong reaffirmation of an enduring faith in the potency of an externally situated and economically viable Black State—the essence of Delany's nationalism. Jerome McGann acknowledges this much in the introduction to his "corrected" edition. Arguing that Delany wrote *Blake* "as part of an argument for Black emigration to Africa and as part of a scheme to raise money for his emigration project," McGann also underlines the religious underpinnings of the novel's plot. As he rightly underscores,

> Everything in Delany's life shows that his revolutionary consciousness was grounded in a Black religious consciousness. In terms of actual history, God's plan is to drive a new birth of human freedom through the agency of an emancipated Black consciousness. Recognizing that plan, hearing God's call, Delany passes it along to his contemporary world. *Blake* is an account of Delany's response to that call, and within the plot of the fiction, we glimpse how this divine scheme will work itself out.[165]

In essence, McGann reiterates "*Blake* is arguing the necessity of emigration from White racist America, Emigrating "to Afraka." Reimagining of an escape to "a world elsewhere" in *Blake* called "Afraka."[166] Robert Carr advances a similar interpretation. He represents *Blake* as the fictional articulation of Delany's overarching agenda of creating "a Pan-African/American nation-state that would undermine Southern slave economy and thus position Africa as the epicenter of a thriving Black commercial empire."[167] Finally, reiterating this interpretation, Grant Shreve writes: "In *Blake*, we can see anew how emigrationist thought expanded the field of view in Black Exodus politics to question what kind of social world order needed to be established to sustain an independent Black nation after liberation."[168]

Conclusion

It is my contention, therefore, that like his notable contemporaries (Douglass, Garnet, and Walker), Delany was ambivalent on violence. While he acknowledged the utility of violence and agreed that violence seemed an appropriate response to the challenges confronting Blacks, the certainty of failure compelled caution. It is also clear from his writings and public utterances that Delany both affirmed the individual's right to self-defense and opposed collective and suicidal acts of violent insurrection. The latter would fail, unless undertaken from a position of strength and with divine guidance. This was consistent with the views of other prominent Blacks, including David Walker, Henry Garnet, and Frederick Douglass. While they endorsed individual acts of violence in self-defense, they discouraged organized and collective acts of violent resistance that had little chance of succeeding.

Delany wrote *Blake* undoubtedly to reiterate the ideas he had unsuccessfully attempted to popularize in his earlier political tracts: that violence was futile; that Blacks lacked the capacity to launch a successful violent resistance; that such resistance would crumble beneath the weight of state power; that though violence seemed justifiable in principle, its indiscriminate application was doomed and morally reprehensible. The only viable option then was emigration, and the political economy of an external Black State, whose success, he hoped, would confirm the capabilities of Blacks and thus negate racist notions of Black inferiority. The "radicalism" in *Blake*, therefore, did not go beyond rhetoric. Henry was undoubtedly bitter and defiant. Yet he was unduly cautious. While he acknowledged the need for violence against slavery, Henry objected on practical and moral grounds and directed his followers instead to the economic potentialities of Africa. Unlike Nat Turner, Henry's alienation did not result in violent revolt. He just couldn't unleash violence against slavery! *Blake*'s ambivalence is unmistakable. On the one hand, Henry, the "militant," is defiant and vows to destroy slavery. He successfully stirred his followers from their hitherto quietist and fatalistic dispositions. On the other hand, however, this same "militant," impelled by ethical considerations and cognizant of the enormity of state power, opted for what some critics perceived as an escapist strategy: emigration. Henry perfectly reflected Delany's ambivalence; he was angry, and seriously considered violence, but was restrained by both moral and pragmatic considerations and faith in divine intervention.

It is worth repeating that *Blake* remains incomplete; the last missing chapters have not been found. This means that we are left with nothing but speculation on what the likely outcome of the planned revolution would have been. Jerome McGann candidly acknowledges, "I may imagine how those missing chapters unfolded, but the truth is that I don't know."[169] Nonetheless, scholars have been very creative in reimagining how the novel ended. While one is free to extrapolate and imagine how the novel ended, what is very much indisputable is that Delany did not leave us in doubt about the likely termination of his novel. As several critics cited here acknowledge, Delany's ultimate goal and vision was to establish a strong case for emigration. Fundamentally, this was why he wrote the novel. Toward the end, the plot left no one in doubt about the impractical and problematic nature of any attempts at hemispheric revolution. If that were to occur at all, Henry made it clear to his followers to wait for divine intercession, just like the Knights of Tabor. I suggest therefore that Delany wrote *Blake* not to instigate a hemispheric rebellion that he knew was doomed, but to demonstrate the challenges of the option, and redirect people toward emigration and the potentialities of a successful African/Black nationality. Though *Blake* clearly mapped the geographical terrain of a hemispheric/Pan-African resistance, it was all in the planning and *imaginary*. Certain factors compelled reconsideration and caution. In the end, Henry Blacus asked his followers to seek divine guidance.

Delany manifested another curious paradox on violence. Though he refused to embrace violence when John Brown presented the opportunity, Delany seemed to cherish the symbolism of violence or what could be characterized as the moral appeal of militancy. Perhaps under certain circumstances, to be associated with violence, or to be seen as someone potentially of violent nature, had its utilitarian appeal. This could possibly explain why, in an address to a gathering of South Carolina Democrats (conservatives) in October 1874, Delany introduced himself as "A John Brown Abolitionist," and advocated reconciliation and reunion with these erstwhile, and many would argue, and with justification, still unrepentant, defenders of slavery.[170] It should be recalled that Delany began his post-Civil War career in South Carolina as a Freedmen's Bureau field agent who developed a reputation for violent rhetoric enough to prompt one White observer to conclude, after listening to one of Delany's public addresses, that he (i.e., Delany) was "a thorough hater of the White race."[171] It is reasonable to infer, therefore, that several, possibly most in the audience in 1874, perceived Delany with trepidation. They saw him as someone who harbored deep hatred of, and potential for violence against, Whites. Therefore, his conciliatory tone and call for reconciliation would seem reassuring and thus comforting to this hitherto hostile constituency. They reciprocated with deafening applause and welcomed him to their movement! Along with Delany, they sang the "Bonnie Blue Flag" (the Confederate anthem)![172] Notwithstanding, it is worth recalling that John Brown's scheme was the antithesis of slavery. Brown's ultimate solution was violence, which Delany refused to endorse.

What then should we make of Delany's self-characterization as "a John Brown abolitionist? What did being a "John Brown abolitionist" mean in nineteenth-century America? The answer leaves no room for ambiguity: a "John Brown abolitionist" would be someone who confronted violence without being restrained by the possibility or certainty of failure. John Brown did not consider the constellation of forces, neither was he discouraged by the likelihood of failure. Self-preservation was not paramount to John Brown, a key element of Delany's worldview. It should also be noted that the South Carolina Democrats with whom Delany, this self-acclaimed "John Brown Abolitionist," sought reconciliation and reunion, pathologically loathed Brown. They most certainly celebrated his failure and demise. To juxtapose Brown with his arch enemies, therefore, was the greatest of contradictions. In death, Brown seemed to have finally found peace with his living detractors! Only the mind of a Martin Delany could have contrived this, and it was obvious that neither he, nor his audience, recognized the contradiction. Of what relevance then was Delany's invocation of John Brown before such anti-Brown audience? Perhaps, Delany's action mirrored the changing political context. In the political climate of late Reconstruction South Carolina, an appeal for reconciliation from an avowed advocate of violence seemed consistent with what some political observers characterized as a changing political context and culture, one that was reconciling erstwhile political opponents. As a correspondent of the *New York Times* reported from South Carolina, "parties are now getting mixed in the South. Other questions than those raised by the War are now making their way into politics . . . which do not leave old party lines clear. . . . Republicans are found acting with Democrats and vice-versa."[173] This would be the only logical explanation for what, at the time, for Delany, was a political blunder of epic proportions.

It should be stressed that though Delany was ambivalent on violence, he was no coward. His courage and willingness to embrace and undertake violence given certain circumstances was attested to by the role he played in organizing resistance to anti-Black violence and vigilantism against the Fugitive Slave Law in Pennsylvania from the late 1830s through the early 1850s. This was also reflected by his commissioning as the first Black combat major in the Union army and his assistance with recruiting and raising several battalions of Colored troops during the Civil War. Furthermore, Delany undoubtedly encouraged one of his sons to enlist in the 54th Massachusetts Regiment. On violence, therefore, one can surmise that Delany, like Frederick Douglass, Josiah Henson, and many others of his generation, would readily undertake violence if it had a chance of succeeding (if their lives were not threatened). It is worth recalling that, in the words of Rollin, "nature marked Delany for combat and victory and not for martyrdom."[174] He would boldly confront any violent situation where victory was certain. The Civil War was one such instance of a violent confrontation that these Blacks believed would succeed, and they all endorsed it. Delany saw the "hand" of God in the Civil War and welcomed it. He saw reckless endangerment in John Brown's scheme, and like Frederick Douglass, kept a respectable distance.

CHAPTER 3

Education

The Why, Which, and How

ASIDE FROM ENGAGING WITH the subject of religion and violence in
the Black struggle, and the creative manner he sought to use religion to
advance both integration and separatism, Delany was also passionate
about education. In fact, he considered education perhaps the most important
force that would enhance the chances of Black elevation and empowerment. As
a crucial component of moral suasion, Delany had to discuss the state of Black
education in his lectures and writings as well as address strategies of ensuring
Blacks would attain the best education. He took considerable time and effort not
only to explain the importance of education but also to theorize on how Blacks
could benefit from education, what type of education to pursue, and the most
effective strategy for accomplishing it. In order to understand the place of education in Delany's thought, it is necessary first to examine the broader historical
context that compelled Delany and many of his peers to prioritize the quest for
knowledge, and for this we have to turn to the beginning in slavery.

Keeping Blacks (slave and free) ignorant and uneducated was a major function of slavery. It enabled slaveholders' justification for enslavement and subordination of Blacks and the denial of the rights, privileges, and opportunities afforded to Whites. It was no coincidence, therefore, that, early in their struggles,
Blacks realized the importance of education, and it assumed preeminence in
their liberation thoughts and strategies. For leading Blacks, gaining knowledge
became a countervailing repertoire of resistance, the antidote for overcoming
subordination and impoverishment, and ultimately achieving true freedom and
equality. The pursuit of knowledge became the lifeline to freedom and equality, an existential goal. This association of education with freedom and equality
prompted many to attempt seemingly insurmountable obstacles in the quest for
knowledge. According to Heather Williams,

Despite laws and customs in slave states prohibiting enslaved people from learning to read and write, a small percentage managed, through ingenuity and will, to acquire a degree of literacy in the antebellum period. Access to the written word whether scriptural or political revealed a world beyond bondage in which African Americans would make themselves free to think and behave as they chose.[1]

One such was David Walker who, Heather Williams contends, "linked literacy to slavery's demise."[2] Walker accused Whites of depriving Blacks education because they were afraid that educated Blacks would expose "their infernal deeds of cruelty" to the world.[3] This desire to prevent Blacks access to education was widespread and not limited to the slaveholding South. There were similar attempts in Connecticut and other Northern states where antislavery laws were passed to complement and reinforce extra-legal measures of restricting Black education.[4] Hilary Green describes how in the aftermath of the bloody Nat Turner insurrection there emerged "a hostile environment for African American education" which prompted introduction of strict laws "that made educating enslaved African Americans illegal."[5]

Fredrick Douglass was one of those who "through ingenuity and will" acquired literacy. In his epic autobiography, Douglass captured a poignant moment of existential epiphany: revelation of the dialectics of education and freedom. Douglass was a slave who escaped, and subsequently published, among many other works, a *Narrative* (1842) of his life. He recalled, with dramatic effects, the moment his master Thomas Auld berated his wife for teaching him (i.e., Douglass) the alphabet. Within earshot of Douglass, Auld pleaded with his wife to terminate the lesson on the ground that it was both "unlawful and unsafe" to teach slaves to read.[6] Auld informed his wife that, "learning would spoil the best nigger in the world . . . if you teach that nigger how to read (referring to Douglass), there would be no keeping him. It would forever unfit him to be a slave. He would at once become unmanageable, and of no value to his master. . . . It would make him discontent and unhappy."[7] Auld's words, according to Douglass, "sank deep into my heart, stirred sentiments within that lay slumbering, and called into existence an entire new train of thoughts. . . . I now understood what had been to me a most perplexing difficulty—to wit, the White man's power to enslave the Black man. It was a great achievement, and I prized it highly."[8] Douglass would not soon forget this moment. He now "understood the pathway from slavery to freedom."[9] Though Mrs. Auld, in deference to her husband, terminated the lessons and became mean-spirited, Douglass's desire for knowledge, once ignited, would not be extinguished. He would go on to self-educate, and Thomas Auld's words would prove prophetic. The attainment of literacy fired Douglass's desire for freedom. Subsequently, he escaped! Such revelation, however, was not a uniquely Douglassean experience. It was an experience shared by many of Douglass's contemporaries. Nationwide, Heather Williams argues, "Blacks, free and slave . . . devised different strategies of subverting those anti-literacy laws."[10]

The quest for education was a burning desire among Blacks (free and slave) in nineteenth-century America, and it would dominate the debate within the leadership of the emerging Black abolitionist movement from the 1830s as represented in the minutes and proceedings of both state and national Negro Conventions. The question, "Why education?" was a recurrent theme in Black liberation thought. Along with the "why" there were also the "which" and the "how" questions: Which form of education would guarantee the desired freedom and meaningful equality? How would that education be accomplished? On these questions, the free Black leadership was divided into two opposing viewpoints: on the one hand, there were those in favor of classical education, also referred to as collegiate or "education of the mind"; and on the other, there were advocates of industrial education, also referred to as practical, normal, or "education of the hand." The minutes and deliberations of the conventions (state and national alike) clearly underscored this division. At times, the delegates seemed to prioritize practical education, and at other times they seemed to prefer collegiate or classical education.[11]

By the late nineteenth and early twentieth centuries, this division had become even more pronounced, especially during those crucial turn-of-the-century controversies over contending strategies of resistance and accommodation. The debate over which education better advanced the cause of Blacks engaged two of the leading nineteenth-century minds: Booker T. Washington and William E. B. Du Bois. The former was associated with practical education and the latter with collegiate or classical education. A Harvard trained historian, Du Bois was an activist, first through the National Association for the Advancement of Colored People (NAACP), of which he was a founding member and, later, in the Pan-African movement. He had very strong views on which education was right for Blacks, one that he believed would better enhance their chances of elevation in America. His ideas sharply contradicted those of Booker T. Washington. A graduate of Hampton Institute and a staunch advocate of practical education, Washington would go on to help establish a trade school that would train generations of Blacks: the Tuskegee Institute.[12]

In this chapter, I hope to analyze and reconstruct the educational thoughts and philosophy of Martin Delany, the one individual who seemed to have anticipated, and theorized about, much of the themes and values that dominated discourses on education among Black Americans from the very earliest of times. Curiously, he is barely acknowledged in the historiography of African American education.[13] Though Delany was not a professional educator, his writings and speeches are suffused with ideas about the importance of education and strategies of enhancing literacy. He underscored the importance of education as critical for achieving meaningful freedom and equality for Blacks in America. His contributions to the discourses on Black education addressed the "why," the "which," and the "how" dimensions. His answers would resurface in the ideas and philosophies of future generations of American educators, most prominently Booker T. Washington.

The "Education" of Martin Delany

As already confirmed, Martin Delany is not counted among African American educators, perhaps because he neither featured prominently in the establishment of schools nor philosophized at length on Black education.[14] On the contrary, he built his reputation largely on his nationalist activities and on his extensive publications, which introduced his political theories and values. Yet, Delany expressed strong opinions on, and concerns about, the education of his people. In all the phases of his life, he held up education as an indispensable factor. Without education, he warned, Blacks had a very slim chance of becoming meaningfully and effectively free and elevated in American society. Though Delany did not write any lengthy works on education, he infused his political writings and speeches with commentaries on the significance of education and its centrality to advancing the future of Blacks in America. His criticisms of nineteenth-century Blacks' responses and orientation to education highlighted certain ideals and values that he insisted should frame any educational measures or policies designed for Blacks. For this, he certainly deserves recognition as an educator.

Delany felt the pinch of educational deprivation as painfully as Frederick Douglass or any other of his contemporaries. The education of Blacks was a crime in Virginian at the time of his birth. Like other slave states, Virginia proscribed the education of slaves. This policy became even more stringent in the aftermath of the bloody Nat Turner revolt of 1830 in Southampton County. The Virginia General Assembly passed more restrictive laws criminalizing teaching slaves and free Blacks to read and write.[15] However, growing up in what seemed like an integrated neighborhood instilled in young Delany a false sense of security and comfort. He mixed freely with the White children of his neighborhood. Sadly, he would be rudely awakened to the ugly realities of his second-class citizenship when he attempted to "help himself" to the Virginia school system. Upon accompanying his White playmates to school one day, he was refused entry to the classroom.[16] It then dawned on him that education was for Whites only.[17]

Delany's opportunity came when his parents acquired a copy of the *New York Primer and Spelling Book* from an itinerant peddler. The family kept the treasured acquisition a secret and held nocturnal study sessions. Soon, every member had attained literacy.[18] Words spread that the Delany family had broken the law, and prosecution seemed imminent. The family escaped to Chambersburg, Pennsylvania, in September of 1822. Chambersburg was little better than Charlestown. Despite a more permissive environment, racism persisted there.[19] Young Delany was, however, able to continue his elementary education in the public school system, where he encountered values that were meant to inculcate acceptance of the prevailing perception of Blacks as inferior and of Africa as a continent of barbarism.[20] The persistence of derogatory images of Africa bolstered his determination to seek the truth.[21] At the completion of his elementary education in Chambersburg, and with no opportunities for further education, Delany moved to Pittsburgh in July of 1831. There, he encountered a thriving, energetic, and equally determined community of free Blacks, mostly migrants like himself, all of whom thirsted for knowledge.[22] Delany enrolled in the Cellar School of the African Methodist Episcopal Church, where he took classes in the arts and humanities. History was his favorite subject, which he considered fundamental to enlightenment and mental emancipation. Delany made tremendous progress at the Cellar School and was promptly promoted to advanced levels. He supplemented his schoolwork with private study and discussions with his roommate, Mollison Clark. The two frequently discussed and debated diverse issues. To encourage similar activities among other Blacks, they founded the Theban Literacy and Debating Society.[23] In January of 1832, six months into his arrival in Pittsburgh, Delany attended a meeting organized by the city's leading Blacks to discuss the state of Black education. They were concerned about the education gap created by White neglect of Black education. This resulted in the founding of the African Education Society of Pittsburgh.[24] In Pittsburgh, Delany found himself amidst other Blacks who were eager to do something about Black education. He enthusiastically embraced the challenge.

In 1837, the Theban Society expanded its scope and became the Young Men's Literary and Moral Reform Society of Pittsburgh and focused on advancing literacy and intellectual development of "rising generations" of Blacks. Delany was elected its first librarian.[25]

After attaining the equivalence of a high school education, Delany turned his attention to choosing a profession. He noticed a troubling "slavish" disposition among free Blacks: the tendency to gravitate toward menial and servile occupations. He deplored this development and insisted that Blacks needed to aspire for better occupations through higher education. Lamenting what he characterized as "the menial position of our people in this country," Delany further denounced "a seeming satisfaction" among Blacks with seeking after menial positions to a degree "unknown to any other people."[26] According to him,

> There appears to be, a want of a sense of propriety or self-respect, altogether inexplicable; because young men and women among us, many of whom have good trades, and homes, adequate to their support, voluntarily leave them, and seek positions, such as servants, washing maids, coachmen, nurses, cooks . . . when they can gain a livelihood at something more respectable, or elevating in character.[27]

Delany was determined not to replicate this self-degradation. Consequently, he rejected the invitation of his friends and colleagues to become a barber (which was then popular among Blacks, but perceived derogatorily as a "nigger job") and chose instead to pursue a career in medicine.[28] After being rejected by the University of Pennsylvania, Jefferson College, and the medical colleges of Albany and Geneva in New York, Delany entered Harvard University in the spring of 1850.[29] That same spring, Harvard also admitted two other Black students sponsored by the American Colonization Society. The tenure of all three Black students ended prematurely after a semester as a result of a protest by several White students who maintained that the admission of Blacks compromised Harvard's academic standards.[30]

Crusading for Black Education: The Why, Which, and How

Notwithstanding the Harvard episode, by 1850 Delany had effectively been freed from the mental shackles of ideological bondage. He had attained a level of education that enabled him to think independently, to question prevailing normative racist ideas about Blacks and Africans, and most significantly, he had developed a critical mindset, which helped him feel much more positive, self-confident, and motivated. He then embarked on a mission to assist other Blacks attain similar self-emancipatory consciousness through education. Like Frederick Douglass, Delany rebelled against the dominant society's attempts to keep him ignorant. The denial of access to education had ignited in Delany as it had in Douglass, a burning desire to unearth the mystery undergirding the obsessions of Whites with keeping Blacks ignorant. Like Douglass, Delany also discovered a fundamental explanation for the obsession: the emancipatory power of education. Delany was inspired and thus determined to challenge the pervasive culture of Black ignorance. He would ultimately spearhead a crusade to popularize education among Blacks.

In the broader struggle to encourage education among Blacks, Delany confronted a dilemma. While there seemed to be a growing awareness of the utility of education, opinions remained sharply divided on the "which" question: which education was best for Blacks? Ironically, Delany found the answer in the very limitations of his own classical-rooted education. Though enlightened intellectually through classical education, Delany remained without an economically viable livelihood.[31] His experiences therefore proved that intellectual emancipation was one thing, "making a living" was a different challenge. On a few occasions, he had to rely on charity for his livelihood. The quests for dignity and self-respect had inspired Delany's desire for knowledge, but the experiences and challenges he encountered raised doubts about the viability of classical education as solution to the problem of Black poverty. He contended that classical education had not advanced the economic development of Blacks. Many Blacks with collegiate education remained as impoverished and marginalized as their less fortunate and illiterate counterparts.[32] The lessons of his experience, and those of other Black professionals, suggested to Delany that something was seriously wrong with an education that only liberated the mind (education of the mind) without arming the "liberated" individual with the means of economic survival (education of the hand).[33] The latter, also referred to as practical education, did not mean education for "industrial" occupations. Encouraging Blacks to aspire for "industrial" training and occupations would have been both unrealistic and problematic. Given the racist context, it would most definitely have provoked bitter resentment. Yet, Delany was unequivocal in opposition to any education that would prepare Blacks for "menial" jobs. By "practical" education, Delany and other advocates, meant education or training that would enable Blacks develop skills with which to "make a living" preferably as an independent entrepreneur.

Delany launched his crusade for Black education during his collaboration with Douglass in 1847. That year, Douglass carved an independent Black abolitionist path, after years of tutelage under the White abolitionist, William Lloyd Garrison and began publishing his newspaper the *North Star* in Rochester, New York, with Delany as coeditor. He hoped this publication would more accurately reflect, articulate and advance the interests and aspirations of Black Americans. Douglass and Delany were eager to use the *North Star* to promote moral suasion as the means of eradicating Black poverty and "moral decadence." Moral and material improvement became indispensable to Blacks' quest for elevation and equality. Education was an important component of moral suasion; but not just any education; the one that prepared Blacks to become *producers*, as opposed to their present status as *consumers*, of wealth.[34]

As a roving lecturer and coeditor of the *North Star*, Delany was in a position to influence and dictate strategies for advancing the moral and material development of Blacks. He quickly noticed two troubling conditions during his travels from Ohio to Pennsylvania, Michigan, New York, and Delaware. First was the depth of poverty and ignorance among Blacks, slave and free, and second, was how this wretchedness had induced self-denigrating consciousness. Furthermore, he found Blacks overwhelmingly in menial/servile occupations, and most disturbingly, they seemed satisfied. Menial occupations and servility had become almost like "second nature." Freedom had apparently not rid Blacks of slavish characteristics.[35] Though Delany acknowledged the efforts of industrious Blacks in several states, he equally lamented the fragile and transient nature of Black entrepreneurship, which he attributed to deficiency in practical education.[36] Delany's faith in moral suasion thrust practical education to the center stage of his philosophy of education. An appreciation for practical education had to begin at the elementary education level.

In his travels and reports, Delany focused attention on Colored elementary schools. His visits to these schools exposed unsettling realities, many of which he addressed in the *North Star*. In several such schools in Pennsylvania, he observed that free Blacks generally prioritized classical education. Students were taught English, Latin, Greek, arithmetic, music, poetry, and dance.[37] He further concluded that Blacks generally possessed a skewed and shallow conception and understanding of the objective of education. They devoted a greater proportion of the school time to preparing pupils for exhibition and entertainment. The ability to sing a few verses and recite a few stanzas of poems usually fooled Black parents into a false sense of satisfaction that their children had "done going to school," resulting in premature termination of the children's education.[38] He also observed that Black parents seemed overly obsessed with classical education as a foundation for preparing their children for professions such as the law and medicine, often without "consulting the children's propensities."[39] Underscoring the need for a practical and pragmatic approach to education, Delany implored parents to know their children's propensity and "direct their education accordingly."[40] He insisted that too much emphasis on the pursuit of collegiate/professional education had resulted in the premature creation of a professional class of lawyers, doctors, journalists, clergies, and other specialists the Black communities could neither patronize nor sustain. He noticed with consternation that Black parents tended to steer their children in the direction of "professional education before the body of people, are ready for it."[41]

Delany advised Blacks to first develop a reliable and stable business foundation that would elevate the race beyond menial and domestic realms. This foundation would in turn create the need for a professional class. He portrayed classical education as "suited for the wealthy, or those who have a prospect of gaining a livelihood by it."[42] Blacks had yet to attain this level of affluence, demonstrated by the marginalization and impoverishment of the few Black professionals who, shunned and rejected by Whites, could not find clientele and sustenance within the Black community.[43] They had pursued professional education without the foundation that would support such a class. Hence the widespread situation he encountered in several Black communities of trained and qualified professionals who were not gainfully employed. Delany characterized this as "one of our greatest mistakes." Blacks had gone in advance of themselves. They had commenced at the "superstructure" of the building instead of the foundation, "at the top instead of the bottom."[44] Blacks therefore needed an education that would develop their practical faculties and thus, their manhood. This is what would enable them to compete successfully and effectively with Whites. He designated a good business education as the foundation that would enable a community to develop the resources and capacity to sustain and nurture such a professional class.

Delany also denounced the approach of free Blacks to education as too theoretical. He observed that teachers made no attempts to teach Black children how to apply the knowledge acquired to their daily activities. For example, he noted that few students were able to apply the arithmetic they learned in school to business purposes.[45] Delany portrayed this lack of synergy between education and the practical realities of life as a critical flaw of classical education. He placed much of the blame on the curriculum and on the teachers who, ill-prepared and trained in antiquated teaching methods, failed to lead their pupils along the path of what Delany termed "reformed and approved schools," which would have developed and enhanced their practical abilities.[46] Consequently, Delany

advised all such teachers to take a one-month leave of absence to acquaint themselves with the practical and applied dimensions of their respective disciplines.
As he put it,

> I could wish that teachers would abandon their old style and method of
> teaching altogether. It would be worth the while if every school-teacher
> who is not conversant with new systems, would suspend their schools for
> a month, and give their whole attendance during that period to making
> themselves acquainted with new and approved methods.[47]

Delany also estimated that almost nine-tenths of Colored children who were
turned out into the world as having "finished education" were miserably deficient in basic and elementary branches of knowledge, such as composition (correct construction of sentence).[48]

The situation in Black schools in Ohio was particularly illustrative of the
racist context of state-run public education. Black Ohioans, who lived under
the most oppressive "Black Law" ever enacted, were taxed to support a public
education system from which they derived little benefits. Ohio legislature introduced a measure authorizing school districts with less than twenty school-
age Black children to admit such children, provided resident White taxpayers
approved. Districts with more than twenty school-age Black children, however, would have to provide funds for separate Black schools. Not surprisingly,
according to Delany, the allocation for Black education in the latter districts
was barely sufficient to educate twenty Black children in any given quarter.[49]
This limitation forced Black Ohioans to assume greater responsibility for the
education of their children. Many established private schools which unfortunately were, Delany maintained, as ineffective and superficial as the state-run
schools.[50]

Regardless of the context, Delany remarked that Black parents were quick
to deem the education of their children "finished" as soon as they could read a
few Bible verses and scribble a few lines of handwriting. They focused attention
instead on what he characterized as marginal disciplines, pushing their children in the opposite and wrong direction. These children were consequently
not only misguided but also often their education was prematurely terminated.
They became "of no use to themselves, nor community."[51] Delany insisted that
what Blacks needed more urgently than anything else was "a good business education." This is the foundation that would develop the resources with which the
community could patronize and support a professional class of doctors, lawyers,

etc.[52] He was therefore troubled by what he witnessed in Cincinnati, Ohio, for example, where intelligent Black children riveted their attention on the study of poetry and oratory with a passion that seemed to shut other options completely out of consideration.[53]

Delany also commented on the morals of the pupils in the Colored schools he visited, and on the quality and relevance of the instructional materials they were given. For example, the standard arithmetic text in Wilmington, Delaware, Colored schools was Pike's *Old Arithmetic*, which he described as unsuitable for a "progressive system" of teaching and incomprehensible to "the tender mind of youth."[54] A "progressive system" ought to emphasize practical applications. Delany's use of the concept "progressive" referred strictly to a curriculum that was comprehensible to Blacks and designed to develop and enhance their practical skills. In that same district, Delany visited a Colored school taught by a White woman who "appears to teach for the salary" and whose pupils were deficient "in the first evidence of well taught school": good manners.[55] He discovered yet another problem in Philadelphia (true as well of most other places, with the possible exception of the Colored schools of Ohio), the conspicuous absence of Black teachers.[56] He noticed that the teachers in all the Colored public schools in Philadelphia were White. He attributed this to the fact that no Black person, however competent or qualified, was allowed to teach in those schools.[57]

Delany discerned a sinister objective in the practice of placing Black children completely under the control of White teachers. He portrayed the objective as "to raise them subservient to pro-slavery will." He concluded that this practice seemed to be succeeding, exemplified by the servile dispositions of free Blacks and their seeming satisfaction with superficial education.[58] Delany wanted to reverse this debilitating condition. He called for a "well-informed" Black population—men and women "well stored with useful information and practical proficiency, rather than the light superficial acquirements, popularly and fashionably called accomplishments. We desire accomplishments, but they must be useful."[59] These "useful accomplishments" would materialize with the jettisoning of the prevailing and almost normative "extravagant idea" among Blacks; namely, the depiction of classical education as the essence of education, indeed, the end of education.[60] His experience, and the many he referenced in his writings, suggested that emphasis on classical education was a fundamentally flawed strategy that could result in economic dependence. It focused the minds of Black children, and the attention of their parents, on superficial and ineffective endeavors that had very little bearing upon the fundamental problems they confronted, which included making a living and conquering poverty and degradation.

Delany was very emphatic and insistent that Blacks desperately needed an education that would "qualify" them "for active practical business."[61] In order not to be misunderstood or misconstrued as someone absolutely opposed to classical education, Delany was quick to affirm that he was not fundamentally opposed to classical and professional training, having had the advantage of one. He disavowed any intention of advocating total abandonment of such pursuits. Rather, his mission was to impress on Blacks the imperative of building upon a solid foundation of practical education. Practical education would generate and create wealth that would then enable Black communities to support and nurture a viable professional class (products of classical education). Delany lamented that "the classical and professional education of so many of our young men, before their parents are able to support them, and community ready to patronize them, only serves to lull their energy, and cripple the otherwise praiseworthy efforts they would make."[62] He expounded on this vital point:

> A classical education, is only suited for the wealthy, or those who have a prospects of gaining a livelihood by it. The writer does not wish to be understood, as underrating a classical and professional education; this is not the intention; he fully appreciates them, having had some such advantages himself; but he desires to give a proper guide, and put a check to the extravagant idea that is fast obtaining, among our people especially, that a classical, or as it is termed, a 'finished education' is necessary to prepare one for usefulness in life.[63]

Delany's objective was to dispel what he characterized as a misguided view of classical education as "finished education." What Blacks critically lacked, and thus urgently needed, was "an education that shall *practically* [emphasis added] develop our thinking faculties and manhood."[64]

Reporting on Delany's visit and lecture, a resident of York, Pennsylvania (who self-identify simply as "M.C.") noted that he advised Colored people to secure a good education for their children—a good practical education. Delany supposedly counselled moderation on classical education (education of the mind). Fundamentally, he had no objections to such education provided it was "attainable" and "not bent on extremes" because "much learning makes men mad."[65] Delany insisted therefore that Blacks had no choice but to redirect efforts and attention toward practical education if they were to become elevated and achieve equality with Whites. Practical education was, he believed, the key that would unlock the gates to economic prosperity and elevation for Blacks; indeed, the "indisputable evidence" of "the enterprise and industry" of Blacks. This "would not admit of controversy. It would bear with it truths as evident as self-existence."[66]

This prioritizing of practical education was not unique to Delany. This was a widespread conviction among Black thinkers and leaders of his time. Proceedings of the national and state conventions held by free Blacks during the 1830, 1840s, and 1850s underscored the centrality of practical education to the success of the Black liberation struggles in the United States.[67] There were hardly any gatherings of free Blacks at which education did not feature in the deliberations. There was, however, disagreement on the exact form and nature of education deemed appropriate to the success of the struggle. For example, delegates at the Second Annual National Negro Convention in Philadelphia in 1832 stressed the importance of both practical and classical education. However, at the Third Convention the following year, members appeared to lean in favor of "manual labor" education. Two years later, at the fifth and final National Negro Convention of the 1830s, classical education assumed preeminence.[68] Similarly, delegates at the State Convention of the Colored Freemen of Pennsylvania, meeting in Pittsburgh in 1841, also recommended practical education.[69] Ten years later, at the State Convention of the Colored People of New York meeting in Albany, the delegates endorsed classical education.[70]

Delany attempted to end the dillydallying on "which" education by highlighting the benefits of practical education. He exhorted Blacks to prepare their children for useful practical business. As he lamented, Blacks were so attached to classical education that they pushed their young ones aimlessly along its narrow path. He also observed, with consternation, that Blacks had a tendency to "move in advance of themselves"; that is, they began education with the classics instead of practical education.[71] He deplored another disposition of free Blacks: they were either totally illiterate, or trained in classical education, and thus unprepared for entrepreneurship and the business world.[72] He insisted that Blacks had thus far "been on the extreme; either no qualification at all, or a Collegiate education. We jumped too far, taking a leap from the deepest abyss to the highest summit; rising from the ridiculous to the sublime; without medium or intermission."[73] Delany theorized that by focusing on and prioritizing classical education Blacks skipped and thus missed a critical intermediate phase of applied training—one that would have prepared them adequately, at least those who were so inclined and talented—for classical education. As a corrective, he proposed a two-tier educational ladder consisting of a *substructure* of practical education, and a *superstructure* of classical education.[74] As he stated, "we should first be mechanics and common tradesmen, and professions as a matter of course, would grow out of the wealth made thereby."[75] In Delany's schema, therefore, practical education constituted the base, the foundation for nurturing of classical culture, the intermediate phase between ignorance and intellectualism.

The subjects at the core of Delany's proposed practical education curriculum underscored a symbiotic relationship between practical and classical education. He identified English, arithmetic, geography, and political economy as the essential disciplines Blacks had to master in order to prepare for practical usefulness.[76] Delany seemed to suggest that practical education was itself inconceivable without a solid "orthographic" foundation. As he declared, "good orthography is the foundation of all scholarship."[77] Blacks had to start with mastery of all the basic rules of grammar and composition. He further held that arithmetic and "good penmanship" were indispensable tools for aspiring Black businessmen and women.[78] Similarly, he stressed the importance of geography, a subject he defined as "knowledge of the world."[79] Finally, for Blacks to develop a vibrant capitalist culture, they needed to study political economy, which he defined as "the science of the wealth of nations—practically, the daily application of industry for the purpose of making money."[80] These are not abstract subjects too difficult to master but "common School Primer learning that everybody may get. And, although it is the very key to prosperity and success in common life, but few know anything about it."[81] Besides the definitions he offered, Delany did not elaborate on the specific contents of each subject. He did, however, stress the need for a utilitarian and practical methodology of education and recommended the adoption of books and materials consistent with "the progressive system of teaching" prescribed earlier.[82] Delany believed that effective classroom materials for Black learners had to be comprehensible to "the undisciplined minds" of their pupils. Furthermore, he urged periodic critique and review of these materials and other teaching aids to ascertain their continued relevance and, if necessary, be revised and updated.[83]

During his lecture travels to numerous Black communities in the Northeast and Midwest, Delany visited Colored schools and reported on his findings. In Cincinnati for example, he reported that he encountered "several young men ... who have talents of the highest order, oratory and poetry being familiar themes in their literacy course."[84] He was concerned however that they were focusing on disciplines that were not consistent with what he characterized as "the spirit of the age." In his view, Blacks lived in a "capitalist age" which required a particular orientation to, and type of, education. These young intelligent Black kids needed an education that would equip them with the practical skills to succeed in a world characterized by enterprises and investments. He called for emphasizing adequate business education. This would bring prosperity to the race and, more importantly, bridge the racial gap.[85] Delany repeatedly blamed Black parents for not properly guiding their children. He observed this troubling trend not only in Cincinnati but also in all other Black communities he visited. He lamented that Black children were being pushed either by their parents or the pressure of society to engage and pursue what Delany derisively called "exhibition displays" education. They riveted the children's interests on the pursuits of subjects such as music and the arts instead of business education and "elements of science."[86] As he reasoned, "Let our young men and women, prepare themselves for usefulness and business; that the men may enter into merchandise, trading, and other things of importance; the young women may become teachers of various kinds, and otherwise fill places of usefulness."[87] He exhorted Blacks to prioritize the education of their children, especially "to educate them for useful practical business purposes. Educate them for the Store and Counting House—to do every day practical business."[88]

Delany was particularly disturbed that Black parents tended to declare the education of their children "finished," even with deficiency in elementary principles of English language and composition. Many of the kids Delany encountered who were declared to have "finished" their education were unable to write a single complete sentence.[89] He was especially troubled that Blacks generally seemed to gravitate toward an education that would not fundamentally alter their subordinate status but rather would enhance and solidify the "superior advantages" Whites enjoyed. He explained this advantage thus: "If knowledge of the arts and sciences, the mechanical occupations, the industrial occupations . . . and all the various business enterprises, and learned professions were necessary for the superior position occupied by Whites, then the same would apply to Blacks."[90] Delany insisted therefore that in order for Blacks to attain equality, their educational choices and preferences would have to change. He introduced a simple albeit racial logic: "If as before stated, a knowledge of the various business enterprises, trades, professions and sciences, is necessary for the elevation of the White, a knowledge of them also is necessary for the elevation of the colored man, and he cannot be elevated without them."[91]

Delany believed that a major explanation for White dominance in America was the "superior advantage" they acquired due to the "attainments" resulting from their "knowledge of the arts and sciences, the mechanical occupations, the industrial occupations, as farming, commerce, and all the various business enterprises, and learned professions."[92] Consequently, he devoted several pages of his book, *The Condition*, to addressing the importance of education, specifically business and practical education. He was unsparing in castigation of Blacks and their seeming inability or unwillingness to prioritize practical education. He ascribed the attainments of Whites, and the superior status they occupied in society, to education. Consequently, he exhorted Blacks to aggressively pursue and prioritize the type of education that would enable them achieve attainments that would in turn transform them from perennial consumers and parasites to producers. Putting it bluntly, and with disregard for whatever Blacks had accomplished, Delany wrote:

> White men are producers—we are consumers. They build houses, and we rent them. They raise produce, and we consume it. They manufacture clothes and wares, and we garnish ourselves with them. . . . By their literary attainments, they are the contributors to, authors and teachers of, literature, science, religion, law, medicine, and all other useful attainments that the world now makes use of. We have no references to ancient time.[93]

This stunning rebuke and condemnation of Blacks, this nullification and abrogation of everything Blacks had done and accomplished by someone widely acknowledged and acclaimed for his antislavery convictions—someone who had built a reputation as a defender and advocate of the rights and privileges of Blacks, deserves contextualizing and further clarification.

In fairness to Delany, this was more a reflection of the depth of his frustration with his seeming inability to convince fellow Blacks of the imperative of becoming more educated, productive, and self-deterministic. In fact, not to be misunderstood, only a few pages later, Delany completely reversed and contradicted himself. Significantly qualifying his earlier contentions, Delany wrote,

> indeed the fitness of men for positions in the body politic, can only be justly measured by their qualification as citizens. And we may safely venture the declaration, that in the history of the world, there has never been a nation, that among the oppressed class of inhabitants—a class entirely ineligible for any political position of honor, profit or trust—wholly discarded from the recognition of citizens' rights—not even permitted to carry the mail, nor drive a mail coach—there never has, in the history of nations, been any people thus situated, who has made equal progress in attainment with the colored people of the United States. It would be as unnecessary as it is impossible, to particularize all the individuals.[94]

Delany then proceeded in several pages to draw attention to prominent Black individuals and their accomplishments. These were hardworking, wealthy, and productive individuals who were contributing to the overall development of their societies and nations; some, like Henry Boyd of Cincinnati, Ohio, a former slave who owned an "extensive furniture manufactory," even employed "some five or six White men" in his business.[95] To dispel any doubts about, or misunderstanding of, how he viewed Black accomplishments, Delany accentuated a crucial point:

> Certainly there need be no further proofs required, at least in this department, to show the claims and practical utility of the colored people as citizen members of society. We have shown, that in proportion to their numbers, they vie and compare favorably in points of means and possessions, with the class of citizens who from chance of superior advantages, have studiously contrived to oppress and deprive them of equal rights and privileges, in common with themselves.[96]

This would not be the first time, and would certainly not be the last, that Delany had gone to extremes in his criticisms of fellow Blacks, and had to reverse his views, or offer clarifications. On a few occasions, he had publicly expressed his disdain for what he discerned to be a natural inclination among Blacks: the seeming satisfaction with, and preference for, menial occupations. In consequence, he had been accused of condescension and insensitivity to the situations of Blacks who were compelled by their circumstances to engage in such occupations. Delany denied such charges and insisted that he was driven by purely altruistic desire to see his race elevated and empowered.[97] The tone and language of one of his reviews of the activities and performances of Blacks in South Carolina during the Reconstruction was so vicious as to prompt this remark from his old friend Frederick Douglass: "Were you not M. R. Delany, I should say that the man who wrote thus of the manners of the colored people of South Carolina had taken his place with the old planters."[98]

In truth, Martin Delany had not taken his place with the old planters, and Douglass knew that. However, in 1871, as in the 1840s and 1850s, Delany invoked and utilized the most vicious vitriol in order to get his message across. He just wanted to impress on fellow Blacks the need to pursue a specific type of education that he was convinced would guarantee them the attainments necessary for elevation in society, one that would secure for them "unqualified equality" with Whites. It had to be an education that imparted knowledge of useful skills that would prepare Blacks for higher level positions.

Delany's blunt and vicious depiction of Blacks as parasitic, noted above, was no doubt meant to awaken them to the dire reality and challenges they confronted, the urgency of the matter, and to induce in them a determination to boldly confront and undertake the task of remedying the situation. He was very emphatic about the primacy of a good business and practical education and urged Black parents to educate their children for everyday practical purposes— skills that would make them productive members of society. While Delany was very adamant on the need for practical education, he was also careful to warn Black parents against forcing their children into professions for which they had no propensity. He urged Black parents to focus on first identifying and helping to develop their children's propensities rather than forcing them into the professions. While a society or community of professions (lawyers, doctors) was admirable and good, Delany reasoned that it was in the interest of Blacks to cultivate talents that the community could adequately support. He deemed it unwise to encourage an education that would produce professionals that the community could not sustain and support.

Delany's travels exposed him to the dark and ugly realities of the lives of free Blacks in America. He presented as a solution an education that would impart the requisite practical skills for survival. This is the remedy that would launch Blacks on an irreversible path to elevation and freedom, one that both freed the mind and empowered the hand. Convinced that the issue of Black education deserved the endorsement and commitment of everyone, Delany sought a national platform to espouse his views. He took his concerns about the state of Black education to the Colored National Convention of 1848 in Cleveland, Ohio. As chair of the Business Committee, he helped craft several resolutions some of which directly addressed his views on education. Resolution 1 was a bold declaration of intent to resist "every action emanating from what source it may, whether civil, political, social or religious, in any manner derogatory to the universal equality of man." Resolution 2 emphasized the importance of industry and mechanical education to Black elevation. This also included knowledge of "mercantile and professional business, wealth and education." Resolution 3 stressed the necessity of obtaining knowledge of mechanical and mercantile trades, agriculture, the learned professions, as well as the accumulation of wealth—all essential to elevation. Resolution 5 stated "That as education is necessary in all deportments, we recommend to our people, as far as in their power lies, to give their children especially, a business education."[99]

Women's Education and Black Liberation

Concern for the condition of Black women was also at the core of Delany's philosophy of education. He bemoaned the subordinate positions occupied by Black women, believing strongly that there was a direct correlation between the status of women and the condition of Blacks in general. Blacks could not advance if Black women were confined to menial and domestic occupations. The degree of Black elevation was therefore heavily dependent on the status of Black women. Delany called for prioritizing women's education which he characterized as the foundation upon which the overall struggles for Black liberation depended. He offered this very simple, yet cogent, logic:

> Our female must be qualified, because they are to be the mothers of our children. As mothers are the first nurses and instructors of children; from them children consequently, get their first impressions, which being always the most lasting, should be the most correct. Raise the mothers above the level of degradation, and the offspring is elevated with them.[100]

Delany used every opportunity he had to highlight the importance of an educated female population. He was very clear and dire in his warning about the risk of neglecting women's education:

> Until colored men, attain to a position above permitting their mothers, sisters, wives, and daughters, to do the drudgery and menial offices of other men's wives and daughters; it is useless, it is nonsense, it is pitiable mockery, to talk about equality and elevation in society.[101]

This concern had existed long before his association with the *North Star*. In an article in the *Pittsburgh Mystery*, Delany highlighted and lamented the wretched condition of Black women in the United States. He ascribed the subordination of the Blacks in general to the appalling condition of their women. As he poignantly noted,

> No people are ever elevated above the condition of their *females*; hence, the condition of the *mother* determines the condition of the child. To know the position of a people, it is only necessary to know the *condition* of their *females*; and despite themselves, they cannot rise above their level. Then what is our condition? Our *best ladies* being washerwomen, chamber-maids, children's travelling nurses, and common house servants, and menials, we are a degraded, miserable people, inferior to any other people as a whole, on the face of the globe [emphasis in original].[102]

Delany was insistent, therefore, that in order for Blacks to be elevated, a priori, the condition of Black women must change. Black women must be prepared for education that would position them above menial, servile, and domestic occupations. His article touched the hearts of many, including that of the White philanthropist, Rev. Charles Avery of Allegheny County, Pennsylvania, who subsequently donated funds for the establishment of a school for Black men and freedwomen: the Allegheny Institute and Mission Church.[103]

Throughout his tours for the *North Star*, Delany found Black women to be the most illiterate, degraded, and subordinated of subjects, confined overwhelmingly to menial jobs. This discovery confirmed his belief that the poor state of female education, or the almost complete lack of it, had seriously limited the ability and capacity of Black women and, ipso facto, Black men, to compete effectively for economically enriching occupations, thus relegating the entire race to the servile domain. He maintained that the elevation and empowerment of the entire Black race was contingent upon an educated and enlightened female population.[104] The ultimate solution for Blacks, therefore, was not in education per se but in the development of an enlightened female class.[105] Delany envisioned a world where young Black women would not be transcribing "recipes for *cooking*" but instead would be "making the transfer of *Invoices of Merchandise* [emphasis in original]."[106] This would not materialize with a predominantly illiterate female population. Women therefore occupied a very special place in Delany's schema for Black liberation. He called on Black women also to learn trades and develop practical skills that would generate wealth. Such a productive and economically viable female class would be the foundation for building an equally productive, potent, and economically successful Black populace. An illiterate female population, he warned repeatedly, would nurture ignorant children, who would in turn become illiterate and slavish adult population. Nothing troubled Delany much more than the specter of Black men seemingly comfortable with their wives, daughters, and sisters engaged in menial and domestic occupations.[107] This orientation and consciousness had to end in order for Blacks to become elevated and empowered.

During his visit to Wilmington, Delaware, Delany encouraged the young Colored women there and elsewhere employed in domestic services, and living in close proximity, to organize small study-group sessions "for the purpose of moral and mental improvement." He suggested that they met periodically to study "books of useful knowledge."[108] He asked them "to commence with the spelling-book, obtaining the most convenient assistance, taking their lessons by columns, until they have mastered English Grammar, at least sufficiently to write sentences correctly."[109] One of such books he recommended, which he believed would give the women a sound orthographic foundation, and thus the ability "to write correct sentences," was Roswell C. Smith's *English Grammar*, which he described as a very "simple" and "comprehensive" book for beginners.[110]

Race and Black Education

There was, however, another dimension to Delany's educational crusade that did not become fully manifest until the 1850s: the racial factor. Though on a few occasions in the 1840s Delany drew attention to, and expressed concerns over, the negative impact of staffing Black schools exclusively with White teachers, he did not advocate the total exclusion of Whites. After all, he shared with Frederick Douglass, and other leading Black abolitionists, an abiding faith in moral suasion: an integrationist ideology. In fact, the moral suasion ideology Delany propagated, and which shaped the Black abolitionist movement in the first half of the nineteenth century, was predicated on the belief that Blacks were enslaved and discriminated against due largely to the deficiencies of their *condition*, rather than their *race*. Change the Black *condition* through self-improvement and moral reform and everything else would fall in place, including the eradication of discriminatory practices.[111] As a critical component of moral suasion, therefore, education became of special interest to Delany and leading Blacks.[112] Due to his faith in moral suasion, until the late 1840s, Delany's critique of education focused not so much on the racial and cultural backgrounds of the teachers but on the curricula and teaching methods, on the materials used in the schools Blacks attended, and on the orientation of Blacks generally toward education. However, this focus changed dramatically in the early 1850s with the failure of moral suasion and the passage of the Fugitive Slave Law (1850). In fact, the failure of moral suasion was evident by the late 1840s. The material, moral, and educational elevation of free Blacks had not induced positive reciprocity from White society, contrary to the expectation of advocates of moral suasion. Instead, Blacks' efforts at self-improvement seemed to provoke violent reactions from Whites in both the North and South, as such efforts were deemed threatening to the status quo.[113]

The failure of moral suasion and the passage of the Fugitive Slave Law ignited Delany's nationalist consciousness. The law had pledged federal support and services for the pursuit and apprehension of fugitive slaves. It threatened the already fragile freedoms of many free Blacks who had in fact won their freedoms legitimately. In response, Delany expounded a strong ideological justification for emigration in his seminal book, *The Condition, Elevation, Emigration and Destiny of the Colored People of the United States* (1852).[114] Here, he stressed the depth and ubiquity of racism and insisted that Blacks could never achieve true freedom and equality in the United States, regardless of how hard they struggled. As an advocate of emigration, Delany's faith in practical education and in the importance of women's education remained strong. Consistent with his pessimistic outlook, however, he theorized both in *The Condition* and in subsequent publications an end to White control of, and influence on, Black lives, especially in education. He exhorted Blacks to assume greater control of their destinies. Also, he angrily condemned what he perceived as the misguided consciousness of many free Blacks, whom he accused of surrendering all their initiatives to Whites and forever looking to Whites for assistance and direction, even on such a crucial subject as education.[115]

Delany's adoption of race and ethnicity as the definitive and substantive construct for analyzing and defining the Black condition resulted in conflict with his former associate Frederick Douglass. When Delany left the *North Star* in 1849, both he and Douglass tried to minimize emerging conflict over their growing ideological estrangement. It was, however, only a matter of time before that conflict became public knowledge. As Delany embraced emigration, Douglass remained steadfastly optimistic. By the mid-1850s, the two had become leaders of opposing ideological movements represented by two national conventions: an integrationist one led by Douglass held in Rochester, New York, in 1853, and an emigrationist one led by Delany held in Cleveland, Ohio, the following year. Though the two conventions represented broad ideological battlegrounds, education provided specific, narrow, and more direct subject of controversy. Like Delany, Douglass conceived of education as the cure for what he characterized as the "triple malady" that inflicted Blacks: poverty, ignorance and degradation.[116] He also considered the pursuit of classical education necessary and viable only after Blacks had built a strong foundation of practical education.

For Douglass, as for Delany, practical education constituted the foundation for classical culture. Again, like Delany, Douglass too maintained that Blacks were not yet in a position to appreciate and utilize the services of professionals. The deliberations of the Rochester convention underscored Douglass's regard for, and prioritizing of, practical education. In its *Report*, the convention's Committee on Manual Labor stressed the importance of manual labor and industrial education.[117] This rapport on practical education notwithstanding, disagreement surfaced on strategies of implementation. To help implement his platform, the integrationist and still-optimistic Douglass solicited the assistance of White abolitionist Harriet Beecher Stowe, author of *Uncle Tom's Cabin* (1853). Stowe had earlier expressed a desire to assist the cause of Black freedom and had sought Douglass's opinion. Douglass wrote to her suggesting education as the most important area and requested her assistance with establishing in New York or some other location, an industrial school to train Blacks in the various mechanical arts.[118]

Delany's reaction was predictably negative. In a strongly worded response, he denounced Douglass's initiative. Although in agreement with the demand for an industrial school, Delany objected to soliciting the involvement of Whites, especially on such a crucial matter as the education of Black children. Inviting Whites was, he believed, both inconsistent and self-destructive.[119] He insisted that the education of Blacks deserved the undivided attention of "intelligent and experienced" Black leaders. Stowe, according to Delany, "KNOWS NOTHING ABOUT US the free Colored people . . . neither does any White person . . . and consequently can contrive no successful scheme for our elevation, it must be done by ourselves."[120] Furthermore, he pondered; "Why, in God's name don't the leaders among our people make suggestions and CONSULT the most competent among THEIR OWN brethren concerning our elevation [emphasis in original]?"[121] Douglass fired back, questioning Delany's spirit of self-confidence and independence. Chronic disunity, Douglass retorted, had rendered Blacks incapable of attaining the complete independence Delany envisioned. He accused Delany of being too theoretical and out of touch with the realities of the Black situation and reaffirmed his own intention to continue to solicit assistance from all quarters.[122] This squabble over the role of Whites in the education of Blacks did not consume much of Delany's attention precisely because he was much more focused on emigration, which he pursued vigorously from 1852 right up to the outbreak of the Civil War.

Freedmen's Education

The theme of Black independence and self-initiative dominated Delany's thought throughout his brief emigrationist phase. The Civil War, however, ushered in a new Delany. It rekindled his optimism, perhaps to an extreme. Like Douglass and many other free Blacks, Delany welcomed the war as the force that would finally destroy slavery. He became a staunch advocate of Black participation. He was commissioned the first combat Black major in the Union army and assisted in recruiting several Colored regiments. However, it was in his capacity as sub-assistant commissioner of the Freedmen's Bureau; a post he assumed after the war, that Delany was able to refocus attention on Black education. He was assigned to Hilton Head Island, South Carolina, and given jurisdiction over several government plantations. Suddenly entrusted with responsibility over the emancipated inhabitants of these plantations, Delany was anxious to develop means of solidifying their new freedom. Two critical and closely related factors presented themselves: economics (i.e., making a living) and education. Developing a viable economic foundation for the freedmen and freedwomen of the South was almost impossible, he acknowledged, without first ridding them of the ignorance that centuries of enslavement and subordination had infused in their consciousness. Freedom was empty and fragile, Delany reasoned, without education. As a Bureau agent, Delany struggled to enhance the economic adjustment of Blacks to freedom through organizing and supervising productive activities on the plantations. He wrote Bureau headquarters arguing that, given the opportunity, the free Blacks in these locales had the ability and intelligence to benefit from schooling.[123] He requested increased attention to, and expenditure on, freedmen's education. He criticized the failure of the Bureau Commissioner to provide "expenditure for school house," noting also that

> good and suitable school houses are very much needed, there has not been good or suitable school house in the whole sub-district of Hilton Head ... teachers being obliged to make use of temporary ill-constructed little 'shanties' in such Churches as they may be permitted to occupy ... either of which is ill-adapted to the purpose of a school.[124]

In his yearly reports to the Bureau, Delany was careful to draw the attention of the government to the dire state of Black education, particularly the children in his plantation district in Hilton Head, South Carolina. While applauding the efforts of the American Missionary Association (AMA) in establishing and funding schools, Delany lamented the lack of sufficient funds for education from the Bureau. He appealed to the Bureau to consider increasing its financial commitments to freedmen's education. He also wanted the Bureau to assist in abolishing a practice that had come to be regarded "as an essential part of training"; that is, the whipping of children as means of correction in schools. He expressed disdain for the prevalence of whipping as a method of disciplining Black students, noting that too many teachers resorted to this method "as the easiest and least troublesome mode of correction."[125] He described corporal punishment as a troubling reminder of the violence and coercion of slavery, one that undermined the ability of students to adapt freely to the school environment. He reiterated that a school "should be a place of the most pleasurable resort and agreeable association of children." Whipping compromised the creation of a school environment that would nurture "agreeable association." Frequent resort to the whip, he averred, betrayed a fundamental deficiency on the part of teachers, namely, the inability to adapt to the technicalities of teaching. Delany believed that well-trained teachers should be able to teach and handle their pupils without resorting to the whip. According to Delany, "A teacher is, or is not adapted to teaching. If properly adapted, they could and should teach without whipping. If they were unable to control and correct their pupils without whipping, then it only proves that such teachers were not adapted to teaching, and all such should seek some other employment."[126] He further reiterated that whipping undermined and compromised the very essence of what the school experience should be. He portrayed a school as

> a place of the most pleasurable resort and agreeable associations to children; but certain it is that in no wise can this be the case, where the great hickory, long, leather strap, or bridle rein meets, as it enters the school house, the child's as it does the eye of the visitor, reminding one, as it must them, of entering the presence of the old plantation overseer, in waiting for his victim.[127]

Delany characterized a school environment that allowed whipping as inappropriate for the education of children. Furthermore, in his next report, he lamented the absence of "good and suitable school house" in his district and urged the Bureau to do more to improve facilities. A school ought to be, in Delany's judgment, "a desirable place of resort" to pupils. This was only possible if it nurtured "pleasurable remembrances." Delany identified the following conditions as prerequisites for nurturing "pleasurable remembrances": "agreeable teachers, pleasant rooms, comfortable seats and desks, with equal playground and scenery."[128]

Delany was, however, powerless to resolve the education problems and challenges he identified, and the Bureau seemed less committed. Fortunately, private religious and philanthropic organizations such as the AMA became active in providing resources for educating freed Blacks in his district.[129] In his periodic reports to Bureau headquarters, Delany continued to emphasize the inadequacy, or more appropriately, the lack of appropriation for education from the Bureau for the schools in his district as well as the sub-district of Beaufort and other places. He highlighted the "plight" of the schools in his district, which he ascribed to the neglect by the Bureau and praised the efforts of private philanthropic organizations in helping to alleviate the situation.

He advocated more active government role in Black education in his, and surrounding, districts.[130]

Delany's persistent efforts to inspire a deeper commitment to Black education failed due to the fact that Bureau officials saw the situation differently. On one occasion, the Bureau school superintendent described Delany's requests as "unnecessary."[131] Denied official support, Delany struck a rapport with the AMA teachers. He paid regular visits to their schools to obtain firsthand knowledge of their operations and their impacts on free Blacks. Determined to help undo the damages of centuries of educational deprivation, he advocated adult literacy and encouraged Blacks in Hilton Head, both young and old, to attend school. The local AMA agent acknowledged Delany's efforts in the area of adult education. In a letter to his superior, the agent wrote, "We succeeded in setting up a day and night school for adults. Major Delany of the Bureau is going to make an effort to arouse the adults and induce them to attend school. I have much faith in his success."[132]

Delany characterized education as much more than the provision of a school setting. He identified certain equally fundamental social, psychological, and environmental conditions—mutual love, admiration, and respect between teachers and pupils; decent accommodations for teachers; comfortable seats and desks for pupils; and adequate recreational facilities for all—as essential elements of the ideal school.[133] Such a school, he maintained, would be a pleasant environment for both teachers and pupils.[134] This conviction prompted Delany to devote considerable attention to the schools in his and surrounding districts. He investigated and assisted in alleviating many of the problems that plagued the schools. He often furnished AMA teachers and agents with much-needed provisions from the meager produce raised by freed Black farmers in his plantation district. Despite official constraints, he readily assisted with the repairs of dilapidated school furniture, buildings, and other infrastructures.[135] Elizabeth Summers, an AMA teacher commissioned to the former Lawton Plantation on Hilton Head, mentioned a Delany visit to her school in one of her letters. Summers reported that Delany inspected the schoolhouses and teacher's "residences to determine what repairs were needed. . . . He is going to fix our school," she concluded with satisfaction.[136]

What is most striking about Delany's view on education in the post-Civil War era is his silence on curricula and the racial identity of teachers. These are matters he had highlighted during late 1840s.[137] During Reconstruction, however, Delany was more focused on ensuring freed Blacks were educated. He was not overly concerned about the racial identity of the teachers. Consistent with his renewed sense of optimism about Blacks attaining full citizenship in the United States, it mattered little by whom, and in what form, that education was transmitted. The Civil War and early reforms of the Reconstruction era seemed to have rekindled Delany's faith in America. Though cognizant of the tense and fragile race relations, especially in the South, Delany remained confident that the fortunes of Blacks would change for the better in an ideal school environment where they not only had unfettered access to learning but also were provided with the essentials that would make such education effective and meaningful. This mirrored the accommodationist philosophy that defined his social, political, and economic worldviews in the aftermath of the war.

Conclusion

There was nothing dogmatic in Delany's philosophy of education. His conception of education changed with changing circumstances. Three distinct phases can be delineated. In the first, which lasted from the 1830s to the end of the 1840s, the dominant abolitionist ethos of moral suasion influenced his views about education. During this phase, Delany advanced practical education as the means of transforming the social and material conditions of Blacks. By the late 1840s, however, he became convinced that *race*, rather than *condition*, deserved priority, and his philosophy of education assumed racial overtone. This phase reflected his pessimistic view of race relations in the United States. Suspicious and distrustful of Whites during this stage, Delany opposed their involvement in any educational scheme meant for Blacks. It should be acknowledged however that in the post-Civil War era, particularly during his Bureau agency, Delany's renewed optimism compelled deemphasizing of the racial and cultural identity factor, and he philosophized instead about the ideal school environment, and the ideal teacher-pupil relationship. This is not to suggest that he jettisoned race and racial analysis. In fact, by the early 1870s, released from the constraints of the Bureau, Delany's ideas assumed strong racial overtone and, to some of his contemporaries, seemed unabashedly separatist. He was heard publicly advocating "Black leaders for Blacks"; a viewpoint he avoided in the late 1860s (more on this in Chapter 4).

What is perhaps most intriguing about Delany's philosophy of education was his approach to the fundamental problem of Black perceptional reorientation, an issue of great interest to modern advocates of Afrocentricity. Delany's own educational odyssey revealed an unrelenting determination to debunk the myths and misrepresentations of Africa and uncover the truths about his people's past and about his heritage, as well as overcome the epistemological limitations of Black education or lack thereof. Toward these goals, he found the liberal arts, particularly history, most helpful. Then, once he had achieved emancipatory consciousness, Delany struggled to induce similar consciousness in other Blacks. Consequently, he devoted much of his writings to refuting racist views of Africa. However, his preoccupation was with the mental and psychological reorientation of Blacks; the "Afrocentric" aspects of his political writings were not a dominant theme in his philosophy of education. This was particularly evident during the moral suasion phase when Delany outlined strategies for an effective Black education. He prioritized education for economic elevation, which he considered of more immediate importance than education for enlightenment. His curriculum reform proposal emphasized subjects that, he thought, would facilitate a speedy integration of Blacks into mainstream middle-class United States.

It should be noted, therefore, that as high as Delany personally ranked history, a subject crucial to his own mental emancipation, it was conspicuously missing in the list of priority academic subjects he subsequently developed. Resolving this apparent ambivalence is not difficult, however, for Delany's educational paradigm did not suggest complete jettisoning of perceptional reorientation. He implied, and in fact believed, that the attainment of economic emancipation and progress would create a foundation for, and facilitate the process of, positive self-perception. "Making a living" was the central tenet of his philosophy of education. Future educators and critics of American education, including Booker T. Washington and Carter G. Woodson, would amplify Delany's insistence that the most rewarding education for Blacks was one geared toward satisfying the fundamental challenge of "making a living." In fact, Woodson would later describe a fundamental shortcoming of Black education in these words: "they have thereby learned little as to *making a living* [emphasis added], the first essential in civilization."[138]

Delany's observations and critique of United States school curricula and the superficial orientation of Blacks to education were undoubtedly pertinent. Nonetheless, he seemed to overestimate the capacity of Blacks and their ability to initiate and sustain the reforms he advocated. Blacks, especially in the 1840s, lacked the financial wherewithal and the ability to institute the type of educational reforms Delany proposed. With very few exceptions, most of the Colored schools he visited were run by Whites and/or were totally dependent on White support. Neither Delany nor any other Black leader was in position to implement a philosophy of education that contradicted mainstream values. On the controversy over Harriet Beecher Stowe, therefore, Douglass seemed more pragmatic. Nonetheless, in the course of his crusade, Delany highlighted some of what he characterized as "egregious" deficiencies in the very limited educational opportunities available to Blacks. He also underlined how years of servitude and enforced ignorance had imposed a superficial and conservative conception of education. Perhaps, most important, he outlined and discussed modalities for a viable and functional Black education. He theorized about the ideal school environment, about curricula reforms, about gender equality and the need to prioritize female education, and about applied education—that is, making education responsive and relevant to the challenges of earning a decent living.[139] These themes continue to dominate contemporary discourses on African American education. Delany was indeed a pioneer Black education theorist/philosopher. His ideas and contributions not only illuminated the challenges of Black education in nineteenth-century America but also advanced solutions appropriated by his contemporaries and future generations of American educators. Long before General Samuel Chapman Armstrong conceived of Hampton Institute or Booker T. Washington dreamt of Tuskegee, Delany had theorized about the dignity of labor and industrial education as foundations for a functional and empowering education for American Blacks.

CHAPTER 4

Politics

Citizenship, Accommodation, and Reconciliation

MARTIN DELANY PUBLISHED BOOKS and articles and delivered hundreds of public speeches with strong political contents and implications. He was a key figure in the racially charged and volatile political terrains of post-Civil War and Reconstruction South Carolina; at one point, he positioned himself as candidate for state senate and lieutenant governor. Furthermore, his writings and speeches, his political ideas, and the decisions he made profoundly impacted the political orientations and consciousness of Blacks from the mid-to-late nineteenth century. Despite his public political pronouncements and prolific political writings, which often contained insightful, if controversial and provocative, political ideas, curiously Delany's political thoughts remain underexplored and unappreciated. Possibly the paradox of paradoxes of Delany's career is that we know so little about the political thought of such a consummate politician. This could be attributed to the fact that he did not become actively involved in politics until late in his career, during Reconstruction. However, the roots of Delany's political thought, as hinted at in an earlier chapter, could be traced back to the 1840s when he helped propagate moral suasion. His moral suasion and antislavery lectures encapsulated deep and profound political ideas, themes, and commentaries about the state of Blacks in America and strategies for their political advancement. Unfortunately, with the exception of an article published in 1984 by Robert Khan, and a more recent article by Tommie Shelby, there has not been much scholarly interrogation of the ideological and philosophical underpinnings of the political eccentricities he displayed during his brief stint as a "politician" in late Reconstruction South Carolina. His nationalist and Pan-Africanist ideas have dominated and shaped scholarly interpretations of his life and thought.[1] This neglect of his political thought could be attributed to a fact acknowledged by just about every Delany scholar: that he defied ideological simplification and compartmentalization. Delany aficionado Victor Ullman underscored this much when he said, "He (Delany) simply cannot be classified with either the 'good guys' or the 'bad guys.'"[2] To interrogate Delany's political ideas and thoughts, therefore, is to enter the realm of political eccentricities; the arena of the proverbial strange bedfellows; where erstwhile political opponents and strangers came together seemingly in pursuit of supposedly shared interests that often turned out to be ephemeral and transient.

Delany is remembered and celebrated as an uncompromisingly militant, anti-establishment (and to some, anti-America) Black nationalist. This is the dominant theme in the Delany historiography to the almost complete obliteration of the conservative aspects of his life and thought. Yet, engaging this conservatism is vital to understanding what Theodore Draper once described as the "dualities" that seemed to define Delany's life and thought or the eccentricities other critics discerned in his postbellum politics.[3] There was much more to Delany than the uncompromisingly radical personality glamorized in nationalist discourses. He once hinted at the peculiar dynamics of his political thought, but unfortunately as I noted earlier, few took notice. He identified this bold and blunt existential philosophy in an article in the *North Star* in 1848, and it is worth repeating here: "I care little for precedent, and therefore, discard the frivolous rules of formality . . . conforming always to principle, suggested by *conscience*, and guided by the light of *reason* [emphasis added]."[4] The statement embodied the conscience-driven philosophy that birthed the controversial conservative ideas Delany espoused during Reconstruction which sharply contradicted those he had earlier defended as a Black nationalist. In this declaration, Delany diminished the importance of precedents and formality, as well as party loyalty or political dogma. He pledged allegiance instead to his *conscience* and *reason*. An inherent problem with Delany's declaration is that the dictates of one's *conscience* and *reason* could often be the most difficult to discern and decipher in political discourses. In this chapter, I examine and analyze the dynamics of the political conservatism of Delany, which surfaced at the very onset of his antislavery activism. Hopefully, this will shed further light on his political ideas and thought. As I hope to demonstrate, it is impossible to delineate Delany's political thoughts from the stark economic and social realities that birthed them. In fact, his political ideas and the ideals he pursued evolved in response and reaction to the overall struggles to improve and change the economic, social, and cultural conditions Blacks encountered.

Delany's political thought could be analyzed within two broad frameworks: the pre-Civil War and post-Civil War/Reconstruction. During the earlier epoch, he analyzed and critiqued the American political tradition, particularly with respect to how Blacks were treated under slavery and more significantly, Blacks' responses or lack thereof. It was a period marked by optimism and hope about Blacks' future in America, one that induced integrationist ideas and aspirations. The ideas and values Delany cherished and espoused during this time were consistent with the prevailing and dominant American middle-class Protestant Work Ethic (thrift, industry, economy, and moral reform). Paradoxically, this optimistic epoch would end with pessimism and frustration. This would launch Delany on the quest for an independent Black nationality abroad. As discussed in an earlier chapter, this phase was short-lived. Delany traveled in search of, but never succeeded in securing, an independent Black nationality. In fact, the outbreak of the Civil War compelled abandonment of this project. He returned to the United States, and with renewed optimism inspired by the war, Delany resurrected his integrationist aspiration. His political ideas during the second period reflected the hopes and optimism inspired by the reforms of the Civil War and Reconstruction. This renewed optimism induced accommodating and compromising political ideas and ideals. In both phases, however, Delany evinced strong conservative ideas, deriving first from his "progressive" representation of American political culture and second from his overly enthusiastic responses to what he perceived to be the "progressive" reforms of Reconstruction, reforms that seemed to broaden the political landscape to accommodate newly enfranchised Blacks. To understand the ideological dynamics of both epochs, one needs to revisit moral suasion, which was the ideology that propelled the early nineteenth-century Black abolitionism—the movement that also launched Delany's antislavery career and birthed his political thoughts.

Moral Suasion: Pursuing/Fulfilling Citizenship (Antebellum)

As John Ernest argues, the denial of citizenship rights and privileges was one of the challenges that galvanized Black abolitionists to create their own institutions and structures that would enhance and strengthen their struggles for real freedom and equality. These institutions symbolized their determination to resist a nation bent on eroding and subverting their humanity.[5] Martin Delany was one of those who spearheaded this response and attempted to formulate a collective outrage in his seminal publication *The Condition* (1852).[6] The book was fundamentally about affirming the claims of Blacks to citizenship rights and privileges. It was also about demonstrating how the denial and subversion of their claims had reduced Blacks to the status of "a nation within a nation."[7]

Delany therefore made the attributes and challenges of citizenship the subject of his book. His definition of citizenship derived from certain fundamental convictions and beliefs about natural rights, and the very nature of American history and political culture. His political beliefs were also informed by what he characterized as the *raison d'être* of his life and struggle: securing for Blacks "*unqualified equality* [emphasis added] with the ruling class of their fellow citizens."[8] This preoccupation developed against the backdrop of Delany's deep-rooted faith in, and optimism about, what he and others characterized as the essential goodness and progressive nature of American political culture. As he explained, "*Equality* of political rights was the *genius of the American government* [emphasis added] and, therefore, like all great principles, will take care of themselves, and must eventually prevail."[9] Delany and many of his contemporaries, including Frederick Douglass, were convinced that America was endowed with an inherently progressive political culture that unfortunately had been subverted and compromised through historical times by human machinations (slavery and racism). That political culture embodied a crucial defining element Delany referred to as the "genius of the American government": equality of rights.[10] This was the essential attribute at the core of American political culture that had been subverted by humans. In other words, humans created slavery and racism, which arrested the evolution of an otherwise progressive political culture. Left uncorrupted, Delany believed that this culture would have matured to where everyone would have achieved full and unrestricted rights of citizenship. The Black struggle in America, therefore, as Delany framed it, was fundamentally about seeking to recapture and actualize this "genius."

One of the greatest challenges Delany and his fellow Blacks in Pennsylvania confronted in the 1830s and 1840s, even as they struggled to promote moral suasion, was that the state did not recognize Blacks as citizens. This was accomplished at a "Reform Convention" in 1837 with the insertion of the word "White" into the Third Article of the constitution, which effectively eliminated Blacks as citizens.[11] From the beginning, therefore, Pennsylvania Blacks focused on affirming their citizenship rights. At a convention in 1841 in Pittsburgh, Delany along with other prominent Blacks like John Vashon and Robert Peck petitioned the state legislature demanding an amendment to the state constitution that would "remove all restriction on account of color."[12] Defending the citizenship rights of Blacks therefore was a major challenge Delany undertook upon arrival in Pennsylvania.

In his *The Condition*, Delany boldly affirmed the citizenship of Blacks, their indisputable and uncontestable claims to rights common to every American. He insisted that Blacks were as entitled to all the rights and privileges of American citizenship as Whites. It was the enactment of the Fugitive Slave Law (FSL) in 1850 that reinforced Delany's resolve on Black citizenship or lack thereof. It also marked his gravitation toward emigration. Delany quickly realized the contradiction of simultaneously advocating citizenship and emigration. If Blacks were truly entitled to citizenship, then to embrace emigration would be tantamount to voluntarily surrendering that right. This was the position Frederick Douglass strongly defended. Delany's advocacy of emigration and implicit abrogation of citizenship rights provoked widespread criticisms and denunciation. In response, and perhaps to better explain his position, Delany devoted much of *The Condition* to unequivocal affirmation of Black citizenship rights. In several of the chapters, he detailed evidence of how Blacks had fulfilled all the criteria for citizenship: natural right, patriotism, contributions to the nation, services, etc.[13] Having established the legitimate considerations for Black citizenship, Delany then addressed the other crucial reality: that Blacks would never be given the opportunity to exercise citizenship rights. He referred to the FSL as evidence of a national resolve to deny citizenship rights to Blacks. Delany was careful to stress that fulfilling the conditions for citizenship did not necessarily confer the rights and privileges. The nation seemed resolved to prevent Blacks from attaining this goal. Consequently, in the last sections of the book, Delany made a strong case for emigration.[14] In 1854, as leader of the emigration movement, he would deliver his four-hour long Presidential address before the convention in Cleveland, Ohio, titled "Political Destiny of the Colored Race on the American Continent."[15] In this address, Delany reminded his audience of the challenges that impeded the realization of citizenship rights and privileges. The thrust of the address was to strengthen the case for emigration. Delany would further deal what could be characterized as the *coup de grâce* on integration in his 1855 address titled "Political Aspect of the Colored People of the United States."[16] In this speech, he reviewed the constitutions of the various states (slaveholding and free) and noticed a national trend: widespread and deep resolve to deny Blacks the exercise of full citizenship.

In all three documents: *The Condition*, "Political Destiny," and "Political Aspect" Delany emphasized one central theme: what he discerned as a "nationalizing" ethos. Regardless of the sectional divide over slavery, he observed a pervasive and shared resolve, across the nation, to restrict Blacks access to the full benefits of citizenship and to keep them permanently as second class subjects, "a nation within a nation."[17] In fact, Delany had taken up this challenge of what Ernest Allen describes as "one of several paradoxes inherent to the 'second-class' status of the Afro-American freedmen" as early as 1847 when he posed the question: "In what manner may I be treasonous to a country which I am not allowed to call mine?"[18] The paradox Delany referred to pertained to the demand for *civic loyalty* on the part of Blacks (implicit acknowledgment of their citizenship), while refusing them access to the rights and privileges. This begs the question: what did it mean to be an American?[19] The answer was simple: being able to exercise the birthright of inalienable freedoms—speech, press, assembly. There was no room for ambiguity; one was either a full citizen or not.[20] This was the question Delany attempted to advance legislative and constitutional answers to in the three documents. Collectively, they underscored the unjustness of the American system. Delany stressed that Blacks in the United States had historically either been completely denied all the constitutionally and legally recognized attributes of citizenship, or, in some places, invested with less-than-full citizenship.[21]

Delany insisted that Blacks had indeed attained and satisfied every conceivable condition upon which Whites based their claims to citizenship, and much more. As he proclaimed, "We are Americans, having a birthright citizenship—natural claims upon the country—claims common to all others of our fellow citizens—natural rights which may, by virtue of unjust laws, be obstructed but never can be annulled."[22] The doctrine of "birthright citizenship," according to Martha Jones, represented affirmation by Blacks of "an unassailable belonging."[23] This sense of belonging had long existed but was suppressed by hopes and optimism inspired by moral suasion. Delany revived this in the 1850s reiterating Black belonging in both cultural and historical terms; in their patriotism, industry, contributions, and services.[24] Aside from natural rights that Delany said were "as immovably fixed as the decrees of the living God," he also invoked constitutional justification for Blacks' claim to equality and citizenship.[25] He contended that "all free nations" established and secured through "constitutional provisions, the fundamental claims of citizenship."[26] In the United States, as in any other such nations, the fundamental basis of claim to citizenship was never in doubt. Delany explained that the "legitimate requirement" for anyone claiming "protection and full enjoyment of all the rights and privileges of an unqualified freeman" is that such person "shall have made contributions and investment in the country. Where there is no investment there can be but little interest."[27] Based on the above principle, Delany then insisted that Blacks were entitled to citizenship.[28]

It should be noted that Delany was not alone in advocating "birthright citizenship." Though his emigration call might have provoked dissenting views, the notion of birthright citizenship was one that other Black leaders, even his ideological opponents, embraced. As Martha Jones argued at the 1853 National Convention in Rochester, New York, Frederick Douglass was part of a committee that issued an address that described Blacks "not as alien nor as exiles" but as "American citizens asserting their rights on their own native soil."[29] Blacks invoked the language of the Declaration of Independence and the Constitution to bolster their claim to citizenship. By claiming birthright citizenship, therefore, Delany tapped into, and reflected, a consensus among Black leaders even as they disagreed on strategies.[30]

Aside from birthright citizenship, Delany also argued that Blacks possessed the legitimate requirements, and met all conditions and criteria for citizenship, political equality and the enjoyment of "all the rights and privileges of an unqualified freeman" through their contributions to, and services for, the country.[31] He contended that it was the ability to invest in, and contribute to, the nation that distinguished a free person and "a citizen of unrestrained rights" who could then be "entrusted fundamentally with the most sacred rights of the country," since there was now a *correspondence* between their interests and the nation's.[32] Delany described this *correspondence* as "the simple but great principle of primitive government" and thus the basis of citizenship in all free countries; and Blacks had satisfied this condition.[33] Blacks fulfilled this condition through their contributions and investments in the country, their sacrifices for the country, and their patriotism, as well as the unbounded love of country they demonstrated.[34] Yet, despite satisfying these conditions, Delany lamented that Blacks were denied due political rights. National political developments seemed to nurture a subversive culture of political segregation that entrenched and bolstered White supremacy.[35]

Along with birthright citizenship, Delany also adduced what Tommie Shelby describes as democratic citizenship, which underlined a person's right to not just equal protection of the law, but as well being able to ascend to positions of honor and public trust.[36] Citizenship therefore also entailed not just "the right to vote for membership of the dominant group but, on possession of the requisite merit, having a fair opportunity to occupy positions of authority."[37] Tied to democratic citizenship was also the right of "self-government."[38] Delany insisted that "true political freedom requires that each adult citizen form an indispensable part of the sovereign authority of the republic."[39] He concluded therefore that in order for freedom to be meaningful, Blacks

> must necessarily be *their own rulers*; that is, *each individual* must, in himself, embody the *essential ingredient*—so to speak—of *sovereign principle*

which composes the *true basis* of his liberty [emphasis in original]. This principle; when not exercised by himself, may, at his pleasure, be delegated to another—his true representative.[40]

Delany also introduced, as a subset of democratic citizenship, the principle of "inherent sovereignty." The ability to vote ("right of suffrage") did not necessarily fulfil "the right of citizenship." Suffrage, when truly enforced and exercised, also implied "acknowledged sovereignty," a principle Delany characterized as "the true basis of his liberty."[41] Fundamentally, this means that Blacks possessed the unqualified rights, just like Whites, to vote (exercise of sovereignty) and to be directly involved in the political decision-making process or to be able to delegate such responsibility to their elected representatives. The ability to fully exercise this right constituted "inherent sovereignty."[42]

Furthermore, Delany defined a free person, politically, as a citizen with "unrestricted rights," one who was able to ascend to the highest position and who was "invested with the highest privileges" including the "most sacred rights of the country" largely because such persons had invested in, and had vested interests in, the country. The interests of the people and those of the nation had to *correspond*. In other words, the progressive nature of American political culture notwithstanding, citizenship was not automatic, but the consequences of fulfilling certain fundamental ideals embedded within the political culture. Based on the above, Delany proceeded to establish the claims of Blacks to citizenship. From slavery (as laborers) to fighting the nation's battles (Revolution and War of 1812), Blacks had hazarded and sacrificed their lives and thus demonstrated unconditional love for the country. This love, which he described as amor patria (love of country), was "the first requisition and highest attribute of every citizen."[43] In essence, all those who so voluntarily risked personal safety for the nation are "patriots of the purest character."[44] Blacks had accomplished and demonstrated all the above as well as in private domains: trade, commerce, business, literary and professional attainments, education, and artistic and cultural contributions.[45] However, despite these conditions and accomplishments, certain historical circumstances had conspired, and continue to conspire, to deny to Blacks the full benefits and advantages of American citizenship they so deserved.

Delany and leading Blacks focused on remedying this situation. However, he did not believe that the establishment was solely responsible for the Black predicament. Blacks shared some culpability. Though America possessed inherently "progressive" political culture, the full maturation and thus actualization of the culture also depended on whether or not everyone who aspired for the benefits fulfilled a certain fundamental ideal embedded within the culture. On this crucial consideration, Delany faulted Blacks. He found Blacks grossly negligent and derelict. According to Delany, Americans were bound by a contractual and existential obligation deeply rooted in the nation's spirit. The strange fact about this contract was that it was neither written down, nor verbally discussed and mutually agreed upon.[46] Nonetheless, its core value established for Americans what needed to be done in order for the nation's ideals to materialize (i.e., genius of the government). As Delany framed it, *"By the regulations of society, there is no equality of persons, where there is no equality of attainments* [emphasis added]."[47] The contract therefore mandated, implicitly if not explicitly, that everyone should seek and accumulate wealth (attainments). Fulfilling this principle would, Delany opined, unleash that *"genius of the American government"* (equality) [emphasis added].

The development of America and equitable distribution of her economic, social, and political resources, therefore, depended on whether or not everyone abided by this core ethos of the national contract. Delany concluded that Blacks had failed to maintain their part of the national contract (more on this later). Given the above predicament and reality of political inequality and marginalization, Delany argued that the fundamental question Blacks needed to address and seek to answer is: "What then is the remedy, for our degradation and oppression? This appears now to be the only remaining question—the means of successful elevation in this our native land?"[48] The answer Delany offered, reflective of his faith in the system during the antebellum period, underscored that Blacks would be the architects of their own salvation. In the spirit of the Protestant Work Ethics, and the promise inherent in the "American Dream," there was a pervasive conviction among leading Blacks that through hard work, industry, economy, thrift, and moral reform Blacks would dismantle the walls of racism and activate that subverted, dormant, but never obliterated "genius" deeply embedded in American political culture.

Much of Delany's political thought and convictions in the early phase therefore reflected his faith in the ideology of moral suasion propagated and defended by leading Blacks, most notably, the Reverend Lewis Woodson and William Whipper, and adopted as a philosophy for the Black abolitionist movement. Woodson and Whipper were two of the highly respected and economically successful members of an emerging Pennsylvania Black middle class as well as founding members of the Black abolitionist movement in early nineteenth-century Pennsylvania. Whipper was one of the wealthiest businessmen in Pennsylvania. He owned a fleet of streetcars and operated a lucrative lumber business in Columbia as well as a free labor and temperance store in Philadelphia.[49] Woodson, on the other hand, owned several barbershops in Philadelphia.[50] They both helped transform Pittsburgh into a bourgeoning hub of antislavery activism. By the beginning of the nineteenth century, the city had a thriving Black community, the vast majority of whom had relocated from other northern and southern states. It was here that Delany gained exposure to the debates about strategies for the emerging Black abolitionist movement spearheaded by Reverend Woodson and William Whipper.[51] Their ideas and writings influenced the exchanges among leading Blacks about the efficacy of moral suasion as abolitionist philosophy. They published extensively on the subject in the columns of the *Colored American* in the 1830s and 1840s. They suggested that any person of upright character who also was hardworking could succeed in America, regardless of race, and in spite of the history.[52] Prejudice would decline and disappear, they reasoned, as Blacks attained material and moral developments. The crux of their arguments was that the challenges Blacks confronted did not emanate from systemic or structural deficiencies. Rather, they attributed these to individual failures and shortcomings, challenges that could be remedied through self-efforts.[53]

As argued earlier, moral suasion defined the contours of the Black abolitionist movement from the founding of the American Moral Reform Society in 1835 through 1850.[54] It taught Blacks to be hopeful and optimistic; to believe in the promises and prospects of the American Dream. More significantly, it also envisioned America as a democratic nation endowed with a progressive political culture which could and would, appearance notwithstanding, ultimately attain perfectibility where everyone, regardless of race and previous condition would be, and feel, accepted and validated.[55] It implied that by becoming more productive and morally upright, Blacks would appeal favorably to the moral conscience of the nation. Advocates believed that the pursuit of moral reform was vital to "the promotion of harmony and accord in society" and would result in "effecting the total abolition of slavery" and the "destruction of vice universally."[56] When Blacks successfully reformed those vices Whites had used as excuses for slavery and racism, America would activate and universalize those inherent, but as yet untapped, progressive and democratic values. Moral suasion, therefore, underscored faith in the redemptive nature of American national conscience—a conscience that, moral suasionists reasoned, could be "persuaded" by exhibitions of attributes that challenged and contradicted prevailing and dominant notions of Black inferiority.[57] Since moral suasion ascribed the challenges Blacks confronted to individual failures and deficiencies, it taught Blacks not to look to, or depend on, the state or the system for succor but to turn inward to themselves for the wherewithal for meaningfully changing their condition. In one of their declarations, referred to in an earlier chapter, delegates at the Second Negro National Convention in 1832 in Philadelphia expressed Blacks' faith in both the redemptive character of American political culture and their (i.e., Blacks') ability to effect change. They envisioned "final redemption" from their trials and tribulations "in the moral strength of this nation."[58]

Delany imbibed this optimism and hope and became actively involved in organizing moral suasion efforts among Pittsburgh youth. By the early 1840s, he had attained the maturity as well as the resources that enabled him to carve a distinct path in the reform efforts in Pennsylvania. In 1843, he founded a newspaper, the *Pittsburgh Mystery*, which became a means of unravelling what he described as the "Mystery" of the Black condition.[59] Consistent with Delany's convictions, the *Mystery* dedicated its pages to condemning slavery and highlighting strategies that would help Blacks improve their condition.[60] In 1847, as indicated earlier, Delany joined Frederick Douglass as coeditor of the *North Star*.[61] The founding of the *North Star* signaled the onset of a more aggressive and independent Black abolitionist movement. Hitherto, Douglass had been closely associated with William Lloyd Garrison's American Anti-Slavery Society.[62] As roving lecturer, Delany traveled to Black communities in the Midwest and Northeast to deliver antislavery lectures and promote moral suasion. Their partnership lasted two years (1847–1849) and opened the first chapter in Delany's abolitionist activism. In his lectures, Delany introduced the concept "Political Economy" (PE) as his strategy for transforming the Black condition in America.[63]

What Delany observed in the communities he encountered during his lecture tours of Pennsylvania, Ohio, New York, Michigan, and Delaware convinced him that Blacks had the capacity to change their condition, and thus change America. He proposed PE, which he defined as "Knowledge of the Wealthy of Nations," or simply, "How to Make Money." This was crucial for Black advancement in America.[64] Like the broader moral suasion ideology, PE stressed Black responsibility and self-efforts. Delany's PE also reflected the prevailing reformist culture of early nineteenth-century America. He seemed to be tapping into the broader national reform impulses and movements as well as the optimistic outlook of Jacksonian America. Surrounded by a plethora of reform initiatives (peace, abolition, women's rights, temperance, and moral reform, etc.) Delany, like other leading Blacks, responded with optimism, envisioning Blacks as agents of change able to reform America for the good of everyone.[65] Before such change could occur, however, Delany insisted that there had to be candid acknowledgment of the primal cause of the glaring racial disparity. Based on his

PE and consistent with moral suasion, Delany did not attribute the disparity solely to systemic deficiency but to the failure of Blacks to fulfil their part of the national contract.

During his lecture tours, Delany observed widespread poverty among Blacks, which he depicted as symptomatic of the failure to adhere to the dictates of the national contract. They had shirked their national obligation. This contrasted with the economic opulence and political dominance of Whites whom he characterized as a people with an aggressive impulse for higher attainments. These poverty-stricken Blacks seemed stymied by what Delany characterized as a pervasive and debilitating providential worldview propagated by several of the leading Black churches. This worldview complicated the moral suasion/PE emphasis on higher attainments and encouraged Blacks instead to prioritize heavenly inheritance.[66] As stated earlier, several of the churches discouraged their congregations from the pursuits of material and secular well-being; thereby constraining the people's drive for self-determination.[67] This worldview, according to Delany, left Whites unchallenged in the quest for, and accumulation of, material wealth. In essence, while Blacks surrendered to providential determinism, Whites sought material attainments which enabled them to fulfil their part of the national contract. Delany was unsparing in denunciation of Blacks for lackadaisical response to moral suasion and thus, found both justification and explanation for Black subordination in their seeming reluctance to seek material prosperity. To escape their present condition, therefore, Blacks had to eliminate the glaring social and economic disparities. There was just one viable strategy for accomplishing this: wealth accumulation and mastering "How to Make Money." He believed that visible displays of Black economic progress would indisputably dispel all doubts about Black capacity for industry and independent initiatives and establish their qualifications for all the rights and privileges accorded other Americans. Delany explained at length how industry and economic empowerment would transform the Black condition:

> You can scarcely imagine the effect it would have over the pro-slavery feeling in this slave holding country, if, in addition to the few business men we have, there were in New York city, Philadelphia, Boston, even Baltimore, Richmond, Norfolk, Washington city, and all other ports of entry where colored men are permitted to trade, and Buffalo (which has one colored mercantile house), Cleveland, Detroit (which has another), Milwaukee, Chicago, Cincinnati, and Pittsburgh, and many other places, but one shipping house, wholesale or retail store, the proprietor or proprietors of

which were colored men, and one extensive mechanic of any description and trade. Such indisputable evidence as this of the enterprise and industry of the colored man, compared with that of the White, would not admit of controversy. It would bear with it truths as evident as self-existence— truths placed beyond the shadow of a doubt.[68]

Delany adduced a compelling argument for developing Black economic power as the foundation for progress. He emphasized that Blacks could justify demands for equality only if they became economically empowered. The quest for "higher attainments" therefore mandated, Delany argued, deemphasizing political rights, and prioritizing instead the pursuits of material wealth (fulfilling the national contract).[69] To reiterate this point, Delany reminded Blacks that they "live in society among men, conducted by men, governed by rules and *regulations* [emphasis added]." One of the *regulations,* and possibly the most important for Blacks in America, mandated wealth-accumulation.[70]

In his antislavery lectures, therefore, Delany urged Black communities to explore avenues of wealth creation. It was simply not enough to "moralize much about equality," or to claim to be "as good as our neighbors, and everybody else," he emphasized.[71] While this might be a reasonable ethical claim, Delany insisted that it would not make a compelling political argument. Such moral arguments alone would not change a political system or culture. Blacks had to move beyond reliance on moral arguments to activating their human agency. They ought to become as driven and as this-worldly as Whites.[72] Delany repeatedly reminded Blacks of the core term of the national contract: "there is no equality of persons where there is not an equality of attainments."[73] Though he stressed the need for "equality of attainments," Delany was quick to clarify that this did not necessarily mean that everyone would actually achieve equal attainments. There would be no absolute equality of attainments. Rather, he meant to underscore that if the pursuit of "attainments" was necessary for the elevation of Whites, then such pursuits should be "necessary for the elevation of the colored man."[74] The problem with Delany's contract theory and PE is the assumption that everyone had equal capacity to seek and accumulate wealth. There was no consideration of how the history of the country had contributed to the inequities and racial imbalances. Neither Delany nor his moral suasion mentors could feign ignorance of this history. In fact, they were living witnesses to the history, and many, like Reverend Woodson, had been drawn to Pennsylvania to escape, or minimize, the debilitating effects of the history. One can only speculate on why they chose to deemphasize the history. Perhaps this was due to their faith in the redemptive power of that "genius of

American government." Undoubtedly, the conviction that America possessed an inherently progressive culture led many Blacks to believe that someday it would attain perfection, the glaring injustices notwithstanding. They placed their hopes for the future on an ideal whose veracity was very much questionable.

By the early 1850s, Delany observed and reported evidence of a significant shift in Black responses to moral suasion and PE. The opposition of several Black churches to material possessions notwithstanding, Blacks increasingly became more self-deterministic and this-worldly. In *The Condition* cited earlier, Delany devoted several chapters to highlighting successful Black enterprises, evidence of a growing Black middle class, and a widening Black economic resource base. He drew attention to numerous examples of Black economic progress and development across several states—evidence that Blacks were adhering to the core principle of the national contract. This was indisputable evidence of Blacks' capacity for industry and self-improvement.[75] Unfortunately, visible manifestations of Black accomplishments, or, to invoke Delany's language, these "truths as evident as self-existence" did not confirm the moral suasionist faith in the malleability and perfectibility of the American political culture. Instead, they exposed the fallacy of the reasoning. Black economic success did little to dent what Delany now perceived and experienced as a frozen wall of American racism.[76] Instead of acknowledgment and validation, Black economic achievements provoked racial intolerance and violence.

In the 1840s, in Pennsylvania, New York, Rhode Island, Ohio, Illinois, and New England, White mobs attacked and destroyed Black institutions and symbols of economic progress. In fact, according to one authority, Philadelphia in the antebellum period was "the race riot capital of the country, if not the world."[77] In several of the so-called free states, legislations were introduced designed either to keep free Blacks out or stymie their drive for self-improvement. There was thus a certain ironic twist to these race riots. As noted earlier, a contemporary observer described them as prime examples "of Whites denouncing Blacks for their degradation while simultaneously destroying those institutions which sought to eradicate that degradation."[78] Similarly, in their "Appeal to the Voters of the Commonwealth of Pennsylvania," delegates at the "Colored Citizens Convention" held in Harrisburg, Pennsylvania, in December 1848 cited earlier expressed disillusionment with the seemingly impregnable racial wall obstructing their path to progress. Their lengthy and poignant declaration is worth quoting:

> The barrier that deprives us of the rights which you enjoy finds no palliative in merit—no consolation in piety—no hope in intellectual and moral

pursuits—no reward in industry and enterprise . . . we may exhaust the mid-
night lamps in the prosecution of study, and be denied the privilege of the
forum—we embellish the nation's literature by our pursuits in science—
the preceptors of a Newton in Astronomy—the dictators of philosophy
to a Locke or a Bacon—the masters of a Montesquieu or a Blackstone on
civil and international law—or could we equal the founder of Christianity
in the purity of our lives . . . yet with all these exalted virtues we could not
possess the privileges you enjoy . . . because we are not 'White.'[79]

As suggested, Delany shared this conclusion which contradicted the optimism
of moral suasion. It had become evident that however hard Blacks struggled,
they would never achieve meaningful change in America. Denouncing America
as irredeemably racist, he urged Blacks to emigrate and seek their destinies in an
external and independent African/Black nationality.

The emigration phase (1850–1863), enabled Delany to rethink, and thus gain
a better understanding of, the racial dynamics of America. Emigration also became the lens through which he reexamined the failed and flawed moral sua-
sion/PE paradigm. As earlier highlighted, the 1850 Fugitive Slave law (FSL) was
the precipitating factor. Among other provisions, the law authorized federal
support for the apprehension and return of fugitives.[80] Delany presented this
as evidence, for anyone still in doubt, of the imminent "nationalization" of slavery; a message to Blacks that they had no future in America. According to him,
Blacks had become, and would remain, "a nation within a nation."[81] Compar-
ing their status to that of Poles in Russia, Hungarians in Austria, Scotch, Irish,
and Welsh in the United Kingdom, Delany described Blacks as "a people who
although forming a part and parcel of the population, yet . . . by the deprivation
of political equality with others, no part, and if any, but a restricted part of the
body politic of such nation."[82] In fact, Delany contended that the very assertion
of White superiority also constituted a denial and deprivation of Blacks' capacity
for self-government.[83] Blacks would have to demonstrate this capacity in an external location. Delany had also lost complete confidence in White abolitionists
whom he suspected of harboring deep racial bigotry despite their public liberal
posturing. He concluded therefore that the nation seemed unified by a consen-
sual perception of Blacks as inferior. He became deeply distrustful of White
abolitionists. On the possible nationalization of slavery, he warned:

The so-called free state, by their acts, are now virtually saying to the south,
'YOU SHALL NOT emancipate; your BLACKS MUST BE SLAVES;
and should they come North, there is no refuge for them'. I shall not

be surprised to see, at no distant day, a solemn convention called by the
Whites in the North, to deliberate on the propriety of changing the whole
policy to that of slave states. This will be the remedy to prevent dissolution;
AND IT WILL COME, MARK THAT! Anything on the part of the
American people to SAVE THE UNION. Mark me—the nonslavehold-
ing states will become slave states [emphasis in original].[84]

Delany was convinced that Blacks confronted clear and unambiguous racial
choice. There was no middle ground. In response, he proclaimed what could
be regarded as the nineteenth-century antecedent of William E. B. Du Bois's
twentieth-century "Color line" dictum:

It would be duplicity longer to disguise the fact that the great issue, sooner
or later, upon which must be disputed the world's destiny, will be a question of Black and White, and very individual will be called upon for his
identity with one or the other.[85]

As Delany interpreted, this "Us vs. Them" binary embodied an existential reality for Blacks. The plain and simple fact was that Blacks were not perceived as
politically coequal of Whites "but alien to the laws and political privileges of
the country. These are truths—fixed facts."[86] He argued that the FSL struck at
the very core of Black existence in America. It constituted a blatant violation of
the constitutional rights of Blacks, further relegating them beneath Whites.[87] It
also obliterated a fundamental dynamic of their struggles: the conviction that
hard work and contribution to national development (the contract) would yield
positive change. On the basis of what Delany witnessed and publicized toward
the end of his travels, Blacks had indisputably established legitimate claims for,
in his words, "protection and full enjoyment of all the rights and privileges of an
unqualified freeman."[88] They had invested in, sacrificed for, and contributed to
building, the nation. Consequently, they had earned the right of "freeman in the
political sense," that is, "a citizen of unrestricted rights . . . being eligible to the
highest position."[89] Unfortunately, the FSL destroyed everything by subverting
"the most prominent provisions of the Constitution of the United States . . . that
every person shall be secure in their person and property; that no person may be
deprived of liberty without due process of law."[90]

   The FSL "degraded" Blacks and made them "liable at any time, in any place,
and under all circumstances, to be arrested" and re-enslaved.[91] It confirmed,
for Delany, the truism of what he characterized as "a great principle of political economy," which states that "no people can be free who themselves do not

constitute an essential part of the *ruling element* of the country in which they live [emphasis in original]."[92] The language and intent of the law clearly did not regard Blacks as full-fledged Americans, let alone constituents of the nation's "ruling element." Instead, Blacks had become, in Delany's words, "Slaves in the midst of freedom."[93] Given this reality, he suggested the development of a distinct national identity as the next logical goal for Blacks. "The claims of no people . . . are respected by any nation," he argued, "until they are presented in a national capacity."[94] In other words, Blacks had to establish an independent Black/African nationality before their cries and tribulations would command serious attention.

Delany's analysis and experience of American political culture had convinced him that by the early 1850s that culture had morphed into a culture of inequality. The embodied "genius" (i.e., equality) had been subverted and compromised. But this was not a uniquely American development. Delany regarded this culture of inequality as a global phenomenon. Inequality (social, political, religious) was global. In all countries and all ages, according to Delany, there had been privileged groups that had oppressed and deprived others of equality and political and social rights—an unjust system of exploitation in which a particular group "due to circumstances" and peculiar positions (i.e., Blacks) were marginalized and excluded from the body polity.[95] This was the status of Blacks in America as a result of America being "unfaithful to her professed principles of republican equality," and thus subverting an essentially progressive political culture, while also denying the natural rights of Blacks.[96] The FSL constituted the ultimate signification of Black betrayal. It violated the most important provisions of the constitution: the guarantee of "personal security," protection of property, and the promise of due process.[97] The FSL essentially excluded Blacks from the body politic. They became aliens denied protection of the law and political privileges.[98]

The discrepancy between the contributions of Blacks to the making of the nation, their existential sacrifices, and unconditional love and the denial of their equality and political right and the subversion of the broader American political culture compelled Delany to spearhead emigration and the search for an external and independent Black nationality in the second half of the nineteenth century. Between 1853 and 1860, Delany gradually turned his attention to emigration and the search for an independent Black nationality. He would lead the 1854 National Emigration Convention in Cleveland, Ohio, after which he embarked on an exploratory journey to the west coast of Africa, visiting Liberia and Nigeria in search of location for the nationality.

Actualizing Citizenship: Utilitarianism, Pragmatism, Accommodation (Postbellum)

Delany returned to the United States in 1860 fully committed to raising awareness of, and resources for, emigration. The onset of the Civil War and subsequent Reconstruction reforms, however, compelled rethinking and revision of his political ideas. Though he had given up on the country and had dismissed the prospect of any meaningful change within, it was difficult for Delany to ignore the growing sectional divide over slavery. He could not ignore the fact that a crisis was brewing over, slavery, the magnitude of which, he reasoned, could be consequential to the future of Blacks. He had argued profusely in the late 1850s that nationalization of slavery was imminent and that slavery would cease to be sectional. Ongoing events belied this prediction. The nation was not unified on slavery, and "nationalization" of slavery did not seem imminent. This compelled Delany to reverse course and embrace the Civil War and the cause of integration. Joining forces with Black leaders like Frederick Douglass and Henry H. Garnet, Delany urged President Abraham Lincoln to make emancipation a war strategy. In this respect, Delany advanced what Maurice Wallace describes as a "masculinist" construction of citizenship. He sought to convince the government that enlisting Blacks was "one of the measures in which the claims of the Black man may be officially recognized, without seemingly infringing upon those of other citizens."[99] In other words, Blacks' claim to citizenship "stood to be settled by the wide visibility of Black men in uniform." Delany thus drew a correlation between nationhood, citizenship and masculinity.[100] Ultimately, they were successful. After prolonged deliberation and hesitation, Lincoln issued the Emancipation Proclamation freeing slaves of the rebellious states effective January 1863. In 1865, Lincoln also approved Delany's commissioning as a combat major in the Union army, becoming the first Black so appointed. For the duration of the war, Delany assisted with raising several Colored regiments. Subsequently, the reforms of the Civil War and Reconstruction, especially the various Constitutional Amendments (Thirteenth, Fourteenth, and Fifteenth), affected a revolution in American political culture, finally undoing and reversing the tradition of subversion of the political culture and bringing the culture much closer to activating its "genius."

The Emancipation Proclamation freed slaves of the rebellious territories; the Thirteenth Amendment abolished slavery and the Fourteenth Amendment (1868) extended citizenship and promise of equal protection of the law to Blacks. These developments convinced Delany that Blacks had now become "part of the ruling element" of the nation, a goal that seemed far-fetched less than a decade ago.[101] Further ratification of the Fifteenth Amendment in 1870 which guaranteed to Blacks unrestricted right to vote and participate in the political process reinforced his growing optimism. Collectively, he concluded that the reforms had finally created opportunity for the American political culture to develop and evolve toward actualizing the embedded "genius." It was this heightened sense of optimism that birthed the political conservatism that defined Delany's thoughts during this period. The reforms fractured his seemingly impregnable late-1850s Black nationality wall. He developed renewed hope in America. In fact, had death struck in 1870, Delany most certainly would have died a happy man. He'd just witnessed a transformation of revolutionary proportions. Less than a decade and half ago, he had given up all hope and had predicted the imminent "nationalization" of slavery and denounced America as irredeemably racist. He'd been proven wrong. Slavery did not become a national institution. Instead, there had been a civil war, in the aftermath of which, the nation had made significant concessions to Blacks. Given these developments, Delany concluded that Blacks, now enfranchised and empowered politically, ought to tread the political landscape with caution, while their political choices and decisions should be guided by the practical demands of their situations rather than ideology, party loyalty, or historical precedent.

Delany's conservative convictions led him to oppose and attempt to contain Black political aspirations. Early in the Reconstruction period, while Black leaders agitated for immediate and increased political rights, Delany voiced restraint and caution. For instance, soon after the assassination of President Lincoln, a delegation of Black leaders including Frederick Douglass approached his successor President Andrew Johnson to demand immediate political reforms and the expansion of Black political rights and privileges.[102] In a letter to the delegation, Delany counseled moderation and gradualism. He implored the delegates to "Be mild . . . be respectful and deferential." He closed the letter with "Be patient in your misery, Be meek in your despair; Be patient, O be patient! Suffer on, suffer on!"[103] To his critics, Delany seemed opposed to radically upstaging the existing culture of political inequality. Fundamentally, his call for gradualism derived from a concern that Blacks would and could destabilize the political climate and culture through what he deemed reckless, premature, and ill-timed political demands. He urged Blacks instead to cultivate a culture of goodwill toward the defeated, angry, and politically humbled Southern Whites. This overture, Delany hoped, would reassure Southern Whites that Black aspirations would not undermine the fundamentals of Southern culture and worldview.

Delany reasoned that such "conservative" concession would guarantee reciprocity from Whites that in turn would afford Blacks the space within which to exercise and enjoy the more crucial economic rights and privileges. In fact, by the mid-1870s, Delany had abandoned any pretense of "radicalism" and focused more intensely on appeasing the alienated and angry state conservatives. He began to openly court the goodwill of the state Democratic Party—the party of former slave-owners—those who had fought the Civil War vigorously and passionately to defend and preserve slavery.[104] Why this shift to a "conservative" position for someone who less than five years earlier was on the camp of the radicals? Why this switch in national political allegiance from radicalism to conservatism? Had Blacks achieved "unqualified equality"? Definitely not, and Delany knew that the political and constitutional reforms notwithstanding, Blacks were far from achieving the goal of "unqualified equality" with Whites. There was however a possible explanation for Delany's willingness to ignore or deemphasize this reality in favor of compromise. This was due largely to his experiences of, and responses to, the political exigencies of post-Civil War and Reconstruction South Carolina.

After the war, Delany settled in South Carolina, first as field agent of the Bureau of Refugees, Freedmen and Abandoned Lands, and after the demise of the Bureau in 1868, he became actively involved in local and state politics. Like many other Blacks, at the onset of Reconstruction, Delany joined the Republican Party—the party of so-called "Radicals." Envisioning himself as someone with much to offer the newly enfranchised Blacks, he wrote a series of essays on citizenship and responsibility titled: *On National Polity* (1870).[105] Blacks needed such information, he felt, given centuries of enslavement, during which they were denied access to education and, ipso facto, knowledge and experiences that would have prepared them adequately for the responsibilities of freedom. Delany became convinced that the American political culture had evolved "an impartial and truly national government" in contrast to the previous (pre-Civil War) practice of slavery, hierarchy, and privilege. Blacks were now enfranchised. However, in order for the newly enfranchised Blacks to fully exercise their rights and privileges under the new dispensation they had to possess informed understanding of what Delany characterized as the "elementary lessons" on political principles, theories on the nature and function of national government, and knowledge of key political documents such as the Constitution.[106] He proceeded to expatiate on these principles in *On National Polity*.

On citizenship, Delany invoked the Roman legal definition of a citizen as someone unrestrained, who possessed inviolable power of political representation.[107] Blacks had long been denied this fundamental citizenship condition in several states. They had only been allowed limited and restricted political rights in some states such as New York and Pennsylvania. They were denied the franchise and thus the rights of representation under the old system.[108] This changed with emancipation, Reconstruction reforms, and Constitutional amendments. These reforms eradicated, in Delany's words, "all legal disabilities and unjust laws," transforming Blacks finally into becoming integral to the "ruling element" of the nation.[109] However, effective and functional political integration and participation required political education, knowledge of how to successfully engage others, as well as clarity on political theory and principles. It was precisely with a view to providing the newly enfranchised, but uninformed, Black electorate such education that Delany wrote and published *On National Polity*.[110]

Delany considered Blacks deficient in knowledge that was crucial for a population just emerging from slavery and entrusted with political responsibilities. And what precisely were the tenets of political education and knowledge Delany deemed essential for the newly enfranchised Blacks? He did not clearly answer this question. However, he expressed concern that, due to ignorance and inexperience, Blacks were likely to be seduced by the defeat of the former slaveholding class, and reversal in roles, into assuming a complacent and triumphalist disposition that would render them oblivious to the fragile and ephemeral nature of their new political status. Living in South Carolina, Delany was aware of the seething resentment and anguish of local Whites over the enfranchisement of Blacks. He was astute enough to know that such resentment was not necessarily local. The former slaveholding class may have been defeated and politically humbled, but the culture of the South, and indeed the entire nation, was not necessarily fully supportive of opening and broadening the social and political spaces to accommodate Blacks. Consequently, Delany urged Blacks to be conciliatory and accommodating and to avoid provocative radical demands and policies.

Delany reminded Blacks of the magnitude of the transformation they had just experienced, stressing that no people could be considered truly free "who do not themselves constitute an essential part of the ruling element of the country in which they live."[111] In essence, real freedom came only when people are "their own rulers" and when each individual is "in himself an essential element of the sovereign power which composes the true basis of his liberty. This right, when not exercised by himself, may, at his pleasure, be delegated to another; his true representative."[112] Here, Delany adduced two political doctrines. First was the doctrine of individual sovereignty, and second, that of political representation.

For anyone to be truly free in the political sense, he/she had to attain two fundamental conditions: first, becoming part of the *ruling element* of the nation and thus in position to exercise, and have access to, without any restraints, all the rights, privileges, and obligations of citizenship, and second, when not able or willing to directly play those roles, he/she also had the power to delegate part of the responsibilities to others (his/her elected representatives). Delany concluded that Blacks had accomplished these conditions. They had not only become part of the "ruling element" of the nation that once enslaved them but also had been invested with the power of sovereignty, which they now exercised directly by contesting for political offices, or indirectly through their elected representatives.

Delany concluded therefore that Blacks had indeed become truly free. Nonetheless, he cautioned that this freedom also implied immense responsibilities. In addition to "having all the rights and privileges," therefore, according to Delany, Blacks "also have all the *responsibilities* [emphasis added] belonging to society."[113] One fundamental *responsibility* derived from "the new life into which we have entered," which required the possession of "such *qualifications* [emphasis added] as to fit us for the high, responsible, and arduous duty."[114] As he elaborated, Blacks "must possess attainments equal to the requirements of the positions" they sought. Otherwise, he affirmed, "we have no right to expect anything."[115] The "attainments" this time, unlike in the 1840s when Delany first broached the idea of "attainment," were not material. Office-holding now required some other qualification besides material attainments. Delany did not elaborate on, or define, the nature of this qualification. Notwithstanding, he considered it reasonable to expect that only "qualified" Blacks assumed positions of responsibility. Freedom was not enough of a qualification for office-holding. There was however another practical reason Delany emphasized qualification. He seemed concerned that entrusting political responsibilities to those Blacks he considered inexperienced would expose them to the machinations of selfish Northern politicians who would exploit their ignorance and gullibility to solidify their political power and promote selfish economic and political agendas. Delany therefore wanted "qualified" Blacks in positions of authority—those he believed could be trusted to make strategic choices and forge alliances that would benefit the race. He contended that such strategic choices could and should include reconciling with their erstwhile oppressors.

Delany was undoubtedly troubled by the political climate in the South, especially in South Carolina, and the implications for Black political rights. He was not convinced that the reforms of the Reconstruction era had actually de-racialized the nation to the degree Blacks could freely assume and exercise their new status and responsibilities unfettered by previous conditions. Though Blacks were now part of the "ruling element," the power dynamics remained fragile. It was clear to Delany that though the former slaveholding class had lost the war, and seemed politically humbled and subdued, it had not been completely neutralized. Delany had the foresight to realize that political change was not permanent. Consequently, he called for compromise with, and concessions to, the defeated and humbled former slaveholding class. He proposed certain political principles that he thought would, if adopted, be most beneficial to Blacks in the circumstance they found themselves sandwiched between a class of Northern politicians whose agenda he distrusted, and the former slaveholding class, who remained bitter and alienated: proportional representation (PR), minority representation (MR), accommodation, compromise, and utilitarianism.

On the 14th of August 1871, a frustrated Delany wrote a strongly worded letter to his long-time friend and now Republican Party stalwart Frederick Douglass. He was particularly troubled by the extent to which he believed Blacks were being exploited and misled by radical politicians for purely personal political gains.[116] As corrective, he called for the adoption of a policy of racial representation: "Black leaders for Blacks."[117] He stressed the imperative of appointing only "qualified" Blacks to leadership positions who could be trusted to better articulate and promote the interests of the race. He was particularly distrustful of the political orientation of the Black political leadership in South Carolina. Black political leaders seemed ignorant, gullible, and easily manipulated by the radical republicans. Delany portrayed Black leaders as inexperienced and easily duped by radical republicans into endorsing policies that ultimately did not directly address the immediate needs and interests of Blacks. On the contrary, these policies only further alienated local Whites, the precise constituency whose goodwill Blacks needed. Delany therefore thought that the Black political leadership needed to be enlightened on appropriate policies that would secure those rights. He was also concerned that Blacks in leadership positions in South Carolina would use their demographic preponderance as a platform for monopolizing and abusing political power. To forestall this, he proposed minority representation (MR) to ensure that no one group, either within the state or nationally, used its majority status as justification for excluding or marginalizing others (in minority) from political participation. If implemented, Delany argued that his MR principle would both guarantee and secure minority rights while enhancing the political image of Blacks.[118] Blacks would be seen as fair and considerate rather than power hungry, domineering, vengeful, and reckless.

Furthermore, with Blacks in the majority in South Carolina, and active in the state legislature, Delany felt compelled to remind the Black political leadership of the fluidity and fragility of the political landscape. Though the former slaveholders had lost the war, the likelihood of their political resurgence should not be discounted. Delany reiterated the imperative for MR in a letter to Black State Chief Justice Jonathan Wright. Alarmed by increased White immigration into South Carolina, Delany warned Blacks of the demographic implication. He predicted that within five years, Blacks would become the minority. In essence, the political rights Blacks now exercised could be compromised and possibly eradicated when Whites assumed the majority. As he informed Justice Wright,

> having prospectively lost the popular preponderance and consequent certainty of representation in all departments of government, local, state and national, our only hope and chance of its future security is in the principle of CUMULATIVE VOTING which secures MINORITY representation as well as majority. Let our legislature be wise enough now, while it is in the power of our race to do so, to take such measures as to secure, by constitutional enactment, the right of minority representation, which, while it immediately secures to the Whites of the state, irrespective of party, a pro rata representation, or representation in proportion to numbers, it secures to the Black race the same ratio of representation in counties where Whites have the majority, and when they shall preponderate in the state, which they most assuredly will, at no distant day [emphasis in original].[119]

The adoption of MR principle, therefore, would allow for participation of the minority (i.e., Whites) in politics in proportion to their population size. It would reassure local Whites, especially conservative defenders of the ancien régime that their needs and interests were not in jeopardy. Delany considered this gesture of political accommodation logical in a fluid political context where roles were easily reversible. The current minority could someday become the majority and vice versa. Thus, despite being the majority and part of the "ruling element" in South Carolina, Delany believed that Blacks stood more to gain by advancing politics of accommodation toward, and concessions to, local Whites. He hoped that they (Whites) too would reciprocate when inevitably they attained demographic and political preponderance.[120] He also advocated nationwide application of the corollary principle of proportional representation (PR) since, according to his estimation, Blacks constituted one-sixth of the American population, they were entitled to executive appointments and congressional representation in proportion to the percentage.[121]

The political principles Delany proposed and defended resonated with the state conservatives some of whom were quick to commend him publicly and amplify his ideas. For example, on Delany's call for MR, a representative of the state conservatives, echoing Delany, had this dire and ominous warning to Blacks:

> Negro supremacy in South Carolina has not been an unmixed blessing, and when Whites obtain the numerical superiority, as they shortly will from immigration, they are not likely to be more liberal in policy than the Blacks have been. Unless the Blacks now permit the Whites their proportionate participation in affairs, they are certainly in their turn to be entirely excluded, and the relations of the two races will thus be always disturbed.[122]

Delany proposed both PR and MR primarily for parity and political equity. He also wanted to reassure the entire nation, and South Carolinians in particular, that Blacks were not seeking political dominance over and above what their population size merited. In numerous writings and speeches, Delany warned of the imminent return to power of South Carolina conservatives and advised Blacks to respond proactively by deemphasizing and disengaging from radical policies and politics. They should instead court and secure the goodwill of the resurging conservatives. He now saw the interests of Blacks better served through reconciliation and affiliation with the conservatives. In the letter to Frederick Douglass, Delany expressed his growing frustration with radical politics. Angrily denouncing radical republicanism, he concluded that radicalism had only misled Blacks, fed them unrealistic expectations and aspirations, exploited their ignorance and gullibility, and further alienated them from the very constituents, he believed, were key to their future development.[123]

By 1873, no longer able to contain his frustrations with radicalism and the Republican Party, Delany veered in the direction of the state conservatives and Democratic Party. Based on his ideas and commentaries, it was becoming clear to perceptive observers that Delany's days as a Republican were numbered. In 1874, he joined a coalition of moderate Republicans and some Democrats to launch the Independent Republican Movement (IRM), created as a means of wresting political control from the ruling Radical Republican Party. The IRM nominated John T. Green, an ex-Confederate officer, for governor and Martin Delany for lieutenant governor. The Green-Delany ticket failed miserably in the ensuing election, and the entire movement collapsed, compelling Delany, politically bruised and humiliated, to return, like the proverbial prodigal son, to a hostile Radical Republican Party fold.[124] Predictably, his return and stay would be short-lived. In 1875, Delany formally renounced radical republicanism, joined the Democratic Party, and became the public face of racial reconciliation, compromise, and accommodation. He did not perceive conservatism as necessarily negative and evil. Judging by the conciliatory tone of the public utterances of leading state Democrats, Delany believed that conservatism now held the future for Blacks and afforded greater opportunities for elevation and eventual empowerment. In their campaign platform and speeches, the Democrats pledged to respect and protect those rights Blacks had won since the end of the war. This was reassuring to Delany, and he urged Blacks to give the state conservatives and conservatism a chance.

From 1875 through the end of radical Reconstruction, Delany was a vocal and public advocate of the conservative option. He actively campaigned for the Democratic Party in the crucial 1876 election. He called on Blacks to give the Democrats a chance; to believe in the Party's campaign pledges to respect and protect their rights and freedom if elected.[125] Not surprisingly, the mainstream Black political leadership did not respond kindly to Delany's ideas, and from the very beginning, he found himself deep in hot water. His speeches and campaign activities on behalf of the Democratic Party ruffled feathers and led to bitter opposition and condemnation and, on one occasion, a violent attempt on his life.[126] The radical Black political leadership rejected and repudiated Delany's ideas and, at every opportunity, he was politically obstructed, intimidated, and victimized. His public repudiation of radicalism in the campaigns leading up to the Compromise of 1876 was considered by many the ultimate act of political betrayal of fellow Blacks, for which he was further ostracized.[127] The vast majority of Blacks in South Carolina did not share Delany's faith in the Democratic Party. They had difficulty believing that those who fought a bloody Civil War to protect and preserve slavery could, in so short a time, have abandoned that worldview. They would be proven right.

Delany was undoubtedly an astute observer of the political scene in South Carolina. His advocacy of minority representation echoed a persistent demand of the state conservatives since the onset of radical Reconstruction. Minority representation had featured in the resolutions of the State Conservative Taxpayers Convention of 1871 in Columbia. South Carolina conservatives and ex-Confederates had persistently called for minority representation since the reforms of the Civil Rights Act and the Fourteenth and Fifteenth Amendments.[128] As noted earlier, Delany had hoped that the adoption of MR by Blacks would resonate with the state conservatives who would reciprocate when they assumed political dominance. He was mistaken. South Carolina state conservatives had a fundamentally different understanding of the utility of MR. For them it was a strategic means of infiltrating and ultimately undermining Radical Reconstruction. Though they dangled "reciprocity" in their pronouncements, it was just all a red herring, as Delany would soon discover.

Delany's political philosophy clearly underscored a utilitarian and perhaps even cynical approach to political ideologies and movements. He believed that political affiliations should not serve as wedges or fences. Rather, they exist to promote the interests of members. Black political affiliation, therefore, should be dictated by this pivotal utilitarian consideration. Delany was convinced that what matters the most in politics was not, and should not be, the ideology. He wanted Blacks to focus more on and prioritize their aspirations and interests; in the pursuit of those aspirations, no strategy should be rejected for purely political or ideological reason, even if it entailed associating and cooperating with erstwhile oppressors and enemies. In this respect, the definition and meaning of an ideology in popular imagination became less significant. What was more relevant, in Delany's views, was its capacity to advance the goals and aspirations of Blacks at any given moment. Therefore, an ideology with negative experiential attributes could potentially yield positive results. The futuristic potentials should trump past negative attributes. Though at some point, in the early years of Reconstruction, Republican Party "radicalism" had coincided with Black aspirations, by the mid-1870s, Delany concluded that the party had become a negative and potentially destructive force. In contrast, conservatism, exemplified by the Democratic Party, and historically associated with slavery and racism had, by the mid-1870s, based on its electoral platform and pledges, become the more promising political party for Blacks.[129]

Furthermore, Delany considered an assessment of the dynamics of power fundamental to political affiliation and ideology. He contended that Black leaders should not be guided solely by ideology, be it radical or conservative, but by determination of the dynamics of power. The choice should be the one position or ideology that was both empowering and had the capacity to advance the cause. Even then, one's loyalty to this option terminated when the power dynamics changed. Delany believed that individuals should be free to switch between ideological positions based on their determination of the power dynamics. A Black leader should never be found enslaved to an ideology of powerlessness and vulnerability. For Delany, no one should be held hostage to a political ideology, principle, or affiliation that could prove detrimental and destructive to one's existential interests. This meant, therefore, that if one's affiliation, informed by utilitarian consideration, became threatening, destructive, and disadvantageous, it was prudent and justifiable to explore other options.[130]

In Delany's judgment, therefore, in order for a political party to command and deserve the loyalty of its members, such a party should not only provide material benefits but also ensure their protection. This was his assessment of the political realities of the mid-1870s, by which time, as some historians and political critics concluded, radical republicanism was radical in name only. Political dynamics and power relations had changed in the South. Martin Delany insisted that radical republicanism had failed in its overarching goal—the nurturing of an atmosphere of reconciliation between Blacks and Southern Whites. Nationwide, angry and alienated Southern conservatives were on the political offensive and with a vengeful disposition toward Blacks. The zeal with which the federal government had once defended Black rights had dissipated. This bore ominous consequences for Blacks. Given this development, therefore, Delany considered it prudent for Blacks to switch political allegiance. Republican Party "radicalism" had ceased to be a positive force.[131]

Along with PR and MR, Delany also advocated politics of compromise and reconciliation. He reasoned that for Blacks to maximize the chances of benefiting from their new status, they had to be willing to reach out to, and find common ground with, the old political class (their former oppressors). He had no doubt that Blacks stood to gain more through compromise than a policy that embittered and alienated this group. Regardless of the reassuring presence of Northern politicians, Delany insisted that the future of Blacks still very much depended on the dynamics of their relationship with local Whites. He was sensitive to the fact that the political changes brought by the Civil War and Reconstruction were most difficult and challenging for local Whites, given the fact that for centuries, they had been accustomed to regarding Blacks as property and excluded from positions of political responsibilities. Furthermore, Delany reminded Blacks that the political reforms, however real, could not magically eradicate the gaps and shortcomings created by centuries of enslavement. In other words, it was difficult to transform overnight a relationship that, for almost three hundred years, was defined by inequality and subordination.[132] He believed, and rightly so, that the sudden change and reversals that came with the Civil War and Reconstruction would be most challenging for local Whites who were accustomed to owning Blacks as property. Consequently, Delany contended that it would help if Blacks who occupied positions of authority were not perceived as vengeful, domineering, and power hungry.

The main thrust of Delany's argument, therefore, was that Blacks should not construe becoming part of the "ruling element" to mean that they had achieved absolute equality in all fields. Though he encouraged Blacks to cherish and appreciate the enormity of the political transformation that had occurred, he also stressed that the system was far from perfect. The transformation of Blacks from *slaves* to *citizens*, however revolutionary, did not obliterate racial inequality. The system remained imperfect, and he urged Blacks to acknowledge and accept this imperfection, especially since they too were fundamentally ill-equipped and ill-prepared for the political roles they had been entrusted. In essence, Delany wanted Blacks to understand the limits of their political power. He considered it imprudent to disregard the interests of the former slaveholding class. Blacks had to be open to making concessions that could possibly give precedence to Whites, which could include Blacks voluntarily sacrificing some of their rights, or even, embracing policies that potentially could erode or circumscribe those rights. As Delany explained it, the decisions and choices Black politicians made should be informed by the critical awareness that Whites, "in conceding rights to us . . . had no intention of surrendering their own."[133] This awareness was vital. Consequently, while exercising their political rights, Blacks should, in Delany's words, "take care not to interfere with the rights of others." Underlining this particular point, Delany warned fellow Blacks, "we must not in finding room for ourselves undertake to elbow the White people out of their own places."[134]

Delany strongly defended accommodation and compromise, strategies that could require Blacks to concede "first rank and . . . the first and choice places" to Whites who, in his words, "gave us what we now possess and who first brought us here."[135] This is quite a stunning concession to White privilege and preem-inence from someone who, in an earlier epoch, had vehemently contested any hints of such concessions. What had changed? In the aftermath of the Civil War and Reconstruction, now persuaded that Blacks no longer constituted "a nation within a nation," but an essential part of the "ruling element," Delany became more focused on political stability and orderly race relations, conditions that he felt would be jeopardized if Blacks projected a triumphalist and vengeful disposi-tion toward local Whites. Delany believed that Blacks needed to be reminded of their history and how far the nation had progressed. In his judgment, regardless of how liberated Blacks felt, and despite emancipation, their decisions and polit-ical choices should be balanced against the fact that slavery and its legacies cast ominous shadow over the country. In other words, Blacks had not completely triumphed over slavery.

The last political idea Delany proposed, deriving from, and closely related to, the previous two, was the doctrine of utilitarian politics. He described politics as "intended for the benefits of the people."[136] Politics was not only about resource allocation (Who gets what?) but also about the dynamics of power. For Blacks, this was existential. Politics was, above all else, about survival. The fundamental question, as Delany framed it was: what political arrangements would secure and enhance the survival of Blacks? This touched on something very crucial in the postbellum period: party affiliation. For Blacks, it was presumed, a priori, that their natural political affiliation would be the Republican Party—the party of Lincoln, of emancipation, and of freedom. In essence, historical precedent and ideological loyalty dictated or predetermined the Republican as the logical Party for Blacks. Delany would challenge this reasoning. He believed that the choice should be determined by something more utilitarian and demonstrably enriching. The choice of political affiliation should be determined not by ideological loyalty, old party alliance, or even historical precedent but by practical determination of how that relationship would advance and enrich Blacks' current situation. A political organization/party could justify its members' unwavering loyalty only if it extended some benefits to them. But benefits alone would not solidify such loyalty unless the party also maintained a favorable image in the community. Put differently, the correlation of forces in the society must be in the party's favor. If the odds were against it, "get away as fast as you can," Delany advised.[137] Speaking at a Black-Republican Party Fourth of July rally in Charleston, Delany stressed, "I want you to stick to them (i.e., Republicans) until you find the odds too heavy against them, then get away as fast as you can."[138] Delany's position was that Blacks should determine what party they endorsed and remained loyal to by how much benefit they derived as well as whether or not such relationship safeguarded their political and physical survival. The party had to offer something tangible, material, and existential. Whenever a political party seemed in conflict with, or about to jeopardize, Black interests, and everything appeared at odds with, or against, that party, Delany counselled abandoning such affiliation.

Throughout his career, true to his convictions, Delany frequently switched political allegiances and affiliations, vacillating between radical and conservative options, and each time, his conviction, his determination of what best advanced the interests of Blacks, informed his choices. It should be noted, however, that Delany's espousal of mainstream conservative values was a strategic means of securing a space for Blacks which, he hoped, would enable them eventually to destabilize and obliterate the entire structure of inequality. In essence, he sought a radical end through a conservative strategy. Delany's political philosophy had no room for irreconcilable zero-sum positions. He believed that the astute politician had to be willing to embrace, and experiment with, diverse, even conflicting options and groups and had to be open to working with anyone with the potential to help achieve positive results, even erstwhile enemies. He stressed the fluidity of politics and the fact that changing circumstances could dictate reconciliation, and even developing common ground, with those with whom one had once bitterly disagreed.

It should be noted at this juncture that the political fluidity Delany emphasized, the pragmatism he espoused, and the seemingly ambivalent choices he made were not unique nor isolated. It has been established that such pragmatism/ambivalence was a widespread trait among nineteenth-century Black leaders. There were other Black leaders who, like Delany, often flip-flopped and compromised with erstwhile ideological opponents. One such was Delany's own fellow "militant nationalist" Henry McNeal Turner, who was "famous for his blistering radical condemnation of the racism of American society." Yet, "he always expressed a surprising sympathy with both the social and political views of Southern White conservatives." According to Peter Eisenstadt,

> After 1880 Turner generally voted Democratic, and he was the first of a series of Black nationalists and separatists—including Marcus Garvey, Elijah Mohammed, and Louis Farrakhan—to seek a quixotic common ground with White segregationists. Turner's ambiguous attitude toward the South and southern democrats was characteristic of southern Black leaders of his generation.[139]

This ambiguity, or more appropriately pragmatism, was central to Delany's political thought. He had no permanent political opponents. His choices were informed by his determination of whether or not they would advance what he, at that critical moment, considered (based on his *conscience* and *reason*) were in the best interests of Blacks. Consequently, while the goals Delany pursued remained fairly constant: freedom, justice, equality; the shifting political contexts dictated reassessment and realignment of political strategies. A shrewd political leader, therefore, had to know when it was strategic to switch between radical and conservative alternatives, and at times, the situation could dictate juggling both ideologies, each reinforcing the other.

Although Delany seemed to embrace conservative ideas and coalitions, his ultimate goal was to destabilize the system. His conservatism embodied radical intents. In this regard, Delany's support of South Carolina Democrats in the late 1870s was not, in his judgment, to uphold their right to subordinate Blacks *ad infinitum*. It derived from a realistic assessment of emerging realignment of political power relations in the entire South—a realignment which a correspondent of the *New York Times* reported raised "other questions . . . which do not leave old party lines clear. . . . Republicans are found acting with Democrats and vice versa."[140] Given this development, Delany concluded that Blacks were better served by deemphasizing radicalism, an ideology that no longer was actively and effectively supportive and nurturing of their rights and privileges. Like future conservatives such as Booker T. Washington, Delany might have been naïve in reposing so much faith in accommodation as a means of radically transforming the status quo of inequality. His choice of a conservative approach, at any given moment, derived from a strong conviction that it was the best option for advancing the cause of freedom and equality.

Delany considered a "radical" posture in the early years of reconstruction prudent because Blacks had on their side the force and authority of the federal government, supporting and guaranteeing the exercise of their rights and privileges. This position of strength made radical republicanism a logical and realistic option. By the mid-1870s, however, that federal power and authority was disappearing, and Delany felt that radicalism was bereft of any positive attributes and thus had become disadvantageous. With the gradual dismantling of federal authority in the South in the late 1870s, Delany became convinced that Blacks would be powerless to confront their erstwhile enemies who had been angered by radical politics. This strategic calculation dictated his switch to the Democratic Party in the mid-1870s. In his opinion, the conservative option now offered Blacks a better chance. As indicated above, this utilitarianism was a defining attribute of Black political leadership during Reconstruction.[141] It seems reasonable, therefore, to suggest that in Black American history, political ideologies (radicalism and conservatism) have not always been mutually exclusive, zero-sum entities. Delany personified political pragmatism, which embodied utilitarian construction of political ideology. He portrayed an astute Black politician as neither consistently conservative nor consistently radical. He/She is at times one and/or the other—someone who does not hesitate to embrace, and be publicly identified with, whichever option promised to advance the interests of Blacks. Today, such a leader would be deemed a charlatan, a political prostitute, or pimp. In Delany's times, however, the ever-shifting terrain of Black political history rendered that leadership typology much more viable.

In post-Civil War South, therefore, Delany theorized that Blacks should not be constrained by past historical or ideological considerations in determining political affiliation. He proposed a utilitarian approach that prioritized what potentially Blacks would benefit from such relationship. This also called for vigilance. It was crucial for Blacks to be aware of the changing political and power dynamics. They should know when a political party was no longer in position to promote and defend their interests and when its power dynamics threatened their survival. Blacks should never blindly adhere to a political party but should retain the latitude of switching positions when their interests or survival were at stake. Under such circumstances, breaking with historical and ideological tradition seemed justifiable. This was the basis of Delany's assessment of the Black-Radical Republican Party relationship in the South. Unlike many leading Blacks who supported the Republican Party due to historical obligation, Delany was initially drawn to the Party not primarily because of historical or ideological tradition, but because he felt that at the time, based on his assessment of prevailing political climate, it was the party better able to promote and defend the interests of Blacks. However, as radical Reconstruction progressed, he concluded that the Republican Party policies benefitted and enriched everyone but the newly enfranchised Blacks. Furthermore, he believed that Radical Reconstruction had nurtured a climate of racial resentment and animosity in the South. It was clear to Delany that not even the lofty rhetoric of radical republicanism could protect Blacks from the seething anger and avenging wrath of the defeated and politically humbled but resurging former slaveholding class.

The pragmatic and utilitarian nature of Delany's political philosophy explained his disillusionment with radical republicanism, and decision to switch to the Democratic Party. In the mid-1870s, he changed party affiliation, and embraced the state conservatives and ex-Confederates. Subsequently, he became a prominent speaker and advocate for the Democratic Party in the crucial election of 1876. Being willing and able to reach out to, and find common cause with, former slaveholders was crucial. Even under the most difficult of circumstances, Delany offered Blacks what, in modern political discourse, is akin to the now discredited concept of political "bipartisanship": the ability and willingness to reach out and function across a party, racial, and ideological divide. Though unpopular with leading Blacks and their Radical Republican allies, Delany's ideas and political decisions reflected the dictates of his *reason* and *conscience*, and they found resonance among South Carolina conservatives. They amplified his ideas and invoked them to corroborate their own discredited and unpopular political views.

It could be argued that Delany's political conservatism developed from what could be characterized as a self-derived relativist and psycho-rationalist political doctrine, the product of his *conscience* and *reason*. Nonetheless, this was not a zero-sum and exclusive doctrine. The dictates of Delany's *conscience* and *reason* acknowledged the prudence of engaging with different, often contradictory (if not conflicting), positions and viewpoints when necessary. This meant being amenable to compromise with, and offer concessions to, political opponents, including erstwhile and known political enemies. Delany seemed to suggest that there were no permanent friends or enemies in politics but interests dictated by one's conviction (*conscience* and *reason*). The problem with Delany's *reasoning*, and the dictates of his *conscience*, however, was the assumption that such compromise and accommodation, in the context of post-Civil War South, would necessarily translate into tangible political gains for Blacks. This proved wrong. Though the Democrats ("Redeemers," as they fondly and proudly self-identified) won the 1876 election and regained political power, the outcome was disastrous for Blacks. It dawned on Delany that he had gambled and lost. His political conservatism had not yielded the outcome and reciprocity he predicted. There would be no reciprocity from the ascendant and vengeful "redeemers." Disappointed, frustrated, and desperate, Delany reverted to his old emigration scheme and immersed himself in a resurging Liberia Exodus movement in South Carolina. He appealed to the American Colonization Society for assistance. His appeal fell on deaf ears. In early 1885, his renewed "African Dream" squashed, a physically and psychologically broken Delany returned to the warmth and comfort of his wife and children in Xenia, Ohio, where he would die shortly thereafter.

Conclusion

During his brief political career, Delany switched political allegiances and ideological positions with a dizzying frequency that often left his supporters and detractors alike dazed, confused, disappointed, and, at times, angry. But he was unmoved. Despite oppositions and resentments, Delany remained steadfast in his political pragmatism. He switched positions and allegiances whenever he deemed it politically prudent. For Delany, radicalism and conservatism were not sacrosanct ideologies but flexible options for promoting the interests of Blacks. Those interests took precedence over the ideology and not the reverse. The individual, guided by his or her determination of what was in the best interest of the Black community, should freely experiment with either conservative or radical options. The astute and savvy Black leader must know when such pragmatism dictated switching ideological positions. There was a certain utilitarianism embedded in Delany's conception of politics. Politics, for Delany, was fundamentally about benefits. In any given political situation or relationship or alliance, one should be guided by considerations of rewards and benefits. This was the theory undergirding his responses to post-Civil War and Reconstruction politics. He assessed every situation based on the needs and interests of the newly emancipated and enfranchised Black population, a group that he believed, due to inexperience and lack of education, was susceptible to being manipulated and exploited. For Delany, politics was of little benefit if not utilitarian. It was this utilitarianism that shaped the compromises and pragmatism that defined his political thought. It informed his willingness and readiness to switch political affiliations, to explore common ground with erstwhile opponents. Politics, for Delany, was always in the making—not a rigidly ideological and compartmentalized realm but a fluid process driven by utilitarian considerations. Politics was about reconciling seemingly irreconcilables, forging relationships and alliances with adversaries, and pursuing and exploring compromise for the interests and benefits of all.

Delany's political thought suggested that he was concerned less with how others felt about his choices. He was more focused on whether those choices reflected *his* convictions about what *he* determined were in the best interest of Blacks. Put differently, the decisions and choices Delany made were dictated more by his *conscience*, guided by the light of his *reason*, and less by dogmatic allegiance to some radical or conservative ideology. Thus, his political thought was rooted in a pragmatism that allowed him the flexibility to make choices and decisions based not on blind allegiance to some dogma or political principles but on his determination of what would best further the interests of his constituency at any given political moment. Though Delany embraced, advocated and experimented with "radical" solutions and strategies, he was not averse to switching and adopting "conservative" solutions and strategies when he deemed it necessary. To reiterate, the ideological strategy/approaches mattered less. The goals were far more profound and consequential and thus dictated the strategies. Delany's conservative strategies underscored both the complexity of Black conservatism and its mutually reinforcing relationship to radicalism. One, therefore, concurs with Peter Eisenstadt that "Black conservatism transcends the usual division of integrationists and nationalists. Those of conservative disposition can be found as much among militant nationalists as among committed assimilationists." In fact, the central theme of the Eisenstadt's volume (echoing August Meier) is the "ambivalence of southern conservatism and its tendency to vacillate between accommodation and radical nationalism." Many of the "distinctive southern Black conservatives" including Turner and Delany tended "to alternate between phases of supine accommodationism and militant nationalism or emigrationism."[142]

At different times in his career, Delany has been tagged a conservative who compromised, and at times, a radical and an uncompromisingly militant leader.

In truth, he exemplified all attributes, often combining and juggling them within contiguous historical contexts and struggles. He rejected any blind allegiance to an ideology or ideal, be it radical or conservative, and seemed opposed to an essentialist conception of political ideology as an absolute category which established boundaries and set values and goals deemed inviolable. Delany was not overly concerned about political labels, whether radical or conservative. He believed that goals trumped ideals and labels: one could be consistent on goals and yet flexible and pragmatic on ideology and strategies. This utilitarian ethos shaped the conservative phase of his career. For Delany, therefore, utilitarian consideration determined political group identity and affiliations. The crucial consideration was whether such affiliation would advance the people's aspirations. As underlined in Howard Rabinowitz's anthology, this utilitarianism characterized Black leadership in the nineteenth century, and Martin Delany was the perfect exemplar.[143] Being "conservative" or "radical" was often a utilitarian, rather than existential, choice. The underlying consideration was not the meaning of, or images embedded in, the ideology, but the possibilities and potentials for achieving the desired goals, which could be radical or moderate, or even conservative.

Conclusion

Ahead of His Time

[M]y mission is to assist in the elevation of the oppressed and down-trodden of our land, in order faithfully to do which we must speak the truth and expose error, and this I shall do though the "heaven fall."

—Martin R. Delany, "Report from Cincinnati, Ohio,
May 20, 1848"

I N HIS JUNE 4, 1848, report to Frederick Douglass on his visit to Cincinnati, Ohio, Martin Delany reminded Douglass: "You know I care little for precedent, and therefore, discard the frivolous rules of formality, conforming always to principle, suggested by *conscience*, and guided by the light of *reason* [emphasis added]."[1] Two weeks later, in the June 18 report from Milton, Ohio, Delany elaborated:

I am aware that I shall be subject to censure, by both friends and foes, for the course I have pursued in thus liberally expressing my opinion, but as I have taken my stand as one of the sentinels on the watch-tower of the liberties of our brethren, I never intend to leave the ramparts, nor suffer an approach of the enemy unmolested, until my colors first be grounded in the hands of the fallen helpless victims, who dared, in the midst of a tempest of oppression, such as now surrounds us, stand upon the citadel, and unfurl its proud drapery to the gaze and dismay of the enemies of our race, and the dearest rights of man.[2]

Delany wrote these statements in 1848 in the course of executing his duties at the *North Star*, which entailed visiting cities across the North, Northeast, and Midwest to promote the paper as well as deliver antislavery lectures and propagate moral suasion. In the statements, Delany introduced three vital attributes of, while also providing insights into, the courage and determination that would define his experiences for the rest of his life. First, he underlined the twin forces or agencies that determined the ideas he promoted as well as the choices and decisions he made. These two forces constituted the existential dynamics of his philosophy of life: *conscience* and *reason*.

The ideas and strategies Delany promoted, the choices he made, and the alliances he embraced would be determined and driven primarily by the agencies of his *conscience* and *reason*. What ideological positions he defended at any given time and the affiliations he identified with derived from these two forces. Second, he underlined the existential dynamics of his thoughts, motivations, decisions, and choices: elevation of the oppressed and downtrodden. Third, he affirmed his awareness and acknowledgment of the probability of censure, opposition, resentment, and rebuke from all quarters (friends and foes alike) and the courage to hold steadfastly to his convictions. Delany would boldly express, espouse, and defend his views, choices, and decisions and would stand firmly by them, as long as his *conscience* and *reason* dictated they were the best for advancing the cause of the oppressed and downtrodden people. This would explain his willingness to advocate controversial and unpopular ideas and choices and the boldness with which he both condemned the prevailing racism and bigotry and defended provocative strategies for bridging the racial, socioeconomic, and education gaps, even when they conflicted with the positions and views of dominant groups. It would also account for his versatility as well as his capacity and willingness to advocate for the underprivileged and powerless and to engage such controversial subjects as the abuses and misuse of religion, the neglect of female education, the need to empower women in a society and culture of patriarchy, and the efficacy and challenges of violence as reform strategy. It also underscored his optimism about the malleability of America, as a result of which he encouraged Blacks to be hopeful even in the context of the most dehumanizing of experiences.

Though the American society Delany fought against was imperfect, nonetheless he was optimistic that it could, and would be, perfected. When this optimism proved wrong, Delany sought for, and was amenable to exploring, whatever strategies and solutions he thought would help advance change. The fundamental question at the core of his thoughts was: what shall we do to better our condition?[3] In the course of answering this existential question, Delany offered insightful ideas and commentaries on some of the strategies his counterparts and the entire nation were debating and experimenting with, including education, violence, religion, and politics. Not only did Delany contribute to the discourses and debates his contemporaries had on these subjects, but also his ideas far outlived him and his times. He could rightly be described as someone who was far ahead of his contemporaries on many of the issues of the time. His ideas and solutions would resurface in those of future generations. For example, in 1863 when General Benjamin Butler founded the Butler School for Negro children, the curriculum then considered ideal for elevating Negro children included subjects such as reading, writing, arithmetic, geography, and grammar were precisely the same subjects Martin Delany had proposed during the 1840s.[4] Furthermore, when General Samuel Armstrong established the Hampton Agricultural and Normal School, the curriculum emphasized industrial education that would impart trade and business skills.[5] This was also the pedagogy Delany advocated again and again in the 1840s that ultimately became the model that produced Booker T. Washington and Tuskegee Institute.

Booker T. Washington is memorialized in American history as the exemplar of compromise and accommodation. He is vilified by some as someone whose ideas set the stage for the "Separate but Equal" Jim Crow culture that emerged in the late 1890s. While it is true that Washington advocated accommodation and compromise, he was not the first prominent Black leader to espouse and defend such policies. Martin Delany preceded him in advancing these ideas by at least two decades. A few excerpts from Delany's book *The Condition* (1852) contain similar ideas and strategies Washington would highlight almost half a century later in his Atlanta Exposition address. For example, in his criticism of Blacks' failure to prioritize practical and business skills Delany observed, "One of our great mistakes—we have gone in advance of ourselves. We have commenced at the superstructure of the building, instead of the foundation—at the top instead of the bottom."[6] He went on to write, "we should first be mechanics and common tradesmen and professions as a matter of course would grow out of the wealth made thereby."[7] Further lamenting what he discerned as overemphasis on Classical education, he wrote, "We as heretofore, have been on the extreme; either no education at all, or a collegiate education.... We jumped too far, taking a leap from the deepest abyss to the highest summit; rising from the ridiculous to the sublime, without medium or intermission."[8] Delany made similar observations in many of his reports for the *North Star* in the 1840s. In addition, his Freedmen's Bureau reports during Reconstruction had specific recommendations for the education of freedmen. Delany's criticisms and recommendations would resonate with, and be trumpeted by, future generations of Black leaders, most notably Booker T. Washington. Delany's influence and legacy were not limited to education. He advocated gradualism in politics, deemphasized social

equality, and insisted that Blacks who aspired for positions of political responsibility be qualified and experienced. Decades later, Washington would amplify
these classic Delanyean ideas in his 1895 epochal Atlanta Cotton Exposition
address. Take for example these excerpts:

First,

> Ignorant and inexperienced, it is not strange that in the first years of our
> new life we began at the top instead of at the bottom; that a seat in Congress
> or the state legislature was more sought than real estate or industrial skill;
> that the political convention or stump speaking had more attractions than
> starting a dairy farm or truck garden.[9]

Second,

> The wisest among my race understand that the agitation of questions of so-
> cial equality is the extremist folly, and that progress in the enjoyment of all
> the privileges that will come to us must be the result of severe and constant
> struggle rather than of artificial forcing. . . . It is important and right that
> all privileges of the law be ours, but it is vastly more important that we be
> prepared for the exercise of these privileges.[10]

There are three classic Delanyean ideas in the above extracts from Booker T.
Washington's speeches: gradualism, prioritizing industrial skills, and deemphasizing social equality. Like Delany before him, Washington also suggested that
Blacks be "prepared" for the exercise of the privileges they sought. The insistence
on Blacks being "prepared" and "qualified" before aspiring for, and ascending
to, positions of political responsibility was a point Delany stressed whenever
he had the opportunity in the early years of Reconstruction.[11] This idea, as this
study has shown, positioned Delany at odds with the mainstream Black political
leadership.

Echoes of Delany's political ideas reverberated beyond the 1890s. They remain
audible even in today's dysfunctional political landscape. Concepts and phrases
such as "bipartisanship," "reaching across the aisle," and "forging biracial alliances" are among the ideals most commonly invoked, but rarely practiced, in
modern political discourses, especially in America. They have become clichés,
empty political slogans. Martin Delany both preached and practiced these ideals. Let us recall the political context. This was after a bloody and divisive Civil
War, when emotions were still very raw over slavery and the entire Reconstruction program. Passions ran high on both sides. It was precisely at this critical
moment when it would have been considered imprudent for a Black leader to

venture across the ideological and racial divide that Delany defied conventions and, propelled by the dictates of his *conscience* and *reason*, reached out to former ideological and racial antagonists and attempted to forge compromise and reconciliation. He exemplified courage propelled by the most intimate and personal of convictions. Booker T. Washington would popularize these approaches almost two decades later. Delany also further demonstrated that it was possible to combine Black nationalism with a conservative economic agenda. In order to empower Blacks, one could and should pursue mainstream middle-class values of self-help, self-reliance, and economic development. In the 1920s, Marcus Garvey, the Jamaican immigrant and leading Black nationalist and Pan-Africanist would combine his vision with Booker T. Washington's brand of conservative economics.[12] Martin Delany manifested this disposition at the onset of his antislavery activism. This was reflected in numerous articles and reports in the *North Star* during the late 1840s. This same consideration would inspire him during Reconstruction to advocate deemphasizing political rights in the pursuance of programs of self-help, self-reliance, and economic elevation.

Delany insisted that Blacks should not be locked into, or limited by, boundaries set by precedent and ideology. He did not view politics as a zero-sum game. On the contrary, he conceived of politics as the arena of accommodation and compromises. He believed that the astute politician had to be willing, open, and ready to explore alternative strategies and approaches and not be held hostage by predetermined ideologies or positions. On religion, Delany clearly argued and demonstrated that religion should be considered a lens through which God revealed to humanity how to be productive and fruitful *here* and not *hereafter*. He insisted that Christianity was not just for spiritual salvation but for secular elevation as well—that it embodied deep concerns for the daily challenges of humanity. He quoted copiously from the scriptures to corroborate the argument that religion should fundamentally be about improving the lives of the poor and needy; the less fortunate. In the scriptures, as Delany argued, God clearly endowed humanity with the earthly resources with which to improve the lives of humans *here* and *now*. He defined Christianity with a human and humane face. It was, he insisted, a religion that was about connecting with the poor and needy and bettering their lives. Long before liberation theology became popular, therefore, Martin Delany had articulated some of its core and defining ideals. It would, therefore, not be far-fetched to identify Delany among the pioneers of liberation theology.

Furthermore, in the nineteenth century when Black women, and indeed American women in general, were not supposed to be seen or heard publicly advancing an opinion or staking a position, Delany challenged and defied that convention. He prioritized the elevation of women. In fact, he premised the elevation and advancement of an entire race on the status of women. How Black women were treated, he argued, would determine and reflect the overall condition and experiences of the Black race. He believed that Blacks would not advance and attain meaningful progress for as long as Black women were oppressed and confined to domestic and menial occupations. This was all in the late 1840s and early 1850s! Delany's critique of the condition of Black women and recommendation for their empowerment began during his brief stint at the *North Star*. He would advance a much more robust advocacy for Black Women's empowerment in the early 1850s in his seminal publication, *The Condition*. In this respect, Delany can reasonably be identified alongside of Sojourner Truth and Harriet Tubman, two courageous and indefatigable abolitionists and champions of Black women's rights in the nineteenth century. On the status of Black women, therefore, it could be argued that Delany was ahead of his time. Also, the educational reforms he proposed during Reconstruction underscore how far ahead of the times he was. For example, his calls to ban corporal punishment, to create a school environment conducive to learning, and to ensure that schools were adequately supplied with resources that would facilitate learning are ideas now associated with modern progressive educational reforms. This all grew out of, and reflected the concerns he felt about, the depth of poverty and misery that plagued Blacks in his Bureau district in Hilton Head Island, South Carolina.

Delany is widely acclaimed and remembered today as the father of Black nationalism. Many represent him as the ideological and philosophical predecessor of the likes of Marcus Garvey, Malcolm X, and Stokely Carmichael. While there is justification for this contention, given the contents of his publications and public pronouncements during the early 1850s emigration phase of his career, an equally compelling case could be made for a counter-viewpoint and narrative. Delany could also be described as the father of modern Black conservatism. As this study highlights, his post-Civil War and Reconstruction political ideas embodied strong conservative ethos which simultaneously endeared him to conservative political interests and alienated him from the more radical elements of the Black political leadership. Delany's conservatism anticipated much that scholars and critics would later associate with, and attribute to, Booker T. Washington. As this book underscores, Delany articulated and experimented with diverse political strategies and ideals. During the early phase of Reconstruction, he identified with the (radical) Republican Party.

By the mid-1870s, convinced that the party no longer reflected the interests of Blacks, Delany switched political affiliation and joined the (conservative) Democratic Party. He worked tirelessly for racial reconciliation and bipartisanship in South Carolina. In this, he found himself at odds with the mainstream Black political leadership. The prospect and probability of political retribution could not deter Delany from acting according to the dictates of his *conscience* and *reason*. That he failed in his predictions should not negate the altruism that infused the decisions and choices he made. The political ideas and strategies he advocated such as bipartisanship, compromise and reconciliation have become much sought after, but elusive, ideals in modern American political discourses.

The twentieth century has gone down in history as a violent era for Black Americans. The anti-Black lynchings that engulfed the country from the late nineteenth through the mid-twentieth centuries; and the more recent frightening and seemingly endless killings of unarmed Blacks by law enforcement and self-appointed vigilantes underscore the entrenched nature and resiliency of America's culture of racial bigotry and intolerance. Despite twentieth-century civil rights reforms, rather than abating, the racial intolerance and violence that historically defined the Black experience in America appear to be growing. Ultimately, the persistence of these racially motivated killings galvanized a movement that has become an embedded aspect of Black resistance—Black Lives Matter. The brazen and public nature of these killings broadened and expanded the scope and character of the resistance, becoming not just a Black resistance but an American resistance.[13]

Martin Delany anticipated this outcome over a century and half ago. America today reflects the world and reality Delany encountered and denounced in the early decades of the nineteenth century. The portraits of America Delany experienced and rendered were remarkable for their ugliness and their moral and racial debasement. That America bore uncanny resemblance to, and prefigured, an America he would not live to see: the America of the twentieth and twenty-first centuries. The chain of racial bigotry and violence extended unbroken from Martin Delany to Emmett Till, Medgar Evers, Trayvon Martin, Michael Brown, Tamir Rice, Eric Garner, Ahmaud Arbery, George Floyd, Rayshard Brooks, and Breonna Taylor, to name but few. To appreciate the magnitude of Delany's foresight, his portraits are worth reproducing in their entirety. Recall the report he transmitted from Pittsburgh, Pennsylvania, in February of 1849 in which he described his disillusionment with moral suasion. In that report, Delany condemned the dissonance between the promises and prospects of Black humanity and the "endless outrage and cruelty" Blacks endured (see Chapter 1).[14] About five weeks after publishing that report, Delany wrote a scathing description of "American Civilization," and lamented that

> Not a place is there in the United States of America, whether city, town, village, or hamlet, in which a colored person resides or has ever been, or may go, that they are not continually subject to the abuse, more or less of the Whites—And though at times this abuse may not be corporeal or physical, yet it is at all times an abuse of the feelings, which in itself is a blasting outrage on humanity, and insufferable to the better senses of man and womanhood.[15]

He made the poignant observation that "American people are remarkable for their readiness and aptitude in the persecution of those weaker in number and means than themselves."[16] All that said, Delany was careful not to be perceived as indicting every American. He made an important acknowledgment and distinction that foreshadowed twenty-first century developments worth quoting at length:

> We repeat ... that there are those good Americans who are utterly opposed to this civil outrage and Christian infamy, even those who make no profession to what is termed abolitionism, many liberal editors of different parties have manfully stepped forth and boldly and freely spoken out against these impositions, ably defending the cause of oppressed humanity; but these are few, comparatively, and least they be charged with "fanaticism" may only speak out when some aggravated outrage is committed, such as to call forth the indignation of public censure [like the murders of Michael Brown, Eric Garner]. It is the colored people who daily witness and experience these moral stabs and civil assassinations, perpetrated in so quiet and mild manner, comparatively, that they are not the subject of public attention, and only become so when the outrage is of such a nature as to become the subject of legal complaint, when, to be which, it must be recognized by the law as a penal offence [such as the horrifying killings of George Floyd, Breonna Taylor, Rayshard Brooks].[17]

Delany then wondered what judgment Americans would have rendered had such atrocities as he described been perpetrated by Blacks elsewhere. As he queried rhetorically, "Did the colored people or their children, anywhere in the world, exhibit such continued evidence of moral baseness, it would be charged against them as the strongest proof of their insusceptibility of an elevated civilization.

Can Americans, as such, lay claim to civilization?"[18] This is a question that many today have asked and continue to ask about America.

Again, foreshadowing the future, Delany called for rallying the "voice of outraged humanity . . . against this intolerable crusade against our rights, and insufferable rioting against liberty—reckless tramping under foot our most delicate, and cherished sense of propriety . . . the weight of a nation grinds us in the dust, and we dare make the effort to cast it off."[19] Everything Delany witnessed and experienced led him to one stark conclusion: "There appears to be a fixed determination on the part of the oppressors in this country, to destroy every vestige of self-respect, self-possession, and manly independence left in the colored people."[20] In both documents, Delany spoke in a language that leading Black activists today utilize in their reactions to the contemporary state of Black America. Delany's words and language captured the ugly dimensions and realities of Black existence in nineteenth-century America. In another sense, Delany vividly captured the America of the future. His portraits bore an uncanny and troubling resemblance to the America of today—the one we are all witnessing—the one that birthed Black Lives Matter.

Acknowledgments

1. Gerald A. Burks, *Partial Genealogy of Martin R. Delany* (Revised. Unpublished manuscript, 2006), 1.

2. Ibid.

3. Gerald A. Burks, "Martin R. Delany," AfriGeneas Genealogy and History Forum Archive, March 25, 2006.

Introduction

1. William E. B. Du Bois, "A Forum of Facts and Opinions," *Pittsburgh Courier*, July 25, 1936.

2. Edna B. McKenzie, "Doctor, Editor, Soldier: On Pittsburgh's Very Own Martin R. Delany," *Post-Gazette*, February 5, 1992.

3. Philip Cash, "Pride, Prejudice, and Politics," *Harvard Medical School Alumni Bulletin* 54 (December 1980): 20–25; Ronald Takaki, "Aesculapius Was a Whiteman: Ante-bellum Racism and Male Chauvinism at Harvard Medical School," *Phylon* 39, no. 2 (1978): 129–134; Cyril Griffith, *The African Dream: Martin R. Delany and the Emergence of Pan-Africanist Thought* (University Park: Pennsylvania State University Press, 1975); Floyd J. Miller, *The Search for Black Nationality: Black Emigration and Colonization, 1787–1863* (Urbana: University of Illinois Press, 1975).

4. "Abraham Lincoln to Hon. E. M. Stanton, Secretary of War, February 8, 1865," in *Life and Public Services of Martin R. Delany*, by Frank A. Rollin (Boston: Lee and Shepard, 1868), 171; Dorothy Sterling, *The Making of an Afro-American: Martin Robison Delany, 1812–1885* (New York: Doubleday, 1971), 230–251.

5. Rollin, *Life and Public Services*, 269–276; Victor Ullman, *Martin R. Delany: The Beginnings of Black Nationalism* (Boston: Beacon Press, 1971), 324–379.

6. Francis Simkins and Robert Woody, *South Carolina during Reconstruction* (Gloucester, MA: Peter Smith, 1966), 473–474.

7. Paul M. Gaston, *The New South Creed: A Study in Southern Mythmaking* (New York: Vintage Books, 1973), 178–179; Joel Williamson, *The Crucible of Race: Black-White Relations in the American South Since Emancipation* (London: Oxford University Press,

1984); Joel Williamson, ed., *The Origins of Segregation* (Lexington, MA: D. C. Heath & Co, 1968); Idus Newby, *Jim Crow's Defense: Anti-Negro Thought in America, 1900–1930* (Baton Rouge: Louisiana State University Press, 1965).

8. Vincent Harding, "Beyond Chaos: Black History and the Search for the New Land," in *Amistad 1: Writings on Black History and Culture*, ed. John A. Williams and Charles F. Harris (New York: Vintage Books, 1970); Sterling Stuckey, "Twilight of Our Past: Reflections on the Origins of Black History," in *Amistad 2: Writings on Black History and Culture*, ed. John A. Williams and Charles F. Harris (New York: Vintage Books, 1971).

9. Sterling, *The Making of an Afro-American*; Ullman, *Martin R. Delany*; Griffith, *The African Dream*; Miller, *The Search for Black Nationality*; Theodore Draper, *The Rediscovery of Black Nationalism* (New York: Viking Press, 1970); see also Draper, "The Father of American Black Nationalism," *New York Times Review of Books*, March 12, 1970.

10. Richard Blackett, "Martin Delany and Robert Campbell: Black Americans in Search of an African Colony," *Journal of Negro History* 60, no. 11 (January 1977); Robert Khan, "The Political Ideology of Martin R. Delany," *Journal of Black Studies* (June 1984); Nell I. Painter, "Martin R. Delany: A Black Leader in Two Kinds of Time," *New England Journal of Black Studies* 8 (1989); Louis Rosenfeld, "Martin Robison Delany (1812–1885): Physician, Black Separatist, Explorer, Soldier," *Bulletin of the New York Academy of Medicine* 65, no. 7 (September 1989); Robert S. Levine, *Martin Delany, Frederick Douglass, and the Politics of Representative Identity* (Chapel Hill: University of North Carolina Press, 1997); Tunde Adeleke, *Without Regard to Race: The Other Martin R. Delany* (Jackson: University Press of Mississippi, 2003).

11. Ira Berlin, *Slaves Without Masters: The Free Negro in the Antebellum South* (New York: New Press, 1992); John Henderson Russell, *The Free Negro in Virginia, 1619–1865* (Baltimore, MD: Johns Hopkins University Press, 1913).

12. Rollin, *Life and Public Services*, 40.

13. Rollin, *Life and Public Services*, 38–42. Delany's parents hastily departed Virginia to escape imminent prosecution for violating Virginia's law criminalizing the education of Blacks. The family had acquired the *New York Primer and Spelling Book* from an itinerant trader with which the children began nocturnal study, and soon every member of the family had gained some literacy. Word got out that the Delanys had committed a crime. Pati escaped with the children to Chambersburg, Pennsylvania.

14. Ullman, *Martin R. Delany*, 22–23; Sterling, *The Making of an Afro-American*, 43–45.

15. Rollin, *Life and Public Services*, 43; Sterling, *The Making of an Afro-American*, 43–45.

16. Rollin, *Life and Public Services*, 43.

17. Ibid.

18. Rollin, *Life and Public Services*, 28. See also Ullman, *Martin R. Delany*, 45–46.

19. Rollin, *Life and Public Services*, 48–67.

20. Howard H. Bell, "The American Moral Reform Society, 1836–1841," *Journal of Negro Education* 27 (Winter 1958); see also Bell, "National Conventions of the Middle

1840s: Moral Suasion VS. Political Action," *Journal of Negro History* 42, no. 4 (October 1957); Richard P. McCormick, "William Whipper: Moral Reformer," *Pennsylvania History* 43 (January 1969).

21. Elizabeth Geffen, "Violence in Philadelphia in the 1840s and 1850s," *Pennsylvania History* 4 (October 1969); Adam D. Simmons, "Ideologies and Programs of the Negro Anti-Slavery Movement, 1830–1861" (PhD diss., Northwestern University, 1983); Bruce Laurie, *Working People of Philadelphia, 1800–1850* (Philadelphia: Temple University Press, 1980).

22. Simmons, "Ideologies and Programs."

23. The Fugitive Slave Law, part of the Compromise of 1850, was designed to defuse the growing sectional divide and animosity over the admission of new states. It now made it a crime to assist or give sanctuary to fugitives and pledged federal resources and support for their apprehension and return. See Stephen E. Maizlish, *A Strife of Tongues: The Compromise of 1850 and the Ideological Foundations of the American Civil War* (Charlottesville: University of Virginia Press, 2018).

24. Martin Delany, "National Disfranchisement of Colored People" in *The Condition, Elevation, Emigration and Destiny of the Colored People of the United States* (Baltimore, MD: Black Classic Press, 1993) 147–158. Originally published in 1852 in Philadelphia; see also Delany, "American Civilization: Treatment of the Colored People in the United States," *North Star*, March 30, 1849, 2.

25. Martin Delany, "Sound the Alarm," *North Star*, January 12, 1849.

26. Ibid.

27. "Minutes of the State Convention of the Colored Citizens of Pennsylvania, Convened at Harrisburg, December 13th and 14th, 1848," in *Proceedings of the Black State Conventions, vol. 2, 1840–1865*, ed. Philip S. Foner and George E. Walker (Philadelphia: Temple University Press, 1979), 124.

28. Delany, "Sound the Alarm" *North Star*, January 12, 1849.

29. Delany, "Sound the Alarm" *North Star*, January 12, 1849, 166–269; Sterling, *The Making of an Afro-American*, 230–299; Ullman, *Martin R. Delany*, 291–380.

30. Simkins and Woody, *South Carolina during Reconstruction*; Alrutheus A. Taylor, *The Negro in South Carolina During the Reconstruction* (Washington, DC: Association for the Study of Negro Life and History, 1924); Thomas Holt, *Black Over White: Negro Political Leadership in South Carolina during Reconstruction* (Urbana: University of Illinois Press, 1977); Joel Williamson, *After Slavery: The Negro in South Carolina During Reconstruction, 1861–1877* (Chapel Hill: University of North Carolina Press, 1965).

31. Adeleke, *Without Regard to Race*, 138, 161.

32. Martin R. Delany, *Trial and Conviction* (Charleston, 1876).

33. William J. Cooper, *The Conservative Regime: South Carolina, 1877–1890* (Baltimore, MD: Johns Hopkins University Press, 1968); Henry T. Thompson, *Ousting the Carpetbagger from South Carolina* (New York: Negro University Press, 1928); Alfred B. Williams, *Hampton and His Red Shirts: South Carolina Deliverance in 1876* (Charleston: Walker, Evans, and Cogswell, 1935).

34. Booker T. Washington, *Up From Slavery: An Autobiography* (New York: Dover Publications, 1995). First published by Doubleday, New York, 1901.

35. Tunde Adeleke, "Martin R. Delany and Booker T. Washington: Ideological Partners Separated by Time and Ideology," in *Booker T. Washington: Interpretative Essays* (London: The Edwin Mellen Press, 1998), 35–80.

36. Ullman, *Martin R. Delany*, ix.

37. Angela Jones, ed., *The African American Political Thought: A Reader from David Walker to Barack Obama* (New York: Routledge, 2013).

38. *North Star*, June 16, 1848.

Chapter 1

1. Frank Rollin, *Life and Public Services of Martin R. Delany* (Boston: Lee and Shepard, 1868), 25.

2. Ibid., 24.

3. Dorothy Sterling, *The Making of an Afro-American: Martin Robison Delany, 1812–1885* (New York: Da Capo Press, 1996). First published by Doubleday, New York, in 1971; Rollin, *Life and Public Services*, 22.

4. William E. B. Du Bois, *The Philadelphia Negro* (Philadelphia: University of Pennsylvania Press, 1899; Philip S. Foner, ed., *The Life and Writings of Frederick Douglass,* vol. 5, *Supplementary 1844–1860.* (New York: International Publishers, 1975), 104.

5. Victor Ullman, *Martin R. Delany: The Beginnings of the Black Nationalism* (Boston: Beacon Press, 1971), 26–27; See also Sterling, *The Making of an Afro-American*, 42–43.

6. Delany started the *Pittsburgh Mystery* in 1843 and ran it up to 1847 when he handed it over to a committee. Subsequently, the African Methodist Episcopal Church bought the *Mystery* and renamed it the *Christian Herald*. In 1852, the AME's publication was moved to Philadelphia and renamed the *Christian Recorder*.

7. Lawrence J. Friedman, *Gregarious Saints: Self and Community in American Abolitionism, 1830–1870* (London: Cambridge University Press, 1982). See also Robert W. Caldwell, *Theologies of the American Revivalists: From Whitefield to Finney* (Downers Grove, IL: InterVarsity Press, 2018).

8. "Letter from Columbiana, August 13, 1848," *North Star*, August 25, 1848.

9. Ibid.

10. Ibid.

11. Ibid.

12. C. Peter Ripley, *The Black Abolitionist Papers*, vol. 3, *The United States, 1830–1846* (Chapel Hill: University of North Carolina Press, 1991), 197.

13. Ibid.

14. Martin R. Delany, "Report from Pittsburgh, January 21, 1848," *North Star*, February 4, 1848.

15. Ibid.

16. Ripley, *The Black Abolitionist Papers*, 198–200.

17. Benjamin Quarles, *Black Abolitionists* (London: Oxford University Press, 1969), 68.

18. Adam D. Simmons, "Ideologies and Programs of the Negro Antislavery Movement, 1830–1861" (PhD diss., Northwestern University, 1983), 34.

19. Ibid.

20. Ibid.

21. Ripley, *The Black Abolitionist Papers*, 198–200.

22. *North Star*, June 27, 1850.

23. Ibid.

24. "Letter from Columbiana, August 13, 1848," *North Star*, August 25, 1848.

25. "Letter from Philadelphia, February 8, 1848," *North Star*, February 25, 1848.

26. Will B. Gravely, "The Rise of African Churches in America, 1786–1822: Reexamining the Contexts," in *African American Religious Studies: An Interdisciplinary Anthology*, ed. Gayraud S. Wilmore (Durham, NC: Duke University Press, 1989), 301–317; Peter J. Paris, *The Social Teaching of the Black Churches* (Philadelphia, PA: Fortress Press, 1985).

27. Howard H. Bell, ed., *Minutes of the Proceedings of the National Negro Conventions, 1830–1864* (New York: Arno Press, 1969), 34.

28. Kellie Carter Jackson, *Force and Freedom: Black Abolitionists and the Politics of Violence* (Philadelphia: University of Pennsylvania Press, 2019), 20.

29. Ibid., 24.

30. Eddie S. Glaude Jr., *Exodus! Religion, Race, and Nation in Early Nineteenth-Century Black America* (Chicago: University of Chicago Press, 2000), 118.

31. Ibid.

32. Ibid.

33. Bell, ed., *Minutes of the Proceedings of the National Negro Conventions*; see also his *A Survey of the Negro Convention Movement* (New York: Arno Press, 1969).

34. James B. Stewart, *Holy Warriors: The Abolitionists and American Slavery* (New York: Hill and Wang, 1976), chapters. 1, 3; Gerald Sorin, *Abolitionism: A New Perspective* (New York: Praeger, 1972), chapters. 1, 4, 6; William Lloyd Garrison, "Declaration of Sentiments of the American Anti-Slavery Society," *Liberator*, December 14, 1833, 198.

35. Howard H. Bell, "The American Moral Reform Society, 1836–1841," *Journal of Negro Education* 27 (Winter 1958); Tunde Adeleke, "Afro-Americans and Moral Suasion: The Debate in the 1830s," *Journal of Negro History* l, xxxiii, no. 2 (Spring 1998); Richard P. McCormick, "William Whipper: Moral Reformer," *Pennsylvania History* 43 (January 1969): 23–46.

36. Glaude Jr., *Exodus!* 131.

37. Ibid.

38. *Colored American*, August 26, 1837.

39. Ibid.

40. Manisha Sinha, *The Slave's Cause: A History of Abolition* (New Haven, CT: Yale University Press, 2016), 299.

41. Ibid.

42. John Ernest, *A Nation within a Nation: Organizing African American Communities before the Civil War* (Chicago: Ivan R. Dee, 2011), 11.

43. Carter Jackson, *Force and Freedom*, chap. 1.

44. William H. Pease and Jane H. Pease, "Boston Garrisonians and the Problem of Frederick Douglass," *Canadian Journal of History* 11, no. 2 (September 1967); Benjamin Quarles, "The Breach Between Douglass and Garrison," *Journal of Negro History* 23, no. 21 (April 1938); Tyrone Tillery, "The Inevitability of the Douglass-Garrison Conflict," *Phylon* 37, no. 2 (June 1976); Friedman, *Gregarious Saints*. Philip S. Foner, *Frederick Douglass: A Biography* (New York: Citadel Press, 1964), 15–172.

45. Sterling, *The Making of an Afro-American: Martin Robison Delany*, 93–106.

46. Adeleke, "Afro-Americans and Moral Suasion"; Bell, "The American Moral Reform Society"; see also Bell, "Negro National Conventions of the Middle 1840s: Moral Suasion vs. Political Action," *Journal of Negro History* 42, no. 4 (October 1957): 247–260.

47. Quarles, *Black Abolitionists*, 68–69.

48. Ibid.

49. *North Star*, February 11, 1848.

50. *North Star*, February 18, 1848.

51. *North Star*, February 10, 1848.

52. *North Star*, November 5, 1848, and February 18, 1848.

53. *North Star*, November 17, 1848.

54. *North Star*, December 1, 1848, and February 16, 1849.

55. Ibid.

56. Ibid.

57. Martin Delany, "Report from Philadelphia, Pennsylvania, January 16, 1849," *North Star*, February 16, 1849.

58. Martin Delany, "Colored Citizens of Pittsburgh," *North Star*, July 13, 1849.

59. Ibid.

60. Ibid.

61. Ibid.

62. *North Star*, November 17, 1848.

63. Martin Delany, "Colored Citizens of Pittsburgh," *North Star*, July 13, 1849.

64. Ibid.

65. Ibid.

66. Martin Delany, "Report from Cleveland, Ohio, July 24, 1848," *North Star*, August 4, 1848.

67. Ibid.

68. Martin Delany, "Report from Hanover, Ohio, March 27, 1848," *North Star*, April 14, 1848.

69. Ibid.

70. Ibid.

71. Ibid.

72. Ibid.

73. Ibid.

74. Martin Delany, "Report from Cincinnati, Ohio, May 20, 1848," *North Star*, June 9, 1848.

75. Ibid.

76. Ibid.

77. Martin Delany, "Report from Cincinnati, Ohio, May 7, 1848," *North Star*, May 26, 1848.

78. Ibid.

79. Ibid.

80. Martin Delany, "Report from Chillicothe, Ohio, April 20, 1848," *North Star*, May 12, 1848.

81. Ibid.

82. Martin Delany, "Report from Milton, Ohio, June 18, 1848," *North Star*, July 7, 1848.

83. Ibid.

84. Ibid.

85. Ibid.

86. Ibid.

87. Ibid.

88. Martin Delany, "Report from Lancaster City, Pennsylvania, December 18, 1848," *North Star*, January 5, 1849.

89. Ibid.

90. *North Star*, July 24, 1848.

91. "Letter from Columbiana, August 13, 1848," *North Star*, August 25, 1848.

92. For information on the views of the "Illiberal" Churches see Delany's reports in *North Star*, particularly those of March 16 and 23, 1849, April 20, 1848, August 4, 1848, February 18, 1848, and April 27, 1849. See also E. Franklin Frazier, *The Negro Church in America* (New York: Schocken Books, 1974), 19–34; Eric Lincoln and Lawrence Mamiya, *The Black Church in the African American Experience* (Durham, NC: Duke University Press, 1990); Henry H. Mitchell, *Black Church Beginnings: The Long-Hidden Realities of the First Years* (Cambridge, UK: William B. Eerdmans Publishing Company, 2004); Paris, *The Social Teachings of the Black Churches*.

93. Ibid.

94. Martin R. Delany, "Domestic Economy," *North Star*, March 23, 1849.

95. Ibid. See also Martin Delany, "Domestic Economy," *North Star*, April 20, 1849.

96. Ibid.

97. Ibid.

98. Quoted in John Ernest, *A Nation Within a Nation*, 72–73.

99. Ibid. See also Glaude Jr. *Exodus!* 19–20.

100. Martin R. Delany, *The Condition, Elevation, Emigration and Destiny of the Colored People of the United States* (New York: Arno Press, 1968), 37–38. First published 1852.

101. Ibid.

102. Martin Delany, "Domestic Economy," *North Star*, March 23, 1849.

103. Martin Delany, "Domestic Economy," *North Star*, April 23, 1849.

104. Martin Delany, "Report from Hanover, March 27, 1848," *North Star*, April 14, 1848.

105. Ibid.

106. Ibid.

107. Martin Delany, "Domestic Economy," *North Star*, April 13, 1849.

108. Ibid.

109. Martin Delany, "Domestic Economy," *North Star*, April 13, 1849.

110. Martin Delany, "Domestic Economy," *North Star*, April 20, 1849.

111. John Ernest, *A Nation within a Nation*, 78.

112. Ibid.

113. Tunde Adeleke, "'Today is the Day of Salvation': Martin R. Delany's Struggles Against Providential Determinism in Early Nineteenth-Century Black Abolitionism," *Interdisciplinary Journal of Research on Religion* 13, no. 4 (2017).

114. Eric Lincoln and Lawrence Mamiya, *The Black Church in the African American Experience* (Durham, NC: Duke University Press, 1990), 11.

115. Ibid., 11–12.

116. Adeleke, "Today is the Day of Salvation." See also Henry H. Mitchell, *Black Church Beginnings*, 46–129.

117. *North Star*, March 31, 1848.

118. "M. R. Delany," *North Star*, May 19, 1849.

119. Ibid.

120. "Letter from York, Pa., November 27, 1848," *North Star*, December 15, 1848.

121. Ibid.

122. Henry H. Mitchell, *Black Church Beginnings*, 48–49.

123. Ibid.

124. Ibid., 49.

125. Ibid.

126. Ibid., 50.

127. Ibid., 60.

128. Simmons. "Ideologies and Programs of the Negro Antislavery Movement," 5–57; Leonard L. Richards, *"Gentlemen of Property and Standing": Anti-Abolitionist Mobs in Jacksonian America* (New York: Oxford University Press, 1970); Mabee Carleton, *Black Freedom: The Nonviolent Abolitionists from 1830 through the Civil War* (London: The Macmillan Company, 1970); Stewart, *Holy Warriors: The Abolitionists and American Slavery* (New York: Hill and Wang, 1976), 50–73.

129. Simmons, "Ideologies and Programs of the Negro Antislavery Movement," chap. 2.

130. David M. Reimers, *White Protestantism and the Negro* (New York: Oxford University Press, 1965), 8; David Brion Davis, *The Problem of Slavery in Western Culture* (Ithaca, NY: Cornell University Press, 1966); Eugene Genovese, *Roll, Jordan Roll: The World the Slaves Made* (New York: Vintage Books, 1976); Joseph R. Washington, *Black Religion: The Negro and Christianity in the United States* (Boston, MA, and Lanham, MD: University Press of America, 1984). First published in 1964; E. Franklin Frazier, *The Negro Church in America*; Albert J. Raboteau, *Slave Religion: The "Invisible Institution" in the Antebellum South* (New York: Oxford University Press, 1978).

131. Martin Delany, "Domestic Economy," *North Star*, March 23, 1849, and April 13 and 20, 1849.

132. "Minutes of the State Convention of the Colored Citizens of Pennsylvania, Convened at Harrisburg, December 13th and 14th, 1848," in *Proceedings of the Black State Conventions, 1840–1865*, vol. 2., ed. Philip S. Foner and George E. Walker (Philadelphia: Temple University Press, 1979), 124.

133. McCormick, "William Whipper: Moral Reformer," *Pennsylvania History* 43, (January 1976): 37.

134. Martin Delany, "Report from Pittsburgh, Pennsylvania, February 24, 1849," *North Star*, March 9, 1849, 1–2.

135. Ibid.

136. Ibid.

137. Ibid.

138. Ibid.

139. Ibid.

140. Martin Delany, "American Civilization: Treatment of the Colored People in the United States," *North Star*, March 30, 1849, 2.

141. Lewis Woodson, "Going West," *Colored American*, May 3, 1838, 4; May 16 and May 2, 1849, 2; October 6, 1838, 2.

142. Lewis Woodson, "Death vs. Expatriation," *Colored American*, November 10, 1837, 2; October 6, 1838, 2; March 13, 1841, 6.

143. Lewis Woodson, "Death vs. Expatriation," *Colored American*, October 27, 1838, 2.

144. Augustine, "For The Colored American, April 19, 1838," *Colored American*, May 3, 1838

145. "Letter from M. R. Delany" in *Frederick Douglass's Paper*, April 11, 1853

146. Grant Shreve, "The Exodus of Martin Delany," *American Literary History* 29, no. 3 (2017): 449.

147. Martin Delany, *The Condition*, chapters 6, 7, 8, 9, 10, 11, 12.

148. Sterling Stuckey, *Slave Culture: Nationalist Theory and the Foundation of Black America* (New York: Oxford University Press, 1987), 226.

149. Ibid., 230.

150. Tunde Adeleke, *UnAfrican Americans: Nineteenth Century Black Nationalists and the Civilizing Mission* (Lexington: University Press of Kentucky, 1998).

151. Martin Delany, "National Disfranchisement of Colored People," in *The Condition*, 147–158.

152. "Letter from M. R. Delany," in *Frederick Douglass's Paper*, April 11, 1853.

153. Delany, *The Condition*, chap. 16. See also Delany, "Political Destiny," in *Life and Public Services*, ed. Frank Rollin, 360; "Letter from Mr. Delany" *Frederick Douglass's Paper*, April 11, 1853.

154. Foner, ed., *The Life and Writings of Frederick Douglass*, 202.

155. "Convention of Colored Persons in Pennsylvania," *Pennsylvania Freeman*, October 23, 1852.

156. "Proceedings of the Colored National Convention, Held in Rochester, July 6–8, 1853," in *Proceedings of the National Negro Conventions, 1830–1864*, ed. Howard H. Bell (New York: Arno Press, 1969), 39.

157. Miles M. Fisher, "Lott Cary: The Colonizing Missionary," *Journal of Negro History* 7, no. 4 (December 1922); Henry N. Sherwood, "Paul Cuffee," *Journal of Negro History* 8 (1928); see also Sherwood, "Paul Cuffee and his Contributions to the American Colonization Society," *Proceedings of the Mississippi Valley Historical Association, 1912–1913* 6 (1913); James Sidbury, *Becoming African in America: Race and Nation in the Early Atlantic* (New York: Oxford University Press, 2007); Howard H. Bell, "Negro Nationalism: A Factor in Emigration Projects, 1858–1861," *Journal of Negro History* 42 (January 1974); Bill McAdoo, *Pre-Civil war Black Nationalism* (New York: David Walker Press, 1983). First published in *Progressive Labor* 5 (June–July 1966); William Pease and Jane Pease, "Black Power: The Debate in 1840," *Phylon* 29 (1968); George Shepperson, "Notes on Negro American Influences on the Emergence of African Nationalism," *Journal of African History* 1, no. 2 (1960); Robert G. Weisbord, "The Back-to-Africa Idea," *History Today* 56 (January 1968).

158. *Voice of the Fugitive*, July 30, 1851, 2; August 13, 1851, 2; September 24, 1851, 2.

159. R. J. M. Blackett, *The Captive's Quest for Freedom: Fugitive Slaves, the 1850 Fugitive Slave Law, and the Politics of Slavery* (Cambridge: Cambridge University Press, 2018), 124–125.

160. Tunde Adeleke, *Without Regard to Race: The Other Martin R. Delany* (Jackson: University Press of Mississippi, 2003). See also Martin R. Delany, "The Moral and Social Aspect of Africa," *Liberator*, May 1, 1863.

161. David Brion Davis, *The Problem of Slavery in the Age of Emancipation* (New York: Alfred A. Knopf, 2014), 124.

162. Delany, *The Condition*, chap. 17. See also Tunde Adeleke, "Religion in Martin R. Delany's Liberation Thought," *Religious Humanism* 27, no. 2 (Spring 1993).

163. Delany, *The Condition*, 159–160.

164. Ibid.

165. Delany, *The Condition*, 172–173 and chap. 1. See also Delany, "Political Destiny," 353.

166. Delany, *The Condition*, chap. 21.

167. Ibid., 183.

168. Ibid., 208.

169. "M. R. Delany to Dr. James McCune Smith (Important Movement)," *The Weekly Anglo-African*, January 4, 1862

170. Delany, *The Condition*, 183; Delany "Political Destiny," 337.

171. Ibid.

172. "Proceedings of the first Convention of the Colored Citizens of the State of Illinois, Chicago, October 6–8, 1853" in *Proceedings of the Black State Conventions, 1840–1865*, vol. 2, ed. Philip S. Foner and George Walker (Philadelphia: Temple University Press, 1974).

173. Ibid.

174. M. R. Delany, "Illinois Convention" in *Frederick Douglass's Paper*, November 18, 1853, 1.

175. Tommie Shelby, "Two Conceptions of Black Nationalism: Martin Delany on the Meaning of Black Political Solidarity," *Political Theory* 31, no. 5 (October 2003): 680. See also Delany, "Political Destiny," 327–367.

176. Shelby, "Two Conceptions of Black Nationalism," 680.

177. Delany, "Political Destiny," 327–367.

178. Ibid., 338.

179. Ibid.

180. *The Provincial Freeman*, June 7, 1856.

181. Ibid.

182. Ibid.

183. Patrick Rael, *Black Identity and Black Protest in the Antebellum North* (Chapel Hill: University of North Carolina Press, 2002) 237–238.

184. Ibid., 238.

185. Delany, "Political Destiny," 342.

186. Ibid.

187. Ibid., 337.

188. Martin Delany, *The Condition*, 214.

189. Ibid.

190. "State Council of the Colored People of Massachusetts Convention, January 2, 1854" in Foner and Walker, eds., *Proceedings of the Black State Conventions*, vol. 2, 93.

Chapter 2

1. Kellie Carter Jackson, *Force and Freedom: Black Abolitionists and the Politics of Violence* (Philadelphia: Pennsylvania University Press), 2019.

2. Ibid., 9.

3. Ibid., 46.

4. Ibid.

5. Frank A. Rollin, *Life and Public Services of Martin R. Delany* (Boston: Lee and Shepard, 1868), 40. Frances Rollin was born in Charleston in 1844, the oldest child of

William Rollin of "French extraction." She first met Delany while he was serving as a Freedmen's Bureau agent. When he heard of her interest in a literary career, he asked her to write his biography. She agreed, and subsequently relocated to Boston, where she wrote and published the book in 1868. She returned to Charleston that same year and married William J. Whipper who was the nephew of William Whipper, the wealthy Pennsylvania businessman who helped start the American Moral Reform Society in 1835. The publisher of her Delany biography, Lee and Shepard, listed her as "Frank A. Rollin" because of the conviction "that the public was not prepared to accept a work by a Black woman." Willard B. Gatewood Jr., "The Remarkable Misses Rollin: Black Women in Reconstruction South Carolina," *The South Carolina Historical Magazine* 92, no. 3 (July 1991): 175, 172–188.

6. Rollin, *Life and Public Services.*

7. "Dred Scott v. Sandford (1857)" in *Civil Rights since 1787: A Reader on the Black Struggle*, ed. Jonathan Birnbaum and Clarence Taylor (New York: New York University Press, 2000), 79.

8. "Convention of the Colored Citizens of Massachusetts, August 1, 1858," in *Proceedings of the Black State Conventions, 1840–1865*, vol. 2., ed. Philip S. Foner and George E. Walker (Philadelphia: Temple University Press, 1980), 97.

9. Ibid.

10. Ibid.

11. Ibid., 104.

12. Ibid.

13. Ibid., 105.

14. Ibid.

15. Howard H. Bell, ed., *Minutes of the Proceedings of the National Negro Conventions, 1830–1864* (New York: Arno Press, 1969).

16. Earl Ofari, *Let Your Motto Be Resistance: The Life and Thought of Henry H. Garnet* (Boston, MA: Beacon Press, 1972), 144–153.

17. Leslie Friedman Goldstein, "Violence as an Instrument for Social Change: The Views of Frederick Douglass," *Journal of Negro History* 61, no. 1 (January 1976): 62.

18. "Report of the Proceedings of the Colored National Convention, Held at Cleveland, Ohio, on Wednesday, September 6, 1848," in Bell, ed., *Minutes of the Proceedings of the National Negro Conventions*, 15–16.

19. Ibid.

20. Ibid. Also, Howard H. Bell, "The American Moral Reform Society, 1836–1841," *Journal of Negro History* 27 (1958) 34–41.

21. George Hendrick and Willene Hendrick, *Black Refugees in Canada: Accounts of Escape during the Era of Slavery* (Jefferson, NC: McFarland & Co. Inc., 2010), 24–43; Kerry Walters, *The Underground Railroad: A Reference Guide* (Denver, CO: ABC-Clio, 2012), 112–113, 140–142. See also H. A. Tanser, "Josiah Henson: the Moses of his People," *Journal of Negro Education* 12, no. 4 (Autumn 1943): 630–632; W. B. Hartgrove, "The Story of Josiah Henson," *Journal of Negro History* 3, no. 1 (January 1918): 1–21.

22. Ibid.

23. Ibid.

24. See IIona Kauremszky, "Uncle Tom Was a Real Person; His Cabin is in Canada," *Christian Science Monitor*, January 26, 2005, 11. See also Tunde Adeleke, "Uncle Tom," *International Encyclopedia of the Social Sciences*, 2008. In African American History, "Uncle Tom" has come to represent a weak and cowardly personality, a racial sell-out—someone who compromises with, and is deferential to, White authority. The 1849 autobiography of Josiah Henson supposedly inspired Harriet Beecher Stowe's epic novel *Uncle Tom's Cabin* (1852). Thus began the historical association of Henson with "Uncle Tom." Stowe was a White abolitionist whose novel helped fan the antislavery flames that ignited the Civil War.

25. Foner and Walker, eds., *Proceedings*, 104.

26. Ibid.

27. Ibid.

28. Ibid.

29. Ibid.

30. Tunde Adeleke, *Without Regard to Race: The Other Martin R. Delany* (Jackson: University Press of Mississippi, 2003), chap. 3.

31. Rollin, *Life and Public Services*, 16.

32. Ibid., 27.

33. Ibid.

34. *North Star*, June 14, 1848.

35. Ibid.

36. Ibid.

37. Ibid.

38. Tunde Adeleke, "Afro-Americans and Moral Suasion: The Debate in the 1830s," *Journal of Negro History* 33, no. 2 (Spring 1998): 127–142.

39. Lewis Woodson ("Augustine"), "The West," *Colored American*, February 16, 1839, March 2, 1839; March 16, 1839; June 15, 1839; and August 31, 1839. Also Woodson, "Going West," July 15, 1839.

40. Lewis Woodson ("Augustine"), "Death vs. Expatriation," *Colored American*, October 27, 1838, 2.

41. Ibid.

42. Ibid.

43. Ibid.

44. *The Colored American*, October 6, 1838, 2; March 13, 1841, 6.

45. William Whipper, "An Address on Non-Violent Resistance to Offensive Aggression," *Colored American,* September 16 and 30, 1837.

46. Ibid.

47. Ibid.

48. Whipper, "An Address on Non-Violent Resistance." See also Richard P. McCormick, "William Whipper: Moral Reformer," *Pennsylvania History* 43 (1976), 23–46

49. Woodson ("Augustine"), "Death vs. Expatriation."

50. Ibid.

51. Adeleke, *Without Regard to Race*, chap. 3.

52. Martin Delany, "Report from Wilmington, Delaware," *North Star*, December 15, 1848; Martin Delany, "Report from Columbus, Ohio," *North Star*, April 28, 1848; Martin Delany, "Report from Cincinnati, Ohio," *North Star*, May 26, 1848.

53. Bruce Laurie, *Working People of Philadelphia, 1800–1850* (Philadelphia: Temple University Press, 1980), 62–64; Elizabeth Geffen, "Violence in Philadelphia in the 1840s and 1850s" *Pennsylvania History* 4 (October 1969). See also Carter Jackson, *Force and Freedom*.

54. Philip S. Foner and George E. Walker, eds., *Proceedings of the Black State Conventions*, vol. 1, *1840–1865* (Philadelphia: Temple University Press, 1979), 113.

55. Rollin, *Life and Public Services*, 44; Victor Ullman, *Martin Robison Delany: The Beginnings of Black Nationalism* (Boston: Beacon Press, 1971), 40.

56. "Proceedings of the Colored National Convention, Cleveland, Ohio, September 6–8, 1848," *North Star*, September 29, 1848.

57. Carter Jackson, *Force and Freedom*, 52.

58. Ibid.

59. Ibid., 53.

60. Ibid., 53.

61. R. J. M. Blackett, *The Captive's Quest for Freedom: Fugitive Slaves, the 1850 Fugitive Slave Law, and the Politics of Slavery* (Cambridge: Cambridge University Press, 2018), 47.

62. Martin R. Delany, *The Condition, Elevation, Emigration and Destiny of the Colored People of the United States* (Baltimore, MD: Black Classic Press, 1993), chap. 16. First published in 1852.

63. Ibid., 154.

64. Rollin, *Life and Public Services*, 76. See also Blackett, *The Captive's Quest for Freedom*.

65. Ibid., 43.

66. "The Case of Alexander Hendrickure (Hendrickson)," *Frederick Douglass's Paper*, June 17, 1853.

67. Manisha Sinha, *The Slave's Cause: A History of Abolition* (New Haven, CT: Yale University Press, 2016), 527–538.

68. Ibid., 527.

69. Ibid., 538.

70. Carter Jackson, *Force and Freedom*, 54–79.

71. Blackett, *The Captive's Quest for Freedom*, 47.

72. Carol Wilson, *Freedom at Risk: The Kidnapping of Free Blacks in America, 1780–1865* (Lexington: University Press of Kentucky, 1994), 115.

73. Delany, *The Condition*, chap. 16.

74. Martin Delany, "Political Aspects of the Colored People of the United States," *Provincial Freeman*, October 13, 1855. Martin Delany, "Political Events," *Provincial Freeman*, July 5, 1856.

75. Blackett, *The Captive's Quest for Freedom*, 307.

76. Ibid., 307.

77. Patrick Rael, *Black Identity and Black Protest in the Antebellum North* (Chapel Hill: University of North Carolina Press, 2002), 238.

78. Blackett, *The Captive's Quest for Freedom*, 124–125.

79. David Brion Davis, *The Problem of Slavery in the Age of Emancipation* (New York: Alfred A. Knopf, 2014), 124–130.

80. Ibid., 130.

81. Davis, *The Problem of Slavery*. See also Blackett, *The Captive's Quest for Freedom*. Also Blackett, "Martin Delany and Robert Campbell: Black Americans in Search of an African Colony," *Journal of Negro History* 60, no. 1 (January 1977).

82. William L. Garrison, "The Letter from Dr. Delany." *Liberator*, May 7, 1852.

83. "The Letter from Dr. Delany," *Liberator*, May 21, 1852.

84. Robert B. McGlone, *John Brown's War against Slavery* (Cambridge: Cambridge University Press, 2009).

85. William E. B. Du Bois, *John Brown* (new edition). New York: International Publishers Co., 2014.

86. Quoted in William W. Hassler, "John Brown: Saint v. Madman?" Undated article in Stanley J. Smith Papers, Regional Room, the Walden Library, the University of Western Ontario, London, Canada.

87. David Blight, ed., *Narrative of the Life of Frederick Douglass, an American Slave, Written by Himself* (New York: St. Martin's Press, 2003), 71–94, 271–291. See also Goldstein, "Violence as an instrument for Social Change," 61–72. See also Frederick Douglass, *Life and Times of Frederick Douglass (Written by Himself)* (New York: Bonanza Books, 1962), 271–275, 302–324. First published in 1892.

88. Douglass, *Life and Times of Frederick Douglass*, 275.

89. Ibid., chap. 10.

90. Ibid., 319.

91. Goldstein, "Violence as an Instrument for Social Change," 65.

92. Ibid., 71.

93. Douglass, *Life and Times of Frederick Douglass*, 319–320.

94. Rollin, *Life and Public Services*, 86.

95. Ibid.

96. Ibid.

97. *Charleston Mercury*, October 12, 1860.

98. Rollin, *Life and Public Services*, 87–88.

99. Rollin, *Life and Public Services*; McGlone, *John Brown's War*, 235–245.

100. Rollin, *Life and Public Services*, 93.

101. McGlone, *John Brown's War*, 397.

102. Rollin, *Life and Public Services*, 355.

103. See Philip S. Foner and George E. Walker, eds., *Proceedings of the Black State Conventions*. See also Bell, ed., *Minutes of the Proceedings of the National Negro Conventions*.

104. Rollin, *Life and Public Services*, 282–283.

105. Adeleke, *Without Regard to Race*, chap. 4. See also Rollin, *Life and Public Services*, 281–283.

106. Rollin, *Life and Public Services*, 282–283.

107. Sean Wilentz, ed., *David Walker's Appeal*. New York: Hill & Wang, 1995, 43.

108. Ibid.

109. Tunde Adeleke, "Violence as an Option for Free Blacks in Nineteenth-Century America," *Canadian Review of American Studies* 35 (2005): 101.

110. Harry A. Reed, "Henry H. Garnet's Address to the Slaves of the United States of America, Reconsidered," *Western Journal of Black Studies* 6, no. 4 (1982), 190.

111. Ofari, *Let Your Motto be Resistance*, 153.

112. Ibid.

113. William H. Pease and Jane H. Pease, "The Negro Convention Movement," in *Key Issues in the Afro-American Experience, Vol. 1, to 1877*, ed. Nathan I. Higgins, Martin Kilson, and Daniel M. Fox (New York: Harcourt Brace Jovanovich, 1971), 191–205.

114. Blight, ed., *Narrative of the Life of Frederick Douglass*, chap. 10. See also Douglass, *Life and Times*, 271–275, 302–324.

115. Martin R. Delany, *Blake, Or, the Huts of America*, serialized in the *Anglo-African Magazine*, January–July 1869, and in the *Weekly Anglo-African Magazine*, November 1861–April 1862. Compiled, edited, and published in 1970 by Floyd J. Miller. See also Jerome McGann, ed., *Blake, Or, The Huts of America: A Corrected Edition* (Cambridge, MA: Harvard University Press, 2017).

116. Ronald Takaki, *Violence in the Black Imagination: Essays and Documents* (New York: G. P. Putnam's, 1972), 12.

117. Vincent Harding, *There Is a River: The Black Struggle for Freedom in America* (New York: Harcourt Brace, 1983), 208.

118. John Zeugner, "A Note on Martin Delany's *Blake* and Black Militancy," *Phylon* 32 (March 1971): 90–103.

119. Ibid.

120. Jean F. Yellin, *The Intricate Knot: Black Figures in American Literature, 1776–1863* (New York: New York University Press, 1972), 197–211.

121. Addison Gayle Jr., *The Way of the World: The Black Novel in America* (New York: Archon Books, 1976), xiii, 13, 21–28.

122. Roger Hite, "Stand Still and See the Salvation: Rhetorical Designs of Martin Delany's *Blake*," *Journal of Black Studies* 5 (December 1976), 194.

123. Judith Madera, *Black Atlas: Geography and Flow in Nineteenth-Century African American Literature* (Durham, NC: Duke University Press, 2015), 75. See also her "Atlantic Architectures: Nineteenth-Century Cartography and Martin Delany's *Blake*," *English Language Notes* 52, no. 2 (Fall/Winter 2014).

124. Martha Schoolman, *Abolitionist Geographies* (Minneapolis: University of Minnesota Press, 2014), 1. See also Katy Chiles, "Within and without Raced Nations: Intertextuality, Martin Delany, and *Blake, Or, The Huts of America*," *American Literature* 80,

no. 2 (June 2008), and her "Defining *Blake*," *American Periodicals: A Journal of History & Criticism* 28, no. 1 (2018).

125. Delany, *Blake*, 16.

126. Ibid., 20.

127. Ibid., 16.

128. Excerpts from Delany's reports are published in Robert Levine, *Martin R. Delany: A Documentary Reader* (Chapel Hill: University of North Carolina Press, 2003)

129. Martin Delany, "Domestic Economy," 1–3, *North Star*, March 23, April 13 and 27, 1849.

130. Levine, *Martin R. Delany*.

131. Delany, *Blake*, part 1.

132. Ibid.

133. Ibid., 105.

134. Ibid.

135. Delany, *Blake*, 122. It should be recalled that Delany first invoked the religious injunction "Stand still and see the salvation" back in the late 1840s during his antislavery lecture tours for the *North Star*. At that time, he was against the injunction, which he considered detrimental to the cause of Black freedom and equality. It reinforced the providential deterministic worldview that he argued misled Blacks into abrogating their responsibility for self-improvement. Instead they focused on heavenly intercession and compensation. By the late 1850s, however, Delany would invoke the religious precept, paradoxically, to convince Blacks who considered violence to seek and hope for divine guidance. The invocation of this injunction in *Blake* underscore the vital point of intersection between religion/politics and nationalism in Delany's thought.

136. Ibid.

137. Ibid., 128.

138. Ibid.

139. Ibid., 306–308.

140. Ibid., 309.

141. Ibid., 313.

142. Ibid., 314.

143. Ibid.

144. Ibid., chap. 74.

145. Ibid.

146. Ibid., chap. 16.

147. Ibid., 290–293.

148. Ibid., 292–293.

149. Ibid.

150. Rev. Moses Dickson, *Manual of the International Order of Twelve of Knights and Daughters of Tabor*, 8th ed. (Glasgow, MO: Moses Dickson, 1911). See also Herbert Aptheker, ed., *A Documentary History of the Negro People in the United States*, vol. 1 (New York: Citadel Press, 1965), 378.

151. Aptheker, *A Documentary History*, 378.

152. Ibid., 378–9.

153. Ibid.

154. Ibid., 379–380.

155. Adeleke, "Violence as an Option for Free Blacks . . . ," 88.

156. Aptheker, *A Documentary History*, 379.

157. Eddie Glaude Jr., *Exodus! Religion, Race, and Nation in Early Nineteenth-Century Black America* (Chicago: University of Chicago Press, 2000), 34.

158. Ibid., 41.

159. Grant Shreve, "The Exodus of Martin Delany," *American Literary History* 29, no. 3 (2017): 452–453.

160. Ibid., 470

161. Delany, *Blake*, 261–262

162. Ibid., 262

163. Ibid.

164. Ibid.

165. McGann, ed., *Blake, Or, The Huts of America*, 24.

166. Ibid., 28.

167. Madera, *Black Atlas*, 112–113. See also Robert Carr, *Black Nationalism in the New World: Reading the African American and West Indian Experience* (Durham: Duke University Press, 2002) 65–67.

168. Shreve, "The Exodus of Martin Delany," 451.

169. McGann, ed., *Blake, Or, The Huts of America*, 28.

170. *News and Courier* (Charleston), October 7, 1874.

171. Edward Magdol, "Martin R. Delany Counsels Freedmen, July 23, 1865," *Journal of Negro History* 56 (1971): 308.

172. *News and Courier*, October 7, 1874.

173. *New York Times*, November 27, 1870.

174. Rollin, *Life and Public Services*, 300.

Chapter 3

1. Heather Andrea Williams, *Self-Thought: African American Education in Slavery and Freedom* (Chapel Hill: University of North Carolina Press, 2005), 7.

2. Ibid., 14.

3. Ibid.

4. Ibid., 16–17.

5. Hilary Green, *Educational Reconstruction: African American Schools in the Urban South, 1865–1890* (New York: Fordham University Press, 2016), 4–5.

6. David W. Blight, ed., *Narrative of the Life of Frederick Douglass, an American Slave, Written by Himself*, 2nd ed. (New York: Bedford/St. Martin's, 2003), 63.

7. Ibid.

8. Ibid.

9. Ibid., 64.

10. Williams, *Self-Thought*, 24–27.

11. Howard H. Bell, *Proceedings of the National Negro Conventions, 1830–1864* (New York: Arno Press, 1964).

12. Booker T. Washington, *Up From Slavery: An Autobiography* (New York: Doubleday), 1901; William E. B. Du Bois, "Of Mr. Booker T. Washington and Others," in Du Bois, *The Souls of Black Folk: Essays and Sketches* (Chicago: A. C. McClurg and Co., 1903), 41–59.

13. J. D. Anderson, *The Education of Blacks in the South, 1860–1935* (Chapel Hill, University of North Carolina Press, 1988); H. A. Bullock, *A History of Negro Education in the South: From 1619 to the Present* (Cambridge, MA: Harvard University Press, 1967); R. E. Butchardt, *Northern Schools, Southern Blacks, and Reconstruction: Freedmen's Education, 1862–1875* (Westport, CT: Greenwood Press, 1980).

14. Ibid.

15. Herbert Aptheker, *American Negro Slave Revolts*, 6th ed. (New York: International Publishers, 1983); Alfred L. Brophy, "The Nat Turner Trials," *North Carolina Law Review* 96 (June 2013), 1818–1880.

16. Dorothy Sterling, *The Making of an Afro-American: Martin Robison Delany, 1812–1885* (New York: Doubleday, 1971).

17. Ibid., 3–34.

18. Sterling, *The Making of an Afro-American*, 3–18. See also Frank A. Rollin, *Life and Public Services of Martin R. Delany* (Boston: Lee and Shepard, 1868), 30–37.

19. Rollin, *Life and Public Services*.

20. Ibid. See also Sterling, *The Making of an Afro-American*.

21. Ibid.

22. Ibid.

23. Rollin, *Life and Public Services*, 39; Sterling, *The Making of an Afro-American*, 42–43. See also A. J. W. Hutton, *Some Historical Data Concerning the History of Chambersburg* (Chambersburg, PA: Franklin Repository, 1930); Victor Ullman, *Martin R. Delany: The Beginnings of Black Nationalism* (Boston: Beacon Press, 1971), 26–27; Dorothy B. Porter, "The Organized Educational Activities of Negro Literary Societies, 1828–1846," *Journal of Negro Education* 5 (October 1936): 573.

24. Ullman, *Martin R. Delany*, 26–27; Sterling, *The Making of an Afro-American*, 42–43.

25. Porter, "The Organized Educational Activities," 173; Ullman, *Martin R. Delany*, 25–26.

26. Martin Delany, *The Condition, Elevation, Emigration and Destiny of the Colored People of the United States* (Baltimore, MD: Black Classic Press, 1997), 197. First published in Pittsburgh, Pennsylvania, 1852.

27. Ibid., 197–198.

28. John H. Russell, "The Free Negro in Virginia, 1819–1865," *Johns Hopkins Studies in Historical and Political Science* 31 (1912): 13–15, 146–151.

29. Sterling, *The Making of an Afro-American*, 122–135. Delany had long manifested an interest in medicine. He had gained crucial experience by apprenticing himself to some of the leading physicians in Pittsburgh (Drs. Samuel McDowell, Joseph P. Gazzan, and Francis J. Lemoyne). From them he mastered the practices of bloodletting, cupping, and leeching, and how to set broken legs, sew wounds, and deliver babies. These experiences enabled him to play such crucial life-saving roles in the cholera epidemic of 1849. These physicians would subsequently strongly endorse and recommend his application to Harvard.

30. Philip Cash, "Pride, Prejudice, and Politics," *Harvard Medical School Alumni Bulletin* (1980): 20–25; Ronald Takaki, "Aesculapius Was a White Man: Antebellum Racism and Male Chauvinism at Harvard Medical School," *Phylon* 39, no. 2 (1978): 129–134; Sterling, *The Making of an Afro-American*.

31. Martin Delany, "Highly Important Statistics, Our Cause and Destiny: Endowment of a Newspaper," *North Star*, October 5, 1849, 4.

32. Delany, *The Condition*, 190–197.

33. Ibid.

34. Tunde Adeleke, "Afro-Americans and Moral Suasion: The Debate in the 1830s and 1840s," *Journal of Negro History* 80, no. 111 (1998); Howard H. Bell, "The American Moral Reform Society, 1836–1841," *Journal of Negro Education* 25, no. 11 (Winter 1958).

35. Delany, *The Condition*, 198–199.

36. Ibid., 190–197.

37. Ibid., 194–197.

38. Martin Delany, "Letter from Harrisburg, Pennsylvania," *North Star*, December 1, 1848, 2.

39. Delany, *The Condition*, 193.

40. Ibid.

41. Ibid.

42. Ibid.

43. Ibid., 193–194.

44. Ibid.

45. Ibid.

46. Delany, "Letter from Harrisburg, Pennsylvania"; Martin Delany, "Letter from Lancaster City, Pennsylvania," *North Star*, January 5, 1849, 2.

47. Delany, "Letter from Lancaster City, Pennsylvania."

48. Ibid. Also, Delany, "Letter from Cincinnati, Ohio," *North Star*, May 26, 1848, 2.

49. Martin Delany, "Letter from Columbus, Ohio," *North Star*, April 28, 1848, 2; Martin Delany, "Letter from Chillicothe, Ohio," *North Star*, May 12, 1848, 2.

50. Ibid.

51. Ibid.

52. Delany, *The Condition*, 195.

53. Delany, "Letter from Chillicothe, Ohio"; Delany, "Letter from Cincinnati, Ohio." See also Delany, "Colored Citizens of Cincinnati," *North Star*, June 15, 1849, 4.

54. Delany, "Letter from Lancaster City, Pennsylvania."

55. Ibid.

56. Delany, "Letter from Pittsburgh, Pennsylvania," *North Star*, March 9, 1849, 2.

57. Ibid.

58. Ibid.

59. Delany, *The Condition*, 195–196.

60. Ibid.

61. Delany, "Letter from Wilmington, Delaware," *North Star*, December 15, 1848, 2. See also Delany, *The Condition*, 190–197.

62. Delany, *The Condition*, 195.

63. Ibid.

64. Ibid.

65. M. C., "Letter from York, Pennsylvania, November 27, 1848," *North Star*, December 15, 1848, 2.

66. Delany, "Letter from Wilmington, Delaware."

67. Howard H. Bell, ed., *Minutes of the Proceedings of the National Negro Conventions, 1830–1864* (New York: Arno Press, 1969); Philip S. Foner and George E. Walker, eds., *Proceedings of the Black State Conventions, 1840–1865*, vol. 1 (Philadelphia: Temple University Press, 1979).

68. Bell, *Minutes of the Proceedings.*

69. Foner and Walker, eds., *Proceedings of the Black State Conventions*, vol. 1, 113–114.

70. Ibid., 73–74.

71. Delany, *The Condition*, 195–196.

72. Ibid.

73. Ibid., 196.

74. Ibid., 193.

75. Ibid.

76. Ibid., 191–193.

77. Ibid.

78. Delany, *The Condition*, 191–193. See also Delany, "Letter from Wilmington, Delaware."

79. Delany, *The Condition*, 194.

80. Martin Delany, "Political Economy" *North Star*, March 16, 1849, 2.

81. Ibid.

82. Ibid.

83. Delany, "Letter from Lancaster City, Pennsylvania."

84. "Report from Cincinnati, Ohio, May 7, 1848," *North Star*, May 26, 1848.

85. Ibid.

86. "Report from Cincinnati, May 20, 1848," *North Star*, June 9, 1848.

87. Delany, *The Condition*, 192–193.

88. Ibid., 193.

89. Ibid.

90. Ibid., 17.

91. Ibid., 45.

92. Ibid., 17–18.

93. Delany, *The Condition*, 44–45. A few pages later, Delany would render a positive review and analysis of Black accomplishments that contradicted this negative and gloomy characterization. Two years later, as leader of the emigration movement, Delany would invalidate the claim that Blacks had "no reference to ancient times." His writings in support of emigration established the antiquity of civilization in Africa as well as Blacks America's rich heritage of history and culture. See his "The International Policy of the World towards the African Race" and "Political Destiny of the Colored People on the American Continent," in *Life and Public Services*, ed. Rollin, 313–367; and "The Moral and Social Aspects of Africa," *Liberator*, May 1, 1863.

94. Delany, *The Condition*, 85–86.

95. Delany, *The Condition*, 85–86, chapters 9, 10, 11, 12. See also "Report from Cincinnati, Ohio, May 20, 1848," *North Star*, June 9, 1848.

96. Delany, *The Condition*, 109–110.

97. "Proceedings of the Colored National Convention, Cleveland, Ohio, September 6–8, 1848," *North Star*, September 29, 1848.

98. Douglass to Delany, *New National Era*, August 31, 1871.

99. "Proceedings of the Colored National Convention, Cleveland, Ohio, September 6–8, 1848," *North Star*, September 29, 1848.

100. Delany, *The Condition*, 196.

101. Ibid., 43.

102. Ibid., 199.

103. Ibid. See also Rollin, *Life and Public Services*, 49–50.

104. Delany, *The Condition*, 198–199.

105. Ibid.

106. Ibid., 196.

107. Ibid., 43.

108. Delany, "Letter from Wilmington, Delaware."

109. Ibid.

110. Ibid.

111. Adeleke, "Afro-Americans and Moral Suasion."

112. Ibid.

113. Elizabeth Geffen, "Violence in Philadelphia in the 1840s and 1850s," *Pennsylvania History* 6, (October 1969); Adam D. Simmons, "Ideologies and Programs of the Negro Anti-Slavery Movement, 1830–1861" (PhD diss., Northwestern University, 1983).

114. Delany, *The Condition*.

115. Delany, *The Condition*. See also Martin Delany, "Political Aspects of the Colored People," *Provincial Freeman*, October 13, 1855, 5. "Political Events," *Provincial Freeman*, July 5, 1856, 5.

116. "Frederick Douglass to H. B. Stowe, March 8, 1853," in *Minutes of the Proceedings of the National Negro Conventions*, ed. Bell, 33–38.

117. "Report of the Committee on Manual Labor School," in *Minutes of the Proceedings of the National Negro Conventions*, ed. Bell, 31–33.

118. Frederick Douglass, "Remarks" *Frederick Douglass's Paper*, April 11, 1853, 3. "Letter to Mrs. H. B. Stowe," in *Proceedings of the National Negro Conventions*, ed. Bell, 33–38.

119. Martin Delany, "Letter to Frederick Douglass," *Frederick Douglass's Paper*, April 11, 1853, 3.

120. Ibid., 4.

121. Ibid.

122. Frederick Douglass, "Remarks."

123. Martin Delany, "Freedmen's Bureau Report, 1867," Microcopy 849, Roll 35. Records of the Assistant Commissioners of the State of South Carolina. Bureau of Refugees, Freedmen, and Abandoned Lands (BRFAL) 1865–1870. Columbia, South Carolina: South Carolina Department of Archives and History.

124. Ibid.

125. Martin Delany, "Freedmen's Bureau Report, September 1867," Records of the Assistant Commissioners of the State of South Carolina. BRFAL 1865–1870. National Archives, Washington, DC, Microcopy 849, Roll 35, 354–362.

126. Delany, "Freedmen's Bureau Report, September 1867."

127. Ibid.

128. Martin Delany, "Freedmen's Bureau Report, May 1868," Records of the Assistant Commissioners of the State of South Carolina. BRFAL, 1865–1870. National Archives, Washington, DC, Microcopy 849, Roll 35, 773–779.

129. J. D. Anderson, "The Education of Blacks in the South, 1860–1935," in *Reading, 'riting, and Reconstruction: The Education of Freedmen in the South, 1861–1870*, ed. R. C. Morris (Chicago, Illinois: University of Chicago Press, 1981).

130. Martin Delany, "Freedmen's Bureau Report, 1868," Microcopy 849, Roll 35.

131. Ibid.

132. E. Wright, "Letter Dated March 17 and 20, 1867," American Missionary Association Papers, Amistad Research Center, Tulane University, New Orleans, Louisiana.

133. Delany, "Freedmen's Bureau Report, May 1868," BRFAL, 773–779.

134. Ibid.

135. R. Wilkins, "Letters dated April 22 and May 17, 1867," The Archives of the American Missionary Association, Amistad Research Center, Tulane University.

136. Elizabeth A. Summers, "Manuscript dated April 11–June 15." Columbia, South Carolina: South Caroliniana Research Library, University of South Carolina.

137. See his reports to the *North Star* in Robert Levine, ed., *Martin R. Delany*.

138. Carter G. Woodson, *The Miseducation of the Negro* (Trenton, NJ: Africa World Press, 1990), 38. First published in 1933.

139. Tunde Adeleke, "Martin R. Delany's Philosophy of Education: A Neglected Aspect of African-American Liberation Thought," *Journal of Negro Education* 63, no. 2 (Spring 1994); Tunde Adeleke, "'Much Learning Makes Men Mad': Classical Education and Black Empowerment in Martin R. Delany's Philosophy of Education," *Journal of Thought* 49, nos. 1 and 2 (Spring–Summer 2015).

Chapter 4

1. Robert Khan, "The Political Ideology of Martin Delany," *Journal of Black Studies* (June 1984); Tommie Shelby, "Two Conceptions of Black Nationalism: Martin Delany on the Meaning of Black Political Solidarity," *Political Theory* 31, no. 5 (October 2003), 664–692.

2. Victor Ullman, *Martin R. Delany: The Beginnings of Black Nationalism* (Boston, MA: Beacon Press, 1971), ix.

3. Theodore Draper, "The Father of American Black Nationalism," *New York Times Review of Books*, March 12, 1970. See also his "The Fantasy of Black Nationalism," *Commentary* 48 (1969).

4. *North Star*, June 16, 1848.

5. John Ernest, *A Nation within a Nation: Organizing African American Communities before the Civil War* (Chicago: Ivan R. Dee, 2011).

6. Martin Delany, *The Condition, Elevation, Emigration and Destiny of the Colored People of the United States* (Baltimore, MD: Black Classic Press, 1993). First published in 1852.

7. Delany, *The Condition*, 12. See also Ernest, *A Nation Within a Nation*, 13–13

8. Delany, *The Condition*, 17.

9. Frank Rollin, *Life and Public Services of Martin R. Delany* (New York: Kraus Reprint Company, 1969), 238. First published in 1868 in Boston by Lee and Shepard.

10. Rollin, *Life and Public Services*, 238; John T. McCartney, *Black Power Ideologies: An Essay in African American Political Thought* (Philadelphia: Temple University Press, 1992), 38–48.

11. Philip S. Foner and George E. Walker, eds. *Proceedings of the Black State Conventions, Vol. 1, 1840–1865* (Philadelphia: Temple University Press, 1979), 113.

12. Manisha Sinha, *The Slave's Cause: A History of Abolition* (New Haven, CT: Yale University Press, 2016), 321.

13. Delany, *The Condition*, chapters 6, 7, 8, 9, 10.

14. Delany, *The Condition*, chapters 16, 17, 18.

15. Martin Delany, "Political Destiny of the Colored Race on the American Continent," in *Life and Public Services*, ed. Rollin, 327–367.

16. Martin Delany, "Political Aspect of the Colored People of the United States," *Provincial Freeman*, October 13, 1855.

17. Delany, *The Condition*, 12.

18. Ernest Allen, "Afro-American Identity: Reflections on the Pre-Civil War Era," in *African American Activism before the Civil War: The Freedom Struggle in the Antebellum North*, ed. Patrick Rael (London: Routledge, 2008), 149.

19. Ibid.

20. Ibid.

21. Allen, "Afro-American Identity," 149–150. See also Delany, "Political Destiny," in *Life and Public Services*, ed. Rollin, 327–329.

22. Martin Delany, *The Condition*, 49.

23. Martha S. Jones, *Birthright Citizenship: A History of Race and Rights in Antebellum America* (Cambridge: Cambridge University Press, 2018), 1.

24. Ibid., 89.

25. Martin Delany, *The Condition*, 49. See also, Martha Jones, *Birthright Citizenship*, 89–90

26. Martin Delany, *The Condition*.

27. Ibid.

28. Ibid., 51.

29. Martha Jones, *Birthright Citizenship*, 90.

30. Ibid., 90.

31. Delany, *The Condition*, chap. 7.

32. Ibid., 50–51.

33. Ibid., 50–51.

34. Ibid., chapters 8, 9, 10, 11, 12.

35. Delany, "Political Aspect."

36. Shelby, "Two Conceptions of Black Nationalism," 669.

37. Ibid.

38. Ibid.

39. Delany "Political Destiny," in *Life and Public Services*, ed. Rollin, 329–330.

40. Ibid.

41. Ibid.

42. Ibid.

43. Martin Delany, *The Condition*, 67.

44. Ibid.

45. Ibid., chapters 10, 11, 12, 14.

46. Ibid., 37–44. See also *North Star*, March 6, 1849.

47. Delany, *The Condition*, 42.

48. Ibid., 39–40.

49. Delany, *The Condition*, 95–96. See also Richard P. McCormick, "William Whipper: Moral Reformer," *Pennsylvania History* 10, no. 11 (January 1976).

50. C. Peter Ripley, ed., *The Black Abolitionist Papers*, vol. 3, *The United States, 1830–1846* (Chapel Hill: University of North Carolina Press, 1991), 129–130, 259–260.

51. Dorothy Sterling, *The Making of an Afro-American: Martin Robison Delany, 1812–1883* (New York: Doubleday and Company, 1971), 39–45; Rollin, *Life and Public Services*, 38–39; Delany, *The Condition*, 95–96.

52. Tunde Adeleke, "Afro-Americans and Moral Suasion: The Debates in the 1830s and 1840s," *Journal of Negro History*, vol. 83, no. 2 (Spring 1998): 127–142. See also *The Colored American*, December 9, 1837, 2; December 16, 1837, 2; February 16, 1839, 2; May 2, 1839, 2; May 3, 1839; Richard McCormick, "William Whipper", 28–29; *Colored American*, September 16, 1837, August 16, 1837, 2; September 9, 1837, 2; January 8, 1837, 2.

53. Ibid.

54. Howard H. Bell, "The American Moral Reform Society, 1836–1841," *Journal of Negro Education* 25, no. 11 (Winter 1958); Richard McCormick, "William Whipper."

55. Ibid. See also Adeleke, "Afro-Americans and Moral Suasion."

56. Howard H. Bell, ed., *Minutes of the Fifth Annual Convention for the Improvement of the Free People of Color in the United States*, Wesley Church, Philadelphia, June 1–5, 1835. (Philadelphia: William P. Gibbons, 1835), 27. Reprinted in his *Minutes of the Proceedings of the National Negro Conventions, 1830–1864* (New York: Arno Press, 1969).

57. Howard H. Bell, "The American Moral Reform Society"; Adeleke, "Afro-Americans and Moral Suasion."

58. "Minutes and Proceedings of the Second Annual Convention for the Improvement of the Free People of Color in These United States, Philadelphia, June 4–13, 1832" (Philadelphia: Benj. Paschal, Theo Butler, and Jas G. Mathews Publishers, 1832), 34. Preprinted in *Minutes of the Proceedings of the National Negro Conventions, 1830–1864*, ed. Howard H. Bell.

59. Rollin, *Life and Public Services*, 48–49.

60. Rollin, *Life and Public Services*, 48–49. See also Martin Delany, *The Condition*, chap. 4. *North Star*, April 7, 1848, 2; October 6, 1849, 2; January 5, 1849.

61. Rollin, *Life and Public Services*, 55.

62. William McFeely, *Frederick Douglass* (New York: W. W. Norton, 1991); William H. Pease and Jane H. Pease, "Boston Garrisonians and the Problem of Frederick Douglass," *Canadian Journal of History* 11, no. 2 (September 1967); Benjamin Quarles, "The Breach Between Douglass and Garrison," *Journal of Negro History* 23, no. 21 (April 1938); Tyrone Tillery, "The Inevitability of the Douglass-Garrison Conflict," *Phylon* 37, no. 2 (June 1976); Philip S. Foner, *Frederick Douglass: A Biography* (New York: Citadel Press, 1964), 15–172.

63. Robert Levine, *Martin R. Delany: A Documentary Reader* (Chapel Hill: University of North Carolina Press, 2003).

64. Martin Delany, *The Condition*, 194.

65. Robert W. Caldwell, *Theologies of the American Revivalists: From Whitefield to Finney* (Downers Grove, IL: InterVarsity Press, 2017); Leon F. Litwack, *North of*

Slavery: The Negro in the Free States, 1790–1860 (Chicago: University of Chicago Press, 1965); Leonard P. Curry, *The Free Black in Urban America, 1800–1850: The Shadow of the Dream* (Chicago: University of Chicago Press, 1985); James O. Horton and Lois E. Horton, *In Hope of Liberty: Culture, Community and Protest among Northern Free Blacks, 1700–1860* (Oxford: Oxford University Press, 1998).

66. Martin Delany, "Colored Citizens of Pittsburgh," *North Star*, July 13, 1849; Martin Delany, "Report from Cleveland, Ohio, July 24, 1848," *North Star*, August 4, 1848; Martin Delany, "Report from Hanover, Ohio, March 27, 1848," *North Star*, April 14, 1848; Martin Delany, "Report from Cincinnati, Ohio, May 7, 1848," *North Star*, May 26, 1848; Martin Delany, "Report from Cincinnati, Ohio, May 20, 1848," *North Star*, June 9, 1848.

67. Ibid.

68. *North Star*, December 15, 1848.

69. Martin Delany, *The Condition*, 42.

70. Ibid., 41.

71. Ibid.

72. Ibid.

73. Ibid., 42.

74. Ibid., 41–42.

75. Ibid., chapters 7, 8, 9, 10, 11, 12.

76. Martin Delany, "American Civilization: Treatment of the Colored People in the United States" *North Star*, March 30, 1849, 2.

77. Adam D. Simmons, "Ideologies and Programs of the Negro Anti-Slavery Movement, 1830–1861" (PhD diss., Northwestern University, 1983), 32.

78. Ibid., 34.

79. Philip S. Foner and George E. Walker, eds., *Proceedings of the Black State Conventions, Vol. 2, 1840–1865* (Philadelphia: Temple University Press, 1979), 124.

80. Martin Delany, "National Disfranchisement of Colored People" in *The Condition*, 147–159.

81. Delany, *The Condition*, 11–12. See also "Letter from Mr. Delany, Pittsburgh, March 22, 1853," *Frederick Douglass's Paper*, April 11, 1853; Rollin, *Life and Public Services*, 359–360.

82. Delany, *The Condition*, 12.

83. Ibid., 13.

84. "Letter from Mr. Delany," *Frederick Douglass's Paper*, April 11, 1853.

85. Rollin, *Life and Public Services*, 335.

86. Delany, *The Condition*, 158.

87. Delany, "National Disfranchisement of Colored People," *The Condition*, chap. 16.

88. Delany, *The Condition*, 49.

89. Ibid., 50.

90. Ibid., 153–154.

91. Ibid., 154.

92. Rollin, *Life and Public Services*, 329.

93. Delany, *The Condition*, 155.

94. Ibid., 210.

95. Ibid., 11–12.

96. Ibid., 14.

97. Ibid., 153–154.

98. Ibid., 157–158.

99. Maurice O. Wallace, *Constructing the Black Masculine: Identity and Ideality in African American Men's Literature and Culture, 1775–1995* (Durham, NC: Duke University Press, 2002,) 69.

100. Ibid., 71.

101. Martin Delany, *Trial and Conviction* (Charleston, 1876), 3.

102. Tunde Adeleke, *Without Regard to Race: The Other Martin R. Delany* (Jackson: University Press of Mississippi, 2003), 91–93.

103. Adeleke, *Without Regard to Race*. See also Rollin, *Life and Public Services*, 283.

104. Adeleke, *Without Regard to Race*, chap. 4.

105. Martin Delany, *A Series of Four Tracts on National Polity* (Charleston, SC: Republican Book and Job Office, 1870).

106. Ibid.

107. Ibid.

108. Ibid.

109. Ibid.

110. Ibid.

111. Ibid., 6.

112. Ibid.

113. Ibid.

114. Ibid., 10.

115. Ibid.

116. Martin Delany, "A Political Review [Letter to Frederick Douglass]," *Daily Republican*, August 15, 1871.

117. Ibid.

118. Ibid.

119. "Delany to Justice Jonathan Wright, Charleston, February 10, 1874," *New York Times*, February 21, 1874.

120. Ibid.

121. Martin Delany, "A Political Review."

122. *New York Times*, February 16, 1874.

123. Adeleke, *Without Regard to Race*, 112–118.

124. "Independent Republican Party: M. P. 1874," Manuscript, South Caroliniana Research Library, Columbia, South Carolina. See also Thomas Holt, *Black Over White: Negro Political Leadership in South Carolina during Reconstruction* (Urbana: University Illinois Press, 1979), chap. 8.

125. Adeleke, *Without Regard to Race*, chap. 5.

126. Blacks first publicly manifested their anger toward, and frustration with, Delany at a joint Republican and Democratic rally on October 4, 1876. While most of the Democratic speakers addressed the rally with minimum of interruptions, Delany was prevented from speaking. As he rose to speak, angry Blacks (men, women, and even children) began cursing and pointing accusingly at him. He was "howled down" and prevented. See Alfred B. Williams, *Hampton and His Red Shirts: South Carolina Deliverance in 1876* (Charleston, SC: Walker, Evans, and Cogswell, 1936), 260–261. Delany narrowly escaped death at another joint rally in Cainhoy, Edgefield County, when a Colored Democrat named McKinlay was mistaken for Delany and fired at by the Black militia. Delany and a few other Democrats sought refuge in an old brick building. Upon learning that Delany was in the building, the crowd stormed it, but he escaped. There were several casualties. See, *Charleston News and Courier*, October 1, 1876, 3; October 17, 18, 1876. See also Henry T. Thompson, *Ousting the Carpetbagger from South Carolina* (New York: Negro University Press, 1926), 120.

127. Adeleke, *Without Regard to Race*, 148–160.

128. Walter Allen, *Governor Chamberlain's Administration in South Carolina: A Chapter of Reconstruction in the Southern State* (New York: Negro University Press, 1969), 284.

129. Adeleke, *Without Regard to Race*, 127–134.

130. *Daily Republican*, July 5, 1870; July 25, 1870, 2.

131. Adeleke, *Without Regard to Race*, chap. 5.

132. Martin Delany, "Citizenship," *National Era*, March 10, 1870.

133. Martin Delany, "Third Offence," in his *Trial and Conviction*, 7.

134. Ibid.

135. "Speech of Col. Delany," *Daily Republican*, August 20, 1870.

136. "A Rousing Ratification Meeting Last Night," *News and Courier*, October 7, 1874.

137. *Daily Republican*, July 5, 1870; July 25, 1870, 2; July 24, 1870; July 15, 1870.

138. *Daily Republican*, July 25, 1870, 2.

139. Peter Eisenstadt, *Black Conservatism: Essays in Intellectual and Political History* (New York: Routledge, 1999), 19.

140. *The New York Times*, November 27, 1870.

141. Howard N. Rabinowitz, ed., *Southern Black Leaders of the Reconstruction Era* (Urbana: University of Illinois Press, 1982).

142. Eisenstadt, *Black Conservatism*, 19.

143. Rabinowitz, ed., *Southern Black Leaders of the Reconstruction Era*.

Conclusion

1. "Report from Cincinnati, Ohio, June 4, 1848," *North Star*, June 16, 1848.

2. "Report from Milton, Ohio, June 18, 1848," *North Star*, July 7, 1848.

3. "Report from Pittsburgh, Pennsylvania, November 5, 1848," *North Star*, November 17, 1848.

4. Veronica Alease Davis, *Hampton University* (Charleston, SC: Arcadia Publishing, 2014).

5. James D. Anderson, *The Education of Blacks in the South, 1860–1935* (Chapel Hill: University of North Carolina Press, 1988), chap. 2.

6. Martin Delany, *The Condition, Elevation, Emigration and Destiny of the Colored People of the United States* (Baltimore, MD: Black Classic Press, 1993), 193. First published in 1852.

7. Ibid.

8. Ibid., 196.

9. Booker T. Washington, "The Atlanta Exposition Address" in *Readings in African-American History*, ed. Thomas R. Frazier, 3rd ed. (Belmont, CA: Wadsworth/Thomson, 2001), 195.

10. Ibid., 197.

11. Tunde Adeleke, *Martin R. Delany's Civil War and Reconstruction: A Primary Source Reader* (Jackson: University Press of Mississippi, 2020).

12. Cary D. Mintz, *African American Political Thought, 1890–1930: Washington, Du Bois, Garvey and Randolph* (New York: M. E. Sharpe, 1996).

13. Ben Crump, *Legalized Genocide of Colored People: Open Season* (New York: HarperCollins Publishers, 2019); Earl Ofari Hutchinson, *The Assassination of the Black Male Image* (New York: Simon and Schuster, 1996).

14. Martin Delany, "Report from Pittsburgh, Pennsylvania," *North Star*, March 9, 1849.

15. Martin Delany, "American Civilization—Treatment of the Colored People in the United States," *North Star*, March 30, 1849.

16. Ibid.

17. Ibid.

18. Ibid.

19. Ibid.

20. Ibid.

BIBLIOGRAPHY

Books

Adeleke, Tunde. "Martin R. Delany and Booker T. Washington: Ideological Partners Separated by Time and Ideology." In *Booker T. Washington: Interpretative Essays*, edited by Tunde Adeleke. London: The Edwin Mellen Press, 1998, 35–80.

———. *Martin R. Delany's Civil War and Reconstruction: A Primary Source Reader*. Jackson: University Press of Mississippi, 2020.

———. *UnAfrican Americans: Nineteenth-Century Black Nationalists and the Civilizing Mission*. Lexington: University Press of Kentucky, 1998.

———. *Without Regard to Race: The Other Martin R. Delany*. Jackson: University Press of Mississippi, 2003.

Allen, Ernest. "Afro-American Identity: Reflections on the Pre-Civil War Era." In *African American Activism before the Civil War: The Freedom Struggle in the Antebellum North*, edited by Patrick Rael. London: Routledge, 2008.

Allen, Walter. *Governor Chamberlain's Administration in South Carolina: A Chapter of Reconstruction in the Southern States*. New York: Negro University Press, 1969.

Anderson, James D. *The Education of Blacks in the South, 1860–1935*. Chapel Hill: University of North Carolina Press, 1988.

Aptheker, H. *American Negro Slave Revolts*. 6th ed. New York: International Publishers, 1983.

———, ed. *A Documentary History of the Negro People in the United States*. Vol. 1. New York: Citadel Press, 1965.

Asante, M. K. *The Afrocentric Idea*. Philadelphia: Temple University Press, 1987.

Bell, Howard H., ed. *Minutes of the Proceedings of the National Negro Conventions, 1830–1864*. New York: Arno Press and The New York Times, 1969.

———. *Proceedings of the National Negro Conventions, 1830–1864*. New York: Arno Press, 1969.

———. *A Survey of the Negro Convention Movement*. New York: Arno Press, 1969.

Berlin, Ira. *Slaves without Masters: The Free Negro in the Antebellum South*. New York: New Press, 1992.

Birnbaum, Jonathan and Clarence Taylor, eds. *Civil Rights since 1787: A Reader on the Black Struggle*. New York: New York University Press, 2000.

Blackett, R. J. M. *The Captive's Quest for Freedom: Fugitive Slaves, the 1850 Fugitive Slave Law, and the Politics of Slavery*. Cambridge: Cambridge University Press, 2018.

Blight, D. W., ed. *Narrative of the Life of Frederick Douglass, an American Slave, Written by Himself*. 2nd ed. New York: Bedford/St. Martin's, 2003.

Bullock, H. A. *A History of Negro Education in the South: From 1619 to the Present*. Cambridge, MA: Harvard University Press, 1967.

Burks, Gerald A. *Partial Genealogy of Martin Robison Delany*. Unpublished manuscript, 2006.

Butchart, R. E. *Northern Schools, Southern Blacks, and Reconstruction: Freedmen's Education, 1862–1875*. Westport, CT: Greenwood Press, 1980.

Caldwell, Robert W. *Theologies of the American Revivalists: From Whitefield to Finney*. Downers Grove, IL: InterVarsity Press, 2017.

Carr, Robert. *Black Nationalism in the New World: Reading the African American and West Indian Experience*. Durham: Duke University Press, 2002.

Cooper, William T. *The Conservative Regime: South Carolina, 1877–1890*. Baltimore, MD: Johns Hopkins University Press, 1968.

Crump, Ben. *Open Season: Legalized Genocide of Colored People*. New York: Harper-Collins, 2019.

Curry, Leonard P. *The Free Black in Urban America, 1800–1850: The Shadow of the Dream*. Chicago: University of Chicago Press, 1985

Davis, David B. *The Problem of Slavery in Western Culture*. Ithaca, NY: Cornell University Press, 1966.

———. *The Problem of Slavery in the Age of Emancipation*. New York: Alfred A. Knopf, 2014.

Davis, Veronica Alease. *Hampton University*. Charleston, SC: Arcadia Publishing, 2014

Delany, Martin R. *Blake, Or, The Huts of America: The Weekly Anglo-African Magazine, 1861–1862*.

———. *The Condition, Elevation, Emigration and Destiny of the Colored People of the United States*. Baltimore, MD: Black Classic Press, 1993. First published in Philadelphia in 1852.

———. "Political Destiny of the Colored Race on the American Continent." In *Life and Public Services of Martin R. Delany*, edited by Frank Rollin, 327–367. Boston: Lee and Shepard, 1868.

———. *Trial and Conviction*. Charleston, SC, 1876.

Dickson, Rev. Moses. *Manual of the International Order of Twelve of Knights and Daughters of Tabor*. 8th ed. Glasgow, MO: Moses Dickson, 1911.

Douglass, Frederick. *Life and Times of Frederick Douglass (Written by Himself)*. New York: Bonanza Books, 1962. First published in 1892 in Boston by De Wolfe & Fiske Co.

Draper, Theodore. *The Rediscovery of Black Nationalism*. New York: Viking Press, 1970.

Du Bois, William E. B. *The Philadelphia Negro*. Philadelphia: University of Pennsylvania Press 1899.

Eisenstadt, Peter. *Black Conservatism: Essays in Intellectual and Political History*. New York: Routledge, 1999.

Ernest, John. *A Nation within a Nation: Organizing African-American Communities before the Civil War*. Chicago: Ivan R. Dee, 2011.

Foner, Philip S. *The Life and Writings of Frederick Douglass*. Vol. 5, *Supplementary, 1844–1860*. New York: International Publishers, 1975.

———. *Frederick Douglass: A Biography*. New York: Citadel Press, 1964.

Foner, Philip S., and George E. Walker, eds. *Proceedings of the Black State Conventions, 1840–1865*. Vols. 1 and 2. Philadelphia: Temple University Press, 1979.

Frazier, E. Franklin. *The Negro Church in America*. New York: Schocken Books, 1974. First published in 1964 by Schochen Books.

Friedman, Lawrence J. *Gregarious Saints: Self and Community in American Abolitionism, 1830–1870*. London: Cambridge University Press, 1982.

Gaston, Paul. *The New South Creed: A Study in Southern Mythmaking*. New York: Vintage Books, 1973.

Gatewood, William B., Jr. "The Remarkable Misses Rollin: Black Women in Reconstruction South Carolina," *South Carolina Historical Magazine*, vol. 92, no. 3, July 1991.

Gayle, Addison, Jr. *The Way of the World: The Black Novel in America*. New York: Archon Books, 1976.

Genovese, Eugene. *Roll, Jordan Roll: The World the Slaves Made*. New York: Vintage Books, 1976.

Glaude, Eddie S. *Exodus! Religion, Race, and Nation in Early Nineteenth-Century Black America*. Chicago: University of Chicago Press, 2000.

Gravely, Will B. "The Rise of African Churches in America, 1786–1822: Reexamining the Contexts." In *African American Religious Studies: An Interdisciplinary Anthology*, edited by Gayraud S. Wilmore. Durham, NC: Duke University Press, 1989.

Green, Hilary. *Educational Reconstruction: African American Schools in the Urban South, 1865–1890*. New York: Fordham University Press, 2016.

Gresson, A. D. *Race and Education Primer*. New York: Peter Lang, 2008.

Griffith, Cyril. *The African Dream: Martin R. Delany and the Emergence of Pan-Africanist Thought*. University Park: Pennsylvania State University Press, 1975.

Harding, Vincent. "Beyond Chaos: Black History and the Search for the New Land." In *Amistad 1: Writings on Black History and Culture*, edited by John A. Williams and Charles F. Harris, 267–292. New York: Vintage Books, 1970.

———. *There Is a River: The Black Struggle for Freedom in America*. New York: Harcourt Brace, 1983.

Hendrick, George, and Willene Hendrick. *Black Refugees in Canada: Accounts of Escape during the Era of Slavery*. Jefferson, NC: McFarland & Co., 2010.

Holt, Thomas. *Black over White: Negro Political Leadership in South Carolina during Reconstruction.* Urbana: University of Illinois Press, 1977.

Horton, James O., and Lois E. Horton. *In Hope of Liberty: Culture, Community and Protest among Northern Free Blacks, 1700–1860.* Oxford: Oxford University Press, 1998.

Huggins, Nathan I., Martin Kilson, and Daniel M. Fox, eds. *Key Issues in the Afro-American Experience, Volume 1 to 1877.* New York: Harcourt Brace, Jovanovich, 1971.

Hutton, A. J. W. *Some Historical Data Concerning the History of Chambersburg.* Chambersburg, PA: Franklin Repository, 1930.

Jackson, Kellie Carter. *Force and Freedom: Black Abolitionists and the Politics of Violence.* Philadelphia: University of Pennsylvania Press, 2019.

Jones, Angela, ed. *The African American Political Thought Reader: From David Walker to Barack Obama.* New York: Routledge, 2013.

Jones, Martha. *Birthright Citizens: A History of Race and Rights in Antebellum America.* Cambridge, UK: Cambridge University Press, 2018.

Keto, T. C. *Vision, Identity, and Time: The Afrocentric Paradigm and the Study of the Past.* Dubuque, IA: Kendall-Hunt, 1995.

Laurie, Bruce. *Working People of Philadelphia, 1800–1850.* Philadelphia: Temple University Press, 1980.

Levine, Robert S. *Martin Delany, Frederick Douglass, and the Politics of Representative Identity.* Chapel Hill: University of North Carolina Press, 1997.

———. *Martin R. Delany: A Documentary Reader.* Chapel Hill: University of North Carolina Press, 2003.

Lincoln, Eric and Lawrence Mamiya. *The Black Church in the African American Experience.* Durham, NC: Duke University Press, 1990.

Litwack, Leon F. *North of Slavery: The Negro in the Free States, 1790–1860.* Chicago: University of Chicago Press, 1965.

Mabee, Carlton. *Black Freedom: The Nonviolent Abolitionists from 1830 through the Civil War.* London: The Macmillan Company, 1970.

Madera, Judith. *Black Atlas: Geography and Flow in Nineteenth-Century African American Literature.* Durham: Duke University Press, 2015.

Maizlish, Stephen E. *A Strife of Tongues: The Compromise of 1850 and the Ideological Foundations of the American Civil War.* Charlottesville: University of Virginia Press, 2018.

McAdoo, Bill. *Pre-Civil War Black Nationalism.* New York: David Walker Press, 1983.

McCartney, John. *Black Power Ideologies: An Essay in African American Political Thought.* Philadelphia: Temple University Press, 1992.

McFeely, William. *Frederick Douglass.* New York: W. W. Norton, 1991.

McGann, Jerome, ed. *Blake, Or, The Huts of America: A Corrected Edition.* Cambridge, MA: Harvard University Press, 2017.

McGlone, Robert B. *John Brown's War against Slavery.* Cambridge: Cambridge University Press, 2009.

Miller, Floyd J. *The Search for Black Nationality: Black Emigration and Colonization, 1787–1863*. Urbana: University of Illinois Press, 1975.

Mintz, Cary D. *African American Political Thought, 1890–1930: Washington, Du Bois, Garvey, and Randolph*. New York: M. E. Sharpe, 1996.

Mitchell, Henry H. *Black Church Beginnings: The Long-Hidden Realities of the First Years*. Cambridge, UK: William B. Eerdmans Publishing Company, 2004.

Morris, R. C. *Reading, 'Riting, and Reconstruction: The Education of Freedmen in the South, 1861–1870*. Chicago: University of Chicago Press, 1981.

Newby, Idus. *Jim Crow's Defense: Anti-Negro Thought in America, 1900–1930*. Baton Rouge: Louisiana State University Press, 1965.

Ofari, Earl. *The Assassination of the Black Male Image*. New York: Simon and Schuster, 1996.

———. *Let Your Motto Be Resistance: The Life and Thought of Henry H. Garnet*. Boston, MA: Beacon Press, 1972.

Paris, Peter J. *The Social Teachings of the Black Church*. Philadelphia: Fortress Press, 1985.

Pease, William H. and Jane H. Pease. "The Negro Convention Movement." In *Key Issues in the Afro-American Experience, Volume 1 to 1877*, edited by Nathan I. Huggins, Martin Kilson, and Daniel M. Fox, 191–205. New York: Harcourt Brace Jovanovich, 1971.

Quarles, Benjamin. *Black Abolitionists*. London: Oxford University Press, 1969.

Rabinowitz, Howard N., ed. *Southern Black Leaders of the Reconstruction Era*. Urbana: University of Illinois Press, 1982.

Raboteau, Albert J. *Slave Religion: The "Invisible Institution" in the Antebellum South*. New York: Oxford University Press, 1978.

Rael, Patrick, ed. *Black Identity and Black Protest in the Antebellum North*. Chapel Hill: University of North Carolina Press, 2002.

Reimers, David M. *White Protestantism and the Negro*. New York: Oxford University Press, 1965.

Richards, Leonard L. *"Gentlemen of Property and Standing": Anti-Abolitionist Mobs in Jacksonian America*. New York: Oxford University Press, 1970.

Ripley, C. Peter. *The Black Abolitionist Papers*. Vol. 3, *The United States, 1830–1846*. Chapel Hill: University of North Carolina Press, 1991.

Rollin, Frank. *Life and Public Services of Martin R. Delany*. Boston: Lee and Shepard, 1868.

Russell, John H. *The Free Negro in Virginia, 1619–1865*. Baltimore, MD: Johns Hopkins University Press, 1913.

Schoolman, Martha. *Abolitionist Geographies*. Minneapolis: University of Minnesota Press, 2014.

Sidbury, James. *Becoming African in America: Race and Nation in the Early Atlantic*. New York: Oxford University Press, 2007.

Simkins, Francis and Robert Woody. *South Carolina during Reconstruction*. Gloucester, MA: Peter Smith, 1966.

Simmons, Adam D. "Ideologies and Programs of the Negro Anti-Slavery Movement, 1830–1861." PhD diss., Northwestern University, 1983.

Sinha, Manisha. *The Slave's Cause: A History of Abolition*. New Haven: Yale University Press, 2016.

Sorin, Gerald. *Abolitionism: A New Perspective*. New York: Praeger, 1972.

Sterling, Dorothy. *The Making of an Afro-American: Martin Robison Delany, 1812–1885*. New York: Doubleday, 1971.

Stewart, James B. *Holy Warriors: The Abolitionists and American Slavery*. New York: Hill and Wang, 1976.

Stuckey, Sterling. *Slave Culture: Nationalist Theory and the Foundation of Black America*. New York: Oxford University Press, 1987.

———. "Twilight of Our Past: Reflections on the Origins of Black History." In *Amistad 2: Writings on Black History and Culture*, edited by John A. Williams and Charles F. Harris, 261–296. New York: Vintage Books, 1971.

Takaki, Ronald. *Violence in the Black Imagination: Essays and Documents*. New York: G. P. Putnam's 1972.

Taylor, Alrutheus A. *The Negro in South Carolina during the Reconstruction*. Washington, DC: Association for the Study of Negro Life and History, 1924.

Thompson, Henry T. *Ousting the Carpetbaggers from South Carolina*. New York: Negro University Press, 1928.

Ullman, Victor. *Martin R. Delany: The Beginnings of Black Nationalism*. Boston: Beacon Press, 1971

Wallace, Maurice O. *Constructing the Black Masculine: Identity and Ideality in African American Men's Literature and Culture, 1775–1995*. Durham: Duke University Press, 2002.

Walters, Kerry. *The Underground Railroad: A Reference Guide*. Denver, CO: ABC-Clio, LLC, 2012.

Washington, Booker T. "The Atlanta Exposition Address." In *Readings in African American History*. 3rd ed., edited by Thomas R. Frazier. Belmont, CA: Wadsworth/Thomson, 2001.

———. *Up from Slavery: An Autobiography*. New York: Dover Publications, 1995. First published by Doubleday, New York, 1901.

Washington, Joseph R. *Black Religion: The Negro and Christianity in the United States*. Lanham, MD: University Press of America, 1984.

Watkins, W. H. *Black Protest Thought and Education*. New York: Peter Lang, 2005.

Watkins, W. H., J. H. Lewis, and V. Chou, eds. *Race and Education: The Role of History and Society in Educating African American Students*. Boston: Allyn & Bacon, 2001.

Wilentz, Sean, ed. *David Walker's Appeal*. New York: Hill and Wang, 1995.

Williams, Alfred B. *Hampton and His Red Shirts: South Carolina Deliverance in 1876*. Charleston: Walker, Evans and Cogswell, 1935.

Williams, Heather A. *Self-Thought: African American Education in Slavery and Freedom*. Chapel Hill: University of North Carolina Press, 2005.

Williamson, Joel. *After Slavery; The Negro in South Carolina During Reconstruction, 1861–1877*. Chapel Hill: University of North Carolina Press, 1965.

———. *The Crucible of Race: Black-White Relations in the American South since Emancipation*. London: Oxford University Press, 1984.

———. *The Origins of Segregation*. Lexington, MA: D. C. Heath and Company, 1968.

Wilmore, Gayraud S, ed. *African American Religious Studies: An Interdisciplinary Anthology*. Durham, NC: Duke University Press, 1989.

Wilson, Carol. *Freedom at Risk: The Kidnapping of Free Blacks in America, 1780–1865*. Lexington: University Press of Kentucky, 1994.

Woodson, Carter G. *The Mis-education of the Negro*. Trenton, NJ: Africa World Press, 1990. First published in 1933 by The Associated Publishers.

Yellin, Jean F. *The Intricate Knot: Black Figures in American Literature, 1776–1863*. New York: New York University Press, 1972.

Articles

Adeleke, Tunde. "Afro-Americans and Moral Suasion: The Debate in the 1830s." *Journal of Negro History* 31, no. 2 (Spring 1998): 127–142.

———. "Violence as an option for Free Blacks in Nineteenth Century America." *Canadian Review of American Studies* 35 (2005): 87–107.

———. "Martin R. Delany's Philosophy of Education: A Neglected Aspect of African-American Liberation Thought." *Journal of Negro Education* 63, no. 2 (Spring 1994): 221–236.

———. "'Much Learning Makes Men Mad': Classical Education and Black Empowerment in Martin R. Delany's Philosophy of Education." *Journal of Thought* 49, nos. 1 and 2 (Spring–Summer 2015): 3–26.

———. "Uncle Tom." *International Encyclopedia of the Social Sciences*, 2008.

———. "Religion in Martin R. Delany's Liberation Thought." *Religious Humanism* 27, no. 2, (Spring 1993): 80–91.

———. "'Today is the Day of Salvation': Martin R. Delany and the Struggle against Providential Determinism in Early Nineteenth Century Black Abolitionism." *Interdisciplinary Journal of Research on Religion* 13, no. 4 (2017): 1–23.

Asante, Molefi K. "The Afrocentric Idea in Education." *Journal of Negro Education* 60, no. 1 (1991): 170–180.

Banks, J. A. "Race, Knowledge Construction, and Education in the USA: Lessons from History." *Race, Ethnicity and Education* 5, no. 1 (2002): 7–27.

Bell, Howard H. "The American Moral Reform Society, 1836–1841." *Journal of Negro Education* 25, no. 11 (Winter 1958): 34–40.

———. "Negro Nationalism: A Factor in Emigration Projects, 1858–1861." *Journal of Negro History* 47 no. 1 (January 1962): 42–53.

———. "National Negro Conventions of the Middle 1840s: Moral Suasion VS. Political Action." *Journal of Negro History* 42, no. 4 (October 1957): 247–260.

Blackett, Richard. "Martin Delany and Robert Campbell: Black Americans in Search of an African Colony." *Journal of Negro History* 60, no. 11 (January 1977): 1–25.

Brophy, Alfred L. "The Nat Turner Trials." (June 18, 2013). *North Carolina Law Review* 96 (June 2013): 1817–1880.

Cash, Philip. "Pride, Prejudice, and Politics." *Harvard Medical School Alumni Bulletin* (1980): 20–25.

Chiles, Katy. "Within and without Raced Nations: Intertextuality, Martin Delany, and *Blake, Or, The Huts of America*." *American Literature* 80, no. 2 (June 2008): 323–352.

———. "Defining *Blake*." *American Periodicals: A Journal of History & Criticism* 28, no. 1 (2018): 75–77.

Delany, Martin R. "Sound the Alarm." *North Star*, January 12, 1849.

———. "American Civilization: Treatment of the Colored People in the United States." *North Star*, March 30, 1849.

———. "Domestic Economy 1-3." *North Star*, March 23, 1849; April 13, 1849; April 27, 1849.

———. "Political Aspects of the Colored People of the United States." *Provincial Freeman*, October 13, 1855.

———. "Political Events." *Provincial Freeman*, July 5, 1856.

———. "Report from Wilmington, Delaware." *North Star*, December 15, 1848.

———. "Letter from Columbiana, August 13, 1848." *North Star*, August 25, 1848.

———. "Report from Pittsburgh, January 21, 1848." *North Star*, February 4, 1848.

———. "Report from Philadelphia, Pennsylvania, January 16, 1849." *North Star*, February 16, 1849.

———. "Colored Citizens of Pittsburgh." *North Star*, July 13, 1849.

———. "Report from Cleveland, Ohio, July 24, 1848." *North Star*, August 4, 1848.

———. "Report from Hanover, Ohio, March 27, 1848." *North Star*, April 14, 1848.

———. "Report from Cincinnati, Ohio, May 20, 1848." *North Star*, June 9, 1848.

———. "Report from Chillicothe, Ohio, April 20, 1848." *North Star*, May 12, 1848.

———. "Report from Milton, Ohio, June 18, 1848." *North Star*, July 7, 1848.

———. "Report from Lancaster City, Pennsylvania, December 18, 1848." *North Star*, January 5, 1849.

———. "Domestic Economy." *North Star*, March 23, 1849.

———. "Domestic Economy." *North Star*, April 20, 1849.

———. "Domestic Economy." *North Star*, April 23, 1849.

———. "Letter from M. R. Delany." *Frederick Douglass's Paper*, April 11, 1853.

———. "M. R. Delany to Dr. James McCune Smith (Important Movement)." *Weekly Anglo-African*, January 4, 1862.

———. "Illinois Convention." *Frederick Douglass's Paper*, November 18, 1853.

———. "The Moral and Social Aspect of Africa." *Liberator*, May 1, 1863.

———. "Letter from Columbus, Ohio." *North Star*, April 28, 1848.

———. "Letter from Cincinnati, Ohio." *North Star*, May 26, 1848.

———. "Letter from Harrisburg, Pennsylvania." *North Star*, December 1, 1848.

———. "Letter from Wilmington, Delaware." *North Star*, December 15, 1848.

———. "Letter from Pittsburgh, Pennsylvania." *North Star*, March 9, 1849.

———. "Colored Citizens of Cincinnati." *North Star*, June 15, 1849.

———. "Highly Important Statistics, Our Cause and Destiny: Endowment of a Newspaper." *North Star*, October 5, 1849.

———. "Political Economy." *North Star*, March 16, 1849.

———. "Letter to Frederick Douglass." *Frederick Douglass's Paper*, April 11, 1853.

———. "A Political Review." *Daily Republican*, August 15, 1871.

———. "Citizenship." *National Era*, March 10, 1870.

Douglass, Frederick. "Remarks." *Frederick Douglass's Paper*, April 11, 1853.

———. "Letter to Mrs. H. B. Stowe" in Howard H. Bell, *Proceedings of the National Negro Conventions, 1830–1935*. New York: Arno Press, 1969. Letter originally written in 1853.

Draper, Theodore. "The Father of American Black Nationalism." *New York Times Review of Books*, March 12, 1970.

———. "The Fantasy of Black Nationalism." *Commentary* 48 (1969).

———. "The Father of American Black Nationalism." *New York Times Review of Books*, March 12, 1970.

Du Bois, William E. B. "A Forum of Facts and Opinions." *Pittsburgh Courier*, July 25, 1936.

Fisher, Miles M. "Lott Cary: The Colonizing Missionary." *Journal of Negro History* 7, no. 4 (December 1922): 380–418.

Garrison, William L. "Declaration of Sentiments of the American Anti-Slavery Society." *Liberator*, December 14, 1833.

———. "The Letter from Dr. Delany." *Liberator*, May 21, 1852.

Geffen, Elizabeth. "Violence in Philadelphia in the 1840s and 1850s." *Pennsylvania History* 36, no. 4, (October 1969): 381–410.

Goldstein, Leslie F. "Violence as an Instrument for Social Change: The Views of Frederick Douglass (1817–1895)." *Journal of Negro History* 61, no. 1 (January 1976): 61–72.

Hartgrove, W. B. "The Story of Josiah Henson." *Journal of Negro History* 3, no. 1 (January 1918): 1–21.

Hite, Roger. "Stand Still and See the Salvation: Rhetorical Designs of Martin Delany's *Blake*." *Journal of Black Studies* 5, no. 2 (December 1974): 192–202.

Kauremszky, Ilona. "Uncle Tom Was a Real Person; His Cabin is in Canada." *Christian Science Monitor*, January 26, 2005.

Khan, Robert. "The Political Ideology of Martin R. Delany" *Journal of Black Studies* 14, no. 4 (June 1984): 415–440.

Madera, Judith. "Atlantic Architectures: Nineteenth-Century Cartography and Martin Delany's *Blake*." *English Language Notes* 52, no. 2 (Fall/Winter 2014): 75–96.

Magdol, Edward. "Martin R. Delany Counsels Freedmen, July 23, 1865." *Journal of Negro History* 56, no. 4, October, 1971: 303–307.

M. C. "Letter from York." *North Star*, December 15, 1848.

McCormick, Richard P. "William Whipper: Moral Reformer." *Pennsylvania History* 43, no. 3 (January 1976): 23–46.

McKenzie, Edna. "Doctor, Editor, Soldier: On Pittsburgh's Very Own Martin R. Delany." *Post-Gazette*, February 5, 1992.

News and Courier, October 7, 1874.

New York Times, November 27, 1870.

Ogbu, John. "Black American Students and the Academic Achievement Gap: What Else You Need to Know." *Journal of Thought* 37, no. 4 (Winter 2002): 9–33.

Painter, Nell I. "Martin R. Delany: A Black Leader in Two Kinds of Time." *New England Journal of Black Studies* 8 (November 1989): 37–47.

Pease, William H, and Jane H. "Black Power: The Debate in 1840."*Phylon* 29, no. 1 (1968): 19–26.

———. "Boston Garrisonians and the Problem of Frederick Douglass." *Canadian Journal of History* 2, no. 2 (September 1967): 29–48.

Quarles, Benjamin. "The Breach between Douglass and Garrison." *Journal of Negro History* 23, no. 2 (April 1938): 144–154.

Reed, Harry A. "Henry H. Garnet's *Address* to the Slaves of the United States of America, Reconsidered." *Western Journal of Black Studies* 6, no. 4 (1982): 186–191.

Rosenfeld, Louis. "Martin Robison Delany (1812–1885): Physician, Black Separatist, Explorer, Soldier." *Bulletin of the New York Academy of Medicine* 65, no. 7 (September 1989): 801–818.

Shelby, Tommie. "Two Conceptions of Black Nationalism: Martin Delany on the Meaning of Black Political Solidarity." *Political Theory* 31, no. 5 (October 2003): 664–692.

Shepperson, George. "Notes on Negro American Influences on the Emergence of African Nationalism." *Journal of African History* 1, no. 2 (1960): 299–312.

Sherwood, Henry N. "Paul Cuffee." *Journal of Negro History* 8, no. 3 (April, 1923): 152–229.

———. "Paul Cuffee and his Contributions to the American Colonization Society." *Proceedings of the Mississippi Valley Historical Association* 6 (1913): 370–402.

Shreve, Grant. "The Exodus of Martin Delany." *American Literary History* 29, no. 3 (Fall 2017): 449–473.

Takaki, Ronald. "Aesculapius Was a Whiteman: Ante-bellum Racism and Male Chauvinism in Harvard Medical School." *Phylon* 39, no. 2 (1978): 128–134.

Tanser, H. A. "Josiah Henson: The Moses of his People." *Journal of Negro Education* 12, no. 4 (Autumn 1943): 630–632.

Tillery, Tyrone. "The Inevitability of the Douglass-Garrison Conflict" *Phylon* 37, no. 2 (June 1976): 137–149.

Weisbord, Robert G. "The Back-to-Africa Idea." *History Today* 56 (January 1968).

Whipper, William. "An Address on Non-Violent Resistance to Offensive Aggression." *Colored American*, September 16 and 30, 1837.

Woodson, Lewis ("Augustine"). "The West." *Colored American*, February 16, 1839; March 2, 1839; March 16, 1839; June 15, 1839; August 31, 1839.

———. "Going West." *Colored American*, July 15, 1839.

———. "Death vs. Expatriation." *Colored American*, October 27, 1838.

———. "Going West." *Colored American*, May 3, 1838.

———. "Going West." *Colored American*, May 16, 1838.

———. "Going West" *Colored American*, October 6, 1838.

———. "Going West." *Colored American*, May 2, 1849.

———. "Death vs. Expatriation 1." *Colored American*, November 10, 1837.

———. "Death vs. Expatriation 2." *Colored American*, October 27, 1848.

———. "For the Colored American, April 19, 1838." *Colored American*, May 3, 1838.

Zeugner, John. "A Note on Martin Delany's *Blake* and Black Militancy," *Phylon* 32, no, 1, July 1973.

Archival Sources

Burks, Gerald A. "Martin R. Delany." AfriGeneas Genealogy and History Forum Archive, March 25, 2006.

Delany, Martin R. Freedmen's Bureau Report, 1867. Microcopy 849, Roll 35; Records of the Assistant Commissioners of the State of South Carolina. Bureau of Refugees, Freedmen, and Abandoned Lands, 1865-1870. Columbia, SC: South Carolina Department of Archives and History.

———. Freedmen's Bureau Report, 1868. Microcopy 849, Roll 35; Records of the Assistant Commissioners of the State of South Carolina. Bureau of Refugees, Freedmen, and Abandoned Lands, 1865-1870. Columbia, SC: South Carolina Department of Archives and History.

Summers, E. A. Manuscript dated April 11–June 15, 1867. Columbia, SC: South Caroliniana Research Library, University of South Carolina, 1867.

Wilkins, R. Letters dated April 22 and May 17, 1867. The Archive of the American Missionary Association, Amistad Research Center, Tulane University, New Orleans, Louisiana.

Wright, E. Letters dated March 17 and 20, 1867. The Archive of the American Missionary Association, Amistad Research Center, Tulane University, New Orleans, Louisiana.

CPSIA information can be obtained
at www.ICGtesting.com
Printed in the USA
BVHW032248100122
625923BV00002B/25